Anonymus

Assunta Howard and other stories and sketches

Anonymus

Assunta Howard and other stories and sketches

ISBN/EAN: 9783741132407

Manufactured in Europe, USA, Canada, Australia, Japa

Cover: Foto ©Thomas Meinert / pixelio.de

Manufactured and distributed by brebook publishing software
(www.brebook.com)

Anonymus

Assunta Howard and other stories and sketches

ASSUNTA HOWARD,

AND OTHER

STORIES AND SKETCHES.

NEW YORK:

THE CATHOLIC PUBLICATION SOCIETY CO.

12 EAST 17TH STREET.

—

1891.

CONTENTS.

ASSUNTA HOWARD.

THE full moon was pouring a flood of light upon the marble pavement of S. Peter's, and, by its weird influence, increased to an almost startling immensity the vastness of that mighty work of art, worthy offspring and expression of the faith which has subdued the world. The soft radiance in the nave seemed to throw into deeper gloom and an almost immeasurable space the ever-burning lamps which, like fixed stars, surround the central point of Christendom—the tomb of the great apostle, to whom was first given the power of the keys. No one could remain unmoved in such an awe-inspiring scene; certainly not two, at least, of the three persons who alone stood within the church, silently receiving impressions which come but seldom in a life-time. And yet, as the same sunbeam, falling upon different objects, will produce different colors, so on these three minds the impressions were stamped according to their preparation to receive them. To the man, in whom the moonlight, bathing him in brightness, revealed the appearance of gentle birth and refined culture, it was merely the human, the miracle of art, the power of man to design and execute; while the pure soul of the fair young girl at his side was struggling through the human up to the divine. The patient old sacristan standing apart, keys in hand, had dwelt for years in the midst of material and spiritual greatness with a faith so simple that he never dreamed it was sublime.

"How grand!" at length exclaimed Mr. Carlisle. "What a power there is in architecture; and how well those master-minds understood and used this power for the elevation of man!"

"Yes," replied his young companion; "and it seems to me that in church architecture every detail should be symbolic, and the whole should convey to the soul the impression of some one of God's attributes. S. Peter's is so truly home of the Christian world, and draws the heart so lovingly to itself, that it always seems to express the paternity of God. But to-night there is more than this. It speaks to my very soul of the Father, but 'the Father of an Infinite Majesty.'"

Mr. Carlisle smiled. "Another of your pretty fancies, Assunta. One would hardly expect to find such grave thoughts beneath this shining hair, which the alchemy of the moonlight is fast turning into gold."

The usual ready answer did not come; for any light conversation was out of harmony with the emotion inspired by such surroundings. Besides, the young girl was struggling with herself and against herself in a contest little suspected by her companion. The wonderful influence of the time and place had brought near the moment of defeat or victory. It is sometimes the way of God with the soul to prepare it gradually for some struggle, and then suddenly and unexpectedly to bring it face to face with the trial, and to permit its whole future to hang upon the decision of a moment. Thank God! to the faithful soul the strength is never wanting. It was such a crisis as this which clouded the bright face and darkened with doubt the mind of one in whom youth and innocence would seem to preclude the possibility of mental conflict.

It was but a few days since she had become convinced that the guardian who had been to her both friend and father had come to feel for her a love which indeed might include that of father and friend, as the greater includes the less, but which was something more than either. And with the consciousness there came a strange yearning of her heart to go forth and meet his heart with an equal love, to trust herself to the protecting care she knew so well, to yield to the happiness which promised to gild her life with a radiance too dazzling to be all of earth. But there arose a barrier between them, and hence the struggle.

Strange how we play the devil's advocate against our conscience! Must she respect that barrier? What if he were almost an infidel; would it not be her sweet mission to take heaven by violence, if need be, and by her importunate prayers obtain for him the light of faith? Dangerous sophistry! And yet on this quicksand how many women wreck themselves, instead of steering the bark freighted with the loved soul into the calm waters of truth!

They two, the guardian and his ward, had entered the church while yet the setting sun was irradiating column and statue with a glowing splendor; and they had continued to walk slowly and almost in silence up and down the long nave until the light had faded and darkness had succeeded the short twilight. They were about to leave the calm influence and the majesty of repose which this vast temple of God ever inspires, when suddenly the moon, rising to a level with the window above the porch, poured its magic-working beams upon the pavement. They paused, and, turning to the sacristan, who was about to close the doors for the night, begged a few moments' delay, which he, with unusual cordiality, granted.

And what were the busy thoughts which induced so prolonged a silence during that hour's walk, until the gathering darkness and then the rising moon warned them how the time was passing, of which they had taken so little note? Suffice it to say that the mind of each was filled with the other. With Assunta Howard, the new sentiments kindled in her heart had conjured up the memory of a scene which, associated with her first sorrow, was a living picture to her imagination. Again, as if it were but yesterday, she, a little child, entered the room of her dying mother, and saw her lying pale and beautiful upon her bed, her crucifix in her hand, and beside her the little table covered with white linen, upon which were the exquisite flowers and the still burning candles placed there in honor of her divine Lord, whom she had just received as the Viaticum of her journey home. The little Assunta thought how much her mamma looked like the beautiful S. Catherine, borne in the arms of the lovely angels, which hung above her own bed; and she wondered if the angels would come before she had time to kiss her mother once again. It was almost with a feeling of awe that she whispered in the ear of the good priest who raised her in his arms, " Is mamma a saint now?"

"My precious child," said the mother, strengthened for this bitter parting by the divine Guest who was reposing in her heart, "mamma must leave her little Assunta, her good little girl. But before long I hope that I shall be with the dear Jesus and his sweet Mother, whom you love so much. So you will be glad for mamma, and always remember how much she loves you. I am not very strong, my darling, but put your arms around my neck, and your curly head close to mine, while I say something to you. You will not understand me now, my poor child, but I know that you will try and remember all, and one of these days you will know what I mean. My darling, when you are grown up to be as tall as mamma, some one will perhaps find a way into that loving little heart. My little daughter, if divine love claims it, and our dear Lord wishes you to be all his own, do not hesitate, but gladly give your life as a sweet offering to him who has chosen you. Give him your whole heart without a fear. But if it is a human love which seeks to make my treasure all its own, think long and well and prayerfully, my child, before you give your heart into its keeping. And, O Assunta! remember, never marry one who does not cherish your faith as you do; who cannot kneel with you before the altar, and love you *in God*, even as you do him. I do not ask you to promise me this, for I feel that it would not be right to bind you by a promise which you cannot understand. Yet it is your dying mother's wish. But I must kiss the wondering expression away from those dear eyes. One of these days dear F. Joseph will remind you of my request when you are old enough to understand—will you not, father? But my little girl can remember that she is to be poor papa's dear comfort, and never forget the little prayer for him every day, that God will give to him— tell me what you ask for papa, my darling?"

The little Assunta answered through her sobs: "I want papa to love my blessed Mother Mary, and I ask God to make him. And, mamma, you said I must say faith; but I don't know what that means, except when I say it in the catechism, and so I ask God to make him as good as mamma is, and a saint just like S. Joseph in my picture; and I think he will, mamma, because you know he heard me once when I asked him to let me go to school to Sister Rose."

The mother smiled, as she replied:

" How earnestly I hope so, my daughter! And papa has promised me to leave you with the good Sisters for a long time; so you must please him by being his good, obedient child. And now, my dear, precious little girl, kiss me—once again, my darling. I am very tired, and must rest. Perhaps, when I wake up, I shall see, instead of my darling's golden curls, the golden gates of the celestial city. When I am gone, Assunta, child of Mary, say every day: ' Dear Jesus, take mamma home soon.' Now call papa."

The priest, who had stood by in silence, came forward and lifted the poor bewildered child down from the bed. He saw that the strength which had until now supported the mother in this time of trial was quite exhausted. She uttered aloud the words, " Thy will, not mine "— words which, since that night beneath the olives in Gethsemane, express both the bitterness of the chalice and the ministry of the angel —then her eyes closed ; and though for a short time consciousness remained, they never opened until the resplendent majesty of the glorious humanity of her divine Lord burst upon her soul's vision.

As the child turned away to obey her mother's request, the priest began to repeat the *Proficiscere, anima Christiana*, with which the church so lovingly speeds her children on their last journey ; and for the first time she realized that her mother was indeed going from her. She crept softly from the room, only to rush away to her own little chamber, where, kneeling before the picture of S. Catherine, evermore associated with that great, first sorrow, she poured out the grief of her loving, childish heart in sobs and tears

And it was this scene which was again before the mental eye of the young girl as she stood there in the moonlight, herself so fair a picture. Her sainted mother, with her look of heavenly repose, and the angel-borne S. Catherine, blended themselves into one image in her mind, while the Holy Spirit was guiding her innocent soul. Suddenly an impulse seized her ; perhaps it was what mystic writers call an inspiration. Turning to her guardian, whose eyes had for some time been wonderingly fixed upon her, she hastily exclaimed : " One moment, my friend," and then walked quickly towards the chapel, where hung the lamp which told of the divine Presence upon the altar.

Mr. Carlisle was quite accustomed to what he was pleased to call her " pretty, graceful piety," and so, without surprise, he turned to exchange a few words with the patient sacristan, while, on her knees before her Lord, Assunta fought and conquered in the first real battle of her life. She realized fully now the love which seemed to offer her such human happiness, and she knew what it would cost her to refuse it. But then came the remembrance of her mother's dying words—" Unless he can love you *in God* "—and her heroic soul gathered up its strength for the consummation of the act of sacrifice. With one appealing, heart-breaking prayer for help, she bowed her head, and made to God the promise which her mother had not required from the child. And those alone who know what it is to offer up the crown and joy of life in sacrifice can understand the peace and rest which came to her troubled heart, even through the vision of a life robbed of its brightness.

Absorbed as she was, she had forgotten the world outside and its distracting claims until her guardian stood beside her.

" *Petite*," he whispered, " in thy orisons be all my sins remembered. But since the list is somewhat long, I think you must not wait to recall them now. Your one moment has lengthened into fifteen by my watch, and I have exhausted my powers of eloquence in my endeavors to charm that good old man into forgetfulness of the flight of time. Can you not leave heaven for earth and us poor mortals? There are so many angels up in heaven, they can afford to spare us our only one."

Rising hastily, Assunta exclaimed: "I have been very thoughtless, and you, as always, kind and patient. We will go at once."

Her gentle apologies to the old sacristan added value to the gift she slipped into his hand; and as he closed and locked the door behind them, he muttered to himself: "She is a saint anyhow, if she is an American."

As they passed down the steps towards the carriage, Mr. Carlisle suddenly stopped, exclaiming: "Why, child, what is the matter? You have the real martyr-look on your face. I read there, as in a book, that combination of suffering and triumph which we see in pictures, representing those times when men were not so chivalrous as now, and inflicted persecutions on account of a devotion which is so natural to your sex, and which," he added, laughing, "is so particularly becoming where the woman is young and pretty. But," he said uneasily, "I cannot see that expression in the face of my *petite.* Sunshine is her element; and the cloud which should cast a shadow upon her life would burst forth in thunder over mine. But what is it? Has the moonlight enchanted you?"

"No, dear friend," replied Assunta, endeavoring to speak gayly. "Enough that you grant me the triumph. The laurel wreath is a woman's ambition. You need not bestow the martyr's palm until it is deserved. And now let us go home."

"Indeed, that is the one thing in this world which I do not intend to do, at least at present. Thanks to my good sister's well-timed headache, we have a rare opportunity to follow out our own sweet will in the most unconventional manner. There is no respect for the world

and the propriety Clara preaches left in me to-night. I, for one, shall take advantage of the absence of that inconvenient third party and her friend Mrs. Grundy to drive to the Colosseum. If you decline to accompany me, I will just remind you that the walk home is somewhat long and the hour somewhat late." Saying which, he gave his order to the coachman, and took his seat beside Assunta in the barouche. After a short silence, he continued:

"The cat-is-away sensation takes me back to my school-boy days. Though I confess dear Clara to be the very best of the tabby race, still she does show her claws sometimes when I propose an escapade that shocks her sense of what is becoming at the advanced age of thirty-five. To see the Colosseum to-night is not to be resisted. There is no dampness whatever in the air, and the moon has risen just high enough to make the shadows perfect."

"I think," said Assunta, "that it must be a very guilty conscience that needs so many words in its justification. I, for my part, am so strong in innocence that I will meet Clara on my return with an unblushing brow—to speak poetically—as far as the Colosseum is concerned. The evening is certainly lovely enough to reduce even your friend Mrs. Grundy to a spirit of meek acquiescence. 'How beautiful is night!' Do you remember the first lines of *Thalaba?* It must have been just such a moon as this that suggested the opening of that remarkable poem."

"Did you not read it to me? How can you ask, then, if I remember? However, I did not hear it then for the first time. The dogs, with their human eyes, made a great impression even upon my boyish mind. But here we are." And jumping down from the carriage, he held out his hand to her.

One moment she hesitated; for, by that instinct which is the shadow of a coming event, she felt that her trial was not yet at an end. But if it must come, why not then? She might never again be so prepared to meet it. There is a fervor of heroism which immediately succeeds a sacrifice that makes us strong to endure. If there is a step to be taken, it is better not to wait until the inevitable reaction is upon us with its enervating influence.

The hesitation was too instantaneous to be remarked, and Assunta allowed her guardian to assist her to alight; and placing her arm within his, they passed the sentinel, and entered the vast amphitheatre. It was indeed a perfect Roman night; and, to an artistic eye, nothing could be more imposing than the strong contrast between the deep gloom beneath those bewildering arches, which threw their dark shadows across the open arena, and the brightness of a winter's moon. The two walked towards the centre, and seated themselves upon the steps of the large cross which rises in the midst of this mighty relic of heathen Rome. Assunta almost shuddered, as if at an evil omen, when she observed that she had unconsciously placed herself so that the shadow of the cross fell directly upon her, and stretched out its unnatural length at her feet. But even had she been superstitiously inclined, she might well have felt that no place could be so safe and sure as beneath the shadow of the cross; it rested so protectingly on her young head, seeming to stand between her and evil. Soon she realized this, and checked the impulse which, alas!

too many of us follow when suddenly we find ourselves close under Calvary—the mount whose crown is a cross, and whose cross is salvation—the impulse to move "out of the shadow into the sun," out of the cloud which wraps us about in love into the sunlight with which the world seeks to dazzle us into forgetfulness.

Gradually they fell into a quiet conversation, the beauty of the scene, the many associations of the past which cling to these ancient walls, furnishing ample topics. At last Mr. Carlisle, turning suddenly to Assunta, said:

"And how many years is it since your poor father summoned me to his bedside, and told me of the troublesome charge I should find in the convent, to be transferred into my hands when the patience of the nuns had reached the limit of endurance, and my young lady the age of eighteen?"

"It is five years since, my most ungracious and ungrateful guardian. But you will soon be released from duty. The fifteenth of next August will be my twenty-first birthday. It was because I came into the world on the Feast of the Assumption that my dear mother gave me the name, at which all her good, practical American friends wondered and held up their hands. Well, on that morning I shall offer you freedom, and I shall expect to hear you exclaim, quoting your favorite Shakespeare, 'For this relief much thanks!'"

"And I suppose you will think," said Mr. Carlisle, somewhat bitterly, "that it will be enough, after all these years, to say, 'You have been kind to me, my guardian, quite like a father; I am very grateful, and hope that we may meet again'; and with a good-by and a pretty courtesy shake off the shackles, and take yourself, with all your sunshine, out into the world to make bright the life of others, forgetting him whose life you alone have the power to darken by absence. Ah! child," he said, his tone changing to tender earnestness, "do you not know with what tie I would bind you to me so that no age could have the right to separate us? Do you think that it is as a father that I love you? That might have been once; but now it is the love of a man of thirty-five, who for the first time has found his ideal of woman realized. Assunta, do I ask too much? When that day comes of which you speak, will you not give me the right to devote my life to you? You were looking forward to the day which was to give you freedom; and you hesitate to put yourself under bondage? If you knew my love for you, you would believe that I ask but the right to love and protect you always. Have I been so severe a guardian that you dare not trust me as a husband? Assunta, you do not speak. If you cannot love me now, will you not at least let me try to win your love?" And as he looked into the face which she now turned towards him, he exclaimed with a mingling of doubt and triumph, "Child, you do love me!"

It was well for Assunta that she had fought her battle beforehand, else she could hardly have hoped to conquer now. "My dear, kind friend," she said sadly, "I would have given much to spare you this. It seems indeed a poor return for all you have been to me to reject the love for which I am very grateful. But it must be so. I cannot marry you, Mr. Carlisle."

The triumph in his face faded;

but, fortunately for his diminishing hope, doubt remained

"*Petite*," he said, "I have taken you by surprise. Do not give me your answer now. Let me take home to-night but a hope and your promise to reconsider your hasty decision, and I will try to be content. But you are so cold, so calm, Assunta. Can it be that I have entirely deceived myself, that perhaps some other"— He paused.

"I am calm, my friend," she answered, "because there is no struggle of indecision in my mind. There is very great regret that I must give you pain, and it costs me more than you know to do so. I entreat you to be generous— more generous than I have been to you—and end this trying conversation."

"I cannot end it without one question more; pardon me if I am wrong in asking it. Assunta, there is something that I do not understand. You do not say that you could not love me, but that you cannot marry me. Who or what is it, then, that comes between us?"

"God!" And she spoke the word so reverently that for one moment Mr. Carlisle was subdued and silent. Then the bitterness which was always latent in his nature gained the ascendency, as he replied:

"Some interference of your church, I suppose."

Assunta was not a saint, and her previous emotion had weakened her powers of self-control, for she spoke with unusual spirit.

"Yes, the church does interfere, thank God, to save her children, else were she no true mother." Then, a little ashamed of her warmth of defence, she continued, without seeming to notice Mr. Carlisle's ironical repetition of her words " *save* her children " :

" You will no doubt consider me fanatical, but you have a right to know why I refuse the love which I value so much, and which, at the same time, I must beg you to forget. I can never marry one who is not of my faith. I believe that, in a true marriage, there must be more than the tie of human love— there must be the union of soul and the blessing of the church. And more than this, there is the insuperable barrier of a solemn promise made to God in consequence of my dying mother's last request. Need I say more? And must I lose my best friend because I can only respect and love him ' as friends love '? I had not looked for so great a sacrifice." And for the first time the tears stood in her eyes and her voice trembled. She waited for a few minutes, but no reply came. Then, noticing that the moon had risen above arch and wall, and, pouring its light full upon the open arena, had sent the shadows back to their hiding-places, she said gently :

" Mr. Carlisle, it is getting late. Shall we go home ?"

He started from his moody silence, and, taking in his the hand that rested on the cross, he said :

" Assunta, you are a noble girl; but," he added with a faint smile, " this conclusion does not make your words easier to bear. But you are shivering. Is it so cold? Come, we will go at once." And as he led the way towards the carriage, he wrapped her shawl closer about her, saying, " My poor child, how thoughtless I have been !"

Once seated, there was again silence until they reached the entrance of the villa. As they ascended the long stair-case, Mr.

Carlisle paused. His old tenderness of manner had all returned, and he was her guardian, and nothing more, as he said :

" Assunta, I have not been generous. I have taken an unfair advantage of my position, and have told you what I had not intended you should know until you were released from all obligation to me. My child, will you trust your friend and guardian to be only that until next August shall make you free ? I cannot promise to give up all hope, but I will not repeat what I have said to-night. Can you forgive me so far as to go back to our old relations? Will you trust me ?"

" Most gladly," said Assunta. " I feel as if my friend, whom I had mourned as lost, has been restored to me. And, Mr. Carlisle, the day will come when we will both look back without regret upon the decision which was made to-night under the shadow of the cross."

" I hope so, even while I doubt, fair prophetess."

But his thought was of the time when he might even yet win that stern conscience to his views, and then indeed he could afford to think without regret of a past disappointment ; while she was thinking of that sweet providence of God which, in compensation for sacrifice, always lets us see in the end that all things are for the best to those who can wait and trust.

Mr. Carlisle opened the drawing-room door, and entered an apartment which had the rare combination of elegance and comfort, of art and home. Mrs. Grey, his pretty, widowed sister, was fond of what she called the " dim religious,' and therefore the candles were not lighted ; but a blazing wood-fire contributed light as well as warmth, while the silver urn upon the side table hissed out an impatient welcome.

Mrs. Grey herself was lying upon the sofa in the most charmingly artistic costume and attitude; and the injured manner she assumed rather added to her fascination. She idolized her only brother; and when, after a short wedded happiness of two years, he had offered the childless widow a home with him, she had gladly accepted; and after a few months of becoming weeds and retirement, she was so far consoled as to mitigate her crape, and allow her brother's visitors to gaze from a distance upon her charms. The mitigating process had gone on until she was now the gayest of the gay, except when an occasional headache reminded her that she was mortal, and others that amiability is not to be found in perfection in this world any more than any other virtue. She was too frivolous to satisfy her brother's deeper nature, but he was as fond of her as her affection for him deserved. She had taken the orphan Assunta into her heart as if she had been a sister; though she insisted that the position of matron to a beautiful young girl was no sinecure.

"Really, Severn," she exclaimed, as he seated himself beside the sofa, "you must have thought it very entertaining for me to stay alone five mortal hours with only my poor head for company."

"Dear Clara, if I had dreamed you would be doomed to such a dearth of companionship, I should not have gone at all."

"Hush! No impertinence," she said. "Where have you left Assunta?"

"Here I am," said the young girl, entering the room at the same moment, and answering for herself. "And how is your head, Clara? I hope you have not been suffering all this time."

"Your sympathy is very pretty and pleasing, Assunta; but, indeed, it is of too mushroom a growth to be very consoling. Confess that this is the first time I have been in your thoughts since you left the house. But," she exclaimed, suddenly recollecting herself, "you have been out alone all this time. Dear me! I hope you did not meet any one you knew, for what would they think? Where have you been?" And as she spoke, she rose from the couch, and went about the womanly occupation of making tea.

"We went to the Colosseum," replied her brother; "and truly the night was so lovely that if it had not been for you and your head, who knows but we might have wandered about until the Roman police lighted upon us, and committed us to the care of the Holy Office as vagabonds?"

"Nonsense! I would risk you with Assunta anywhere, as far as that is concerned. She is Papal protection in herself. She is wrapped about in the yellow and white, metaphorically speaking. Besides, I believe it is not exactly the province of the Holy Office to deal with vagabonds, but with heretics."

"And what am I?"

"Oh! I don't know anything about religion. Has Assunta been calling you a heretic?"

"Assunta never calls me hard names," he answered, and he could not forbear adding under his breath: "But she has made me count the cost of unbelief."

"Has she been trying to convert you?" asked his persistent sister.

"She has offered me every in-
ducement," was his reply.

"Assunta, here is your tea,"
called Mrs. Grey; for the young
girl had been arranging her music
in another part of the large drawing-room during the conversation.

"Yes; and she needs it very
much, poor child," said Mr. Carlisle, placing a chair for her. " I
was so selfish that I did not even
notice it was cold until she was
quite chilled through. You find
your own head such poor company
that you must go with us next
time, Clara, and take better care
of us."

And then they relapsed into a
quiet tea-drinking; after which,
and the removal of the various articles which constitute the tea service, Mrs. Grey returned to her
sofa, while Assunta went to the
piano, and played some of Mendels-
sohn's "Songs without Words," and
Mr. Carlisle sat in deep thought before the fire.

It was a state of things which
Clara could not endure long. Anything like constraint gave her the
sensation of a caged bird, and she
began at once to beat her wings
against imaginary bars.

" I never knew such stupid people. Severn, do please light my
candle. I am sure I trust my
dreams will be more agreeable, or I
shall die of *ennui.* Good-night,
dear Assunta. Do not fatigue me
by your efforts to rival the larks in
early rising, if you have any mercy."
And looking the very picture of
lovely discontent—if so paradoxi-
cal an expression may be allowed
—she retired to her own room.

Assunta extended her hand as
usual to her guardian. He held it
a moment, and then said : " Good-
night, *petite ;* we will begin anew to-
morrow "; and then he returned to
his arm-chair, which he did not
leave for many hours. Assunta
was very tired; but it was rather
with the weight of the cross she
had lifted upon her shoulders than
from any physical fatigue. She
soon dismissed her maid, and, like a
victorious soldier wearied with the
conflict, she fell into a dreamless
sleep, not, however, until she had
returned thanks for the victory to
the God of battles.

II.

COR CORDIUM.

It was an established custom of
the household of Villa Moroni to
be quite independent of each other
until the twelve o'clock breakfast
afforded occasion for an agreeable
reunion. However pleasant an
early family gathering may be in
many home circles, where the
habits and pursuits of all are entirely dissimilar and incongruous
we escape much of the roughness
of life by not attempting too early
an interchange of forced courtesy.
Indeed, in Mr. Carlisle's family it
would have been difficult to effect
an earlier meeting than the one
which suited all parties so well
Mrs. Grey declared that the morning hours with Morpheus were absolutely necessary to her peace of
mind. And certainly the drowsy
god must have been lavish of
bright visions during those hours
when the sun was so carefully excluded from the apartment of the
fair sleeper; for when at last he
permitted the pretty lady to awake
from her dreams, she came from
the hands of her maid into the
outer world the very quintessence

of amiability and freshness. Who would feel assured of such a result had she seen the sun rise? True, it might occur to some persons who take severe views of life to wonder what her soul was doing all that time; but it never did to her. The supernatural was to her a *terra incognita*. She had skimmed over her sorrow as sea-birds over the waves of the ocean, scarcely bearing away a drop on their spread wings. The waters had never gone over her soul and forced her to cry from out of the depths to the God whom she acknowledged in theory, but persistently ignored in practice. Yet she was so lovely and affectionate, and besides, when she chose to exert herself, she had so much good sense withal, by all means let her enjoy life's sunshine, and pluck its sweetest roses, carefully guarding her dainty fingers from contact with the hidden thorns. But why waste our time in moralizing over one who would smile in unconsciousness of our meaning if we uttered our thoughts aloud, and charm the frown from our brow by some pretty petulance?

Mr. Carlisle understood as little of the supernatural as his frivolous sister. But he had a deep, earnest nature, which could not be satisfied with the mere outside of life. Mental food he must have, though it may be a question whether the mind is ever fully nourished when the soul is starving. He therefore, after taking his coffee and smoking his cigar, devoted his morning hours to reading or writing in the cosey little room he used as a library.

The carriage was thus left at Assunta's disposal ; and she usually availed herself of it to assist at Mass, accompanied by her maid; and often an errand of mercy or charitable visit was accomplished before her return. It was her guardian's wish that she should never walk about the city, unless accompanied by himself, else she would many times have preferred to show her American independence by taking a morning stroll with her faithful Marie.

The morning after the eventful visit to the Colosseum was Friday, and on that day Assunta was accustomed to make her confession and receive Holy Communion. She awoke with a stunned feeling, as if recovering from a blow. It was still very early, but, remembering the duties before her, she arose quickly. She was so glad that it was Friday ; for good F. Joseph would certainly be in the confessional, as he always expected her and she felt the need of his counsel. It was the same F. Joseph du Pont who had placed her beside her dying mother, but who had shortly afterwards returned to Rome. When, a few weeks since, she had arrived in the Eternal City, he had welcomed her as a dear child, and she loved and respected him as a true spiritual father. The sun was just rising when she entered the carriage and drove to the Gesù. Her confession was soon made, and after the Precious Blood had poured its healing drops upon her soul through the words of the absolution, she said : " Father, can you spare me a few minutes more this morning? I want your advice."

" Certainly, my child," answered the good priest. " It is nearly an hour before my Mass. How can I help you ? "

" Last evening," said Assunta in a low voice, " I did what I believed to be right ; but the morning light has only confused my mind, and I see nothing clearly. Father, Mr. Carlisle, my guardian, asked me to marry him."

"And you, my child?" questioned the priest somewhat anxiously.

"I had been prepared somewhat to expect it. I had thought of my mother's request, and remembered that it was in accordance with the teaching of the church, and I was impelled to fortify myself by a promise to Almighty God to fulfil to the letter my dear mother's wish. Therefore, when the question came, I could only refuse."

"It cost you something to do this, I can see, my poor child, and this morning you are suffering from the revenge our human nature takes upon us when we have done it violence. Let us look at the matter calmly before God. I believe that you are right, but it will help you to look at both sides of the question. It is a reasonable service that God requires of us; and, be very sure, he never leads us to the altar of sacrifice without bestowing upon us the strength and generosity we need to place our offering upon it. Perhaps you were a little too impulsive in binding yourself by anything like a vow. We must always be very careful not to mistake impulse for inspiration. However, as I understand you, your mind was already decided, and the promise to God was to act as a protection to yourself against your own human weakness. Am I right?"

"Partly, father," replied Assunta "and yet, as I knelt before the Blessed Sacrament, I felt that the sacrifice was required of me in a way I thought I could not mistake."

"Then, my child, doubtless the Holy Spirit has inspired it for some end that we do not now see. But, aside from that, without that additional and conclusive obstacle in the way of such a marriage, I think you acted rightly. Our holy mother, the church, is very wise, as well as very lenient; and it is with great reluctance that she risks the soul of one of her precious children by placing it under the constant influence of one without faith. It is very true that while there is wisdom in knowing how to keep a rule, there is still greater wisdom in knowing when judiciously to make the exception. And I confess that, from a human point of view, yours would seem to be an exceptional case. You are quite alone in the world; and your guardian has been, and no doubt would always be, a faithful friend. As a man, I esteem him highly for his many noble qualities. The world will unquestionably look upon such a marriage as eminently fitting; and so it would be, but for the one thing which is so important. We, however, cannot act upon human principles, as if this world were all. It was not without reason, my child, that your poor mother said those last words to you. When she was married, her faith was as strong, her life as true and pure, as yours. But your father's intellect was powerful, and her love for him so great that she yielded to him until she nearly lost her soul. God be blessed for his mercy, she had the grace to die as a saint, and is now, as I hope, in heaven. But I have seen her in an agony of remorse such as I should grieve indeed to witness in this dear child of hers. The last two years of her life after her return to her faith were truly years of martyrdom, passed in the struggle to reconcile those duties which never should conflict—her love of God and duty to her husband. It was from the very depths of her own sad experience that she pleaded with her little girl. My child, that mother is praying for you now."

"I believe it, father," said Assunta, deeply moved by this story of her beloved mother, which she heard for the first time.

"So, my child, the past is all as it should be; and now for the future. May God grant you the grace to be always as good and brave as you were last night! I would not discourage you, and yet I must remind you that the sacrifice is only begun. It is not likely that your guardian, with only human motives to urge him, will give up so easily where his heart is engaged. He will, of course, do all he can to turn you from your purpose, and no doubt your own heart will sometimes plead on his side. Here lies your further trial. And yet I cannot, as under other circumstances I should do, advise you to shun the temptation. You cannot leave your guardian's care until you are of age; therefore you must face the trial. But I trust you entirely, my child—that is, I trust to the purity of your heart and the power of grace that is in you to guide your actions, even your very thoughts. You must try to be as you have been before; try to forget the lover in the guardian. Avoid coldness of manner as a safeguard; for it would only place you in an unnatural position, and would inevitably strengthen in the end the feelings you would conquer. It is not easy to give an exact rule of conduct. Your own good sense will teach you, and God will be with you. And, my child, you must pray for your guardian, and at the same time it must be without any future reference to yourself in connection with him. Is this too

hard for you? Do your best, and grace will do the rest. By remembering him before God you will learn to purify your feelings towards him—to supernaturalize them; and by committing your future unreservedly to the loving providence of God, your prayer will be a constant renewal of the act of sacrifice you have made. Make it heroic by perseverance. Do I explain myself clearly, my child?"

"Yes, father, perfectly so; and I feel so much comforted and strengthened."

"Well, these are but the words of your father, spoken out of his love for you. Go now, child, and prepare to receive your divine Lord, and listen for the words of peace and comfort he will speak to your soul. To him I commend you with all confidence. One thing more—remember that there is nothing which helps us so much in such a trial as acts of charity towards the poor and the suffering. I know that you never fail in this respect; but now especially I would urge you to forget yourself in sympathy for others as occasion offers, though you must always recognize those claims which your position in society entails upon you. Come to me freely whenever you feel that I can help you. God bless you! I shall remember you in the Holy Sacrifice."

The good priest went to vest himself for Mass, while the young girl returned to the place before the altar where Marie was patiently awaiting her. She was herself a pious woman, and time spent in church never seemed long to her.

When the Mass was over and her thanksgiving ended, Assunta returned home with her heart lightened of its burden. She dressed herself for breakfast with her usual care and taste, and, finding that it still wanted half an hour or more before the great gun of Sant' Angelo would boom out the mid-day signal, she seated herself at the piano, and song and ballad followed each other in quick succession. Her voice and manner were in harmony with herself. Her music soothed, but never excited. It had not the dangerous power to quicken the pulse and thrill the heart with passionate emotion, but it roused the better feelings, while it conveyed to the listener a restful, satisfied impression which ambitious, brilliant performers rarely impart. She was just beginning Cherubini's beautiful Ave Maria when Mr. Carlisle entered the room.

"Here is our early bird welcoming us in true songster fashion. Do not stop yet, *petite,*

" My soul in an enchanted boat,
Which, like a sleeping swan, doth float
Upon the silver waves of thy sweet singing."

But as Assunta had already left the piano to greet her guardian and his sister, he continued :

"By the way, Clara, my quotation has suggested to me an answer to your question. Assunta, my fickle sister, who a week ago was ready to live and die in a picture-gallery, has just now assured me that the very mention of a picture or statue is a fatigue to her ; and she has mercilessly compelled me to find some new and original bit of sight-seeing for to-day. We cannot, of course, visit any church, since the Holy Father is, unfortunately for her, not an iconoclast. But, Clara, what do you say to making a Shelley day of it ? We will take *Prometheus Unbound* with us to the Baths of Caracalla, and there, on the very spot which inspired the poem, we can read parts of it. And when we are tired, we can prolong our

drive to the cemetery, and visit Shelley's grave, as a proper conclusion. How do you like the plan ?"

"Oh !" said Mrs. Grey, "it will be deliciously sentimental ; only breakfast is announced, and I am in a famished condition. I was up so early this morning. It must have been before eleven when that stupid girl called me, and it is an hour since I took my coffee."

"Poor Clara !" said Mr. Carlisle, "your condition is truly pitiable. I should think you might find the almshouse a pleasant change." Mrs. Grey seemed only amused at her brother's sarcasm, when suddenly she checked her silvery laugh, and, springing from the table, at which she had just seated herself, she went towards Assunta with such a pretty, penitential air that she was quite irresistible.

"My dear child," she exclaimed, "speaking of almshouses reminds me of something you will never forgive. Promise me not to scold, and I will devote myself henceforth to the cultivation of my memory."

"What is it ?" asked Assunta, smiling at her earnestness. "I am sure such a pleading look would force forgiveness from a stone."

"Well, then, for my confession, since you absolve me beforehand. While you were out yesterday morning that miserable woman of yours sent word that she was sick, and something about not having a mouthful of bread in the house. I forget the whole message. My maid saw the girl who came, and I promised to tell you. But you remember my wretched headache. You forgave me, you know."

Assunta looked both grieved and vexed for a moment, and then she controlled herself enough to say :

"I must attach a condition to my forgiveness, Clara. Will you let me drive to the house on oux way to the baths ? I will only detain you a few minutes."

"Heavens ! Assunta, you will not go there yourself?" exclaimed the astonished Clara. "I dare say it is some filthy hole, and perhaps the woman may have fever. Send a messenger with some money. I'll give her five dollars."

"Thank you. I will take the five dollars to her willingly," replied the young girl; "but I will take myself too. I can easily walk," she added, looking for permission to her guardian, as the occasion was exceptional.

Displeasure at his sister's thoughtlessness was evident in Mr. Carlisle's tone, as he said :

"You will go in the carriage, Assunta, and I will accompany you. We will return for Clara after the visit. Giovanni, order a basket of provisions to be put up before one o'clock, and be ready yourself to go with us and take charge of it ; and now that the matter is settled, we will have some breakfast."

Poor Mrs. Grey looked disconcerted ; but she thought it her duty to make a further protest.

"You surely will not wear that dress, Assunta ? It will never be fit to put on again."

Mr. Carlisle laughed outright at this new objection, while Assunta said with a smile :

"Why, Clara, have you so soon forgotten your admiration of Mrs. Browning's *Court Lady*, who put on her silks and jewels, and went to the hospital as to the court of the king? On the same principle I should be arrayed in purple and fine linen, for I am going to the court of the King of kings; and if I am not very much mistaken, this same poor woman, whose contact you fear so much, will find her

place very near to the throne in the ranks of the celestial nobility. However, I should be sorry to ruin my new dress, as you predict, and I will be very careful."

The breakfast was soon despatched, the carriage came punctually to the door, and Mr. Carlisle and his ward drove rapidly towards the miserable home of the poor woman, who, in the midst of her poverty, possessed a faith at which Assunta often wondered.

"You are very kind, Mr. Carlisle," she said. "I am sorry I have given you so much trouble."

"In this case," he replied, "the trouble is not altogether disinterested. I must myself find out what the sickness is before I can allow you to enter the house. I cannot let you run the risk of fever or any other malignant disease. You see I came as a sort of police."

"But," said Assunta, touched by his thoughtful care of her, at the same time anxious not to be prevented making what amends she could, "I am so accustomed to visiting the sick, I do not think there can be any danger."

"My child," he said, "as long as your life can be guarded by me, it shall be done. You are under obedience still, you know." She dared not insist ; and, indeed, at the same moment they reached the wretched dwelling. After exacting from her the promise to remain in the carriage, Mr. Carlisle ascended the broken stair-case. In a few moments he returned, and, without saying a word, he took the basket from Giovanni, and again went up the stairs. As he reappeared, he said to the coachman :

"Drive on slowly. I will walk a little. You must not go in, Assunta."

He continued to follow the carriage at a quick pace for a quarter of a mile; then he hailed the driver, and took his seat beside the wondering girl, saying:

"I thought it would be best to give myself an airing after leaving that room. *Petite,* the poor woman died two hours since of a terrible fever. You could have done nothing, and, as usual, Clara was mistaken in the message. They sent word to their 'guardian angel,' as they are pleased to call a certain little friend of mine, of their suffering and need, but with the particular warning that she should on no account direct her flight that way, lest she should expose the unangelic part of her nature to contagion. I left the basket, and money enough to supply all the temporary wants of the children; but it was a dreadful scene," he added with a shudder.

He had striven to speak lightly at first, because he saw the distress in Assunta's anxious face and tearful eyes. But his own feelings were strangely stirred, and he forgot his self-control, as he continued, in a voice low and husky from the very intensity of emotion:

"Child, I am in an agony of terror at the bare thought of what might have been the result had you been exposed to that atmosphere, whose every breath was poison. My God! when I think of the danger you have so narrowly escaped. Oh! if I might always shield this dear life at any risk to mine."

"My life is in God's hands," said Assunta coldly, as she gently disengaged the hand which her guardian had clasped in his, as if he would show, by the action, the power of his love to avert any and every evil which might threaten her.

Poor child! she longed to ask more about the woman's death, and especially to express her gratitude to Mr. Carlisle for his kindness; but she dared not face his present mood. However, as they again reached the villa, she said hurriedly and in a tone full of anxiety:

"Mr. Carlisle, you have exposed yourself to great danger, and I do not forget that it was for my sake. I shall not be satisfied unless you promise me that you will take every possible precaution to avoid any future evil consequences. I should never forgive myself if any harm came to you."

Her eyes lowered beneath the look he for one moment fixed upon her appealing face; then, with the exclamation, "An unblessed life is of little consequence," he sprang from the carriage, and, saying to Giovanni, "I will summon Mrs. Grey," he dashed up the stone staircase.

Assunta sank back with a feeling almost of despair at the task before her. Even if she had not to struggle with her own heart, it would have been hard enough to steer the right, straight course between these contradictory moods in her guardian; one moment so tender and thoughtful, the next so full of bitterness. How could she reconcile them? How should she ever be able to bear her burden, if this weight were added to it day by day?

Assunta possessed the gift—which, advanced to a higher degree, might be termed the natural science of the saints—of receiving religious impressions and suggestions from the natural objects about her. Now, as in a listless manner she looked around, her eyes fell upon the snow-crowned hills which bound the Roman horizon, and rested there. She had no thought of the classic associations which throng those mountain-sides and nestle in the valleys. She needed strength, and instantly the words were present to her mind: " I have lifted up my eyes to the mountains, from whence help shall come to me." And following out the consoling train of thought, she passed from those peaceful Roman hills to Jerusalem and the mountains which surround it, even " as the Lord is round about his people." Then, by a natural transition, she turned her thoughts to the poor woman who had just left behind her poverty, privation, and suffering, and, accompanied only by that hope and love which had endured and survived them all, had entered, so she confidently hoped, into the possession of God—the Beatific Vision. What a contrast between the temporal and eternal!

Her silent requiem for the departed soul was interrupted by Mrs. Grey's bright presence and merry voice.

" I cannot imagine what you have been doing to Severn," she said; " but he is in one of his unaccountable conditions of mind, and declares that he will not go to drive—pressing business, etc. I am sure we can do without him very well, all but the reading part, which had been assigned to him. It is so late, at any rate, that perhaps we had better give up the baths, and drive at once to the cemetery. You see I have secured an excellent substitute for our recreant cavalier," she added, as a gentleman emerged from the massive doorway. " Come, Mr. Sinclair, we are waiting for you."

There was just a shade of stateliness in Assunta's manner as she greeted the somewhat elegant man of the world, who seated himself opposite to her. She would gladly

have been dispensed from the drive altogether, feeling as she did then; nevertheless, she submitted to the necessity which could hardly be avoided.

" Truly, Miss Howard," said Mr. Sinclair, as they drove away, " I begin to believe the ancient goddesses no myths. Flora herself would find in you a worthy rival. It is not often that I have the happiness to be placed opposite two such lovely ladies."

" Very good for a *finale*, Mr. Sinclair," replied Mrs. Grey; " but if you were to speak your mind, you would be calling me Ceres, or something else suggestive of the ' sere and yellow leaf.' "

" That is a gross injustice, not only to me, but to yourself," answered Mr. Sinclair in his most gallant tone. " Have not the poets ever vied with each other in disputes as to the respective merits of spring, with its freshness, and the rich bloom of early summer? And permit me to add that neither has yet been able to claim a victory. In such a presence it would be rash indeed for me to constitute myself a judge."

" Unwise, certainly," rejoined Mrs. Grey, " to take into your hand such an apple of discord. Women and goddesses are pretty much alike, and the fate of Paris might be yours. Remember the ten years' siege."

" Ah!" said Mr. Sinclair, " there you do not frighten me. Welcome the ten years' siege, if during that time the fair Helen were safe within the walls. After ten years one might perhaps be reconciled to a surrender and a change of scene, since even the lovely Trojan's beauty must have lost the freshness of its charms by that time."

" O faithless men!" said Mrs.

Grey, very much as if she were pronouncing an eulogy.

"Miss Howard," said Mr. Sinclair, "you are silent. Does our classic lore fail to enlist your interest, or are you studying antiquities?"

"Pardon me," replied Assunta; "it was rude in me to be so abstracted. I must excuse myself on the ground of sympathy for suffering which I have been unable to alleviate."

"By the way, Assunta," exclaimed Mrs. Grey, "how did you find your *protégée?*"

"She is dead," replied the young girl, softly.

"Oh! I am so sorry. How very sudden! Mr. Sinclair, you were telling me about the Braschi ball when Severn interrupted us. When did you say it is to be?"

"In about three weeks," replied the gentleman. "I hope that you ladies will be there. Our American blondes are greatly in demand among so many black eyes. You are going, are you not?"

"Most certainly we shall," answered Mrs. Grey with ready confidence, the future being to her but a continuation of to-day. The cloud that might appear on her horizon must be much larger than a man's hand to turn her attention to it from the sunshine immediately about her.

And so, between pleasantry and gossip, the time passed until the carriage stopped at the gate of the cemetery.

"You have chosen a very serious termination to your afternoon's drive, Mrs. Grey," said Mr. Sinclair, as he assisted the ladies to alight. "I always carefully avoid whatever reminds me of my latter end."

"Let me play Egyptian coffin, then, for once," replied Mrs. Grey, but with a merry laugh that belied her words. "I will lead you to a contemplation of the fate of genius. I dote on Shelley, and so we have made a pilgrimage to his grave."

"You have every appearance of a pilgrim about to visit some sacred shrine," said Mr. Sinclair with an echo of her bright laugh. "Lead on, fair pilgrim princess; we humble votaries will follow wherever your illustrious steps may guide."

A small, horizontal slab, almost hidden beneath the pyramid of Caius Cestus—itself a tomb—is all that marks the resting-place of the gifted, ill-fated Shelley.

"Here is your shrine, my lady pilgrim," said Mr. Sinclair, as he removed some of the green overgrowth from off the inscription.

"Somebody make a suitable quotation," said Mrs. Grey. "You know we ought to be sentimental now."

Assunta at once rejoined:

"'How wonderful is Death—
Death and his brother, Sleep!'

Poor Shelley! But I do not like the inscription, Clara; or rather, I do not like such an expression on such a grave."

"What do you mean, dear Assunta?" said Mrs. Grey, looking at her as if she were talking Sanscrit.

"I think it is lovely. *Cor cordium*—the heart of hearts, is it not? I am sure nothing could be more appropriate."

"It does not seem to me appropriate," answered Assunta; "but then you know I always do have strange ideas—so you say. Why should *Cor cordium* be written over the ashes of one who was burned in true pagan fashion, and who, as I think, should rather be pitied for what he did not do, with his marvellous gifts, than loved for anything he has done?"

As she paused, a voice beside her exclaimed, "I am sure I cannot be mistaken. Is not this Miss Howard?"

Assunta turned and welcomed with a pleased surprise the young man who appeared so unexpectedly, then she presented him to her companions as Mr. Percival, of Baltimore, the brother of her only intimate school friend. He was tall and slender, not handsome, but with a manly and at the same time spiritual face. His eyes were his finest feature, but their beauty was rather that of the soul speaking through them. Assunta had not seen him since her school days at the convent, and then she had known him but slightly; so she was herself surprised at her ready recognition of him.

"And what has brought you so far away from my dear Mary?" she asked after the first greetings were over.

"I am on that most unenviable of expeditions—health-seeking," was his reply. "After graduating at college, the physician doomed me to a year of travel; and so we meet again at Shelley's grave!"

"Yes," said Mrs. Grey, "and Assunta and I were in the midst of an amiable quarrel when you found us out. I engage you on my side, Mr. Percival. It is about the inscription, which I like and Assunta does not, for reasons which are Greek to me."

"I was just going to say," said Assunta, "that *Cor cordium* seemed to me a sacred phrase wholly misapplied, though I have no doubt the irreverence was unintentional." And turning to Mr. Percival with that sort of spiritual instinct which teaches us where to look for sympathy even in a crowd, she continued:

"I hope that I am not guilty of the same want of reverence in thinking that if those words are to be inscribed on any grave, they should be written upon that stone which was rolled against the opening of the new sepulchre in the garden, and sealed with the Roman seal; for there the true *Cor cordium* was enclosed."

"Mr. Percival, I see that you have gone over to the ranks of the enemy," said Mrs. Grey; "and if Mr. Sinclair deserts me, I shall never be able to stand my ground against two such devotees."

"I am yours to command, Mrs. Grey," replied Mr. Sinclair with an expression of contempt in his tone. "But perhaps it might be well to transfer our operations to another battle-field. Allow me to offer you a souvenir of the occasion." And he handed to each of the ladies a sprig of green from beside the marble tablet.

Assunta quite simply shared hers with Mr. Percival at his request, and then they retraced their steps. As they approached the carriage, Mrs. Grey very cordially begged Mr. Percival to occupy the fourth seat, which he reluctantly declined, as also the invitation to visit them.

"For," said he, "to-morrow I start for Jerusalem; and, Miss Howard, when I am kneeling, as I hope to do, in the Chapel of the Holy Sepulchre, I shall remember you and those suggestive words of yours."

"You could not do me a greater kindness," replied Assunta, "than to remember me there. And when you return, what do you intend to do in the way of a profession? You see I am interested for Mary's sake. I know what her desire is."

An hour before, if this question had been proposed to him, Augustine Percival would have been able to give a probable answer. Though he had not yet decided, his few days' sojourn in Rome had stirred up within him a feeling which had been latent even in his boyhood, and from the depths of the Catacombs and beneath the lofty domes he had thought he heard an interior voice which whispered to him, "Follow me." And now a fair young face had made him hesitate, though, in justice to him, it must be added that no mere charm of beauty would have touched him for a moment. It was the purity and beauty of mind and soul, which he read and appreciated, that caused him to reply to Assunta's question:

"The matter of my future vocation will be left, I think, until my return."

Then, with many pleasant farewell words, they parted; and, except to mention the meeting to her friend in her next letter, Assunta thought no more of the thread of another life which had for a moment crossed hers.

That evening there were guests at the villa; and, as usual, Assunta's amiability was taxed by the repeated demands for music. As she sat absently turning over the leaves before her in one of the intervals, Mr. Carlisle came and stood beside her.

"*Petite*," he said, "I have been to see the authorities about the family of that poor woman who died to-day, and everything will be arranged comfortably for them; so you need feel no further anxiety!"

"How good you are, dear friend!"

she replied. "God bless you for it!"

"It is your blessing that I want," said he. "It was for you that I took the little trouble you are pleased to magnify into something deserving of gratitude."

"Please do not say so, Mr. Carlisle," said Assunta earnestly. "You do such noble acts, and then you spoil them by your want of faith."

The word was unfortunately chosen.

"If by faith," Mr. Carlisle replied, "you mean your Catholic faith, I cannot force myself to accept what does not appeal to my reason. I can respect an honest conviction in others when I am in turn treated with equal liberality; but," he added in a low tone, "I could hate the faith, so called, which comes between me and the fulfilment of my dearest wish."

There was a call for more music, and so there was no opportunity, even had there been inclination, for a reply. But as Assunta was passing wearily to her room after the last guest had departed, Mr. Carlisle stopped her, and, after his usual good-night, he said: "Forgive me, child. I have not been myself to-day."

Two weeks afterwards, when her guardian lay prostrate on his bed in the delirium of fever, Assunta remembered those few words, which at the time had given her pain, with that agony of sorrow which can only be aroused by the knowledge that the soul of one beloved may at any moment be launched upon the immeasurable ocean of eternity, rudderless and anchorless.

III.

IN EXTREMIS.

How slowly and drearily the time drags on, through all the weary length of hours and days, in a household where one has suddenly been stricken down from full life and health to the unconscious delirium of fever—when in hushed silence and with folded hands the watchers surround the sufferer with a loving anxiety; whose agony is in their helplessness to stay for one moment the progress of the disease, which seems possessed of a fiend-like consciousness of its own fatal power to destroy; when life and death hang in the balance, and at any moment the scale may turn, and in its turning may gladden loving hearts or break them; and, oh! above and beyond all, when through the clouding of the intellect no ray from the clear light of faith penetrates the soul, and the prostrate body, stretched upon its cross, fails to discern the nearness of that other cross upon this Calvary of suffering, from which flows in perennial streams the fountain of salvation! Oh! if in the ears, heedless of earthly sounds and words, there could be whispered those blessed words from Divine lips, "This day thou shalt be with me," what heart that loves would not rejoice even in its anguish, and unselfishly exclaim, "Depart, O Christian soul! I will even crush down my poor human love, lest its great longing should turn thy happy soul away from the contemplation of its reward, exceeding great—to be in Paradise, to be with Christ"? But, alas! there were two crucified within reach of those precious, saving drops, and one alone said, "Lord, remember me."

When the family of Mr. Carlisle first realized that the master of the house had indeed been prostrated by the fever which had proved so fatal in its ravages, they were stunned with surprise and grief. It was just the calamity, of all others the least expected, the heaviest to endure.

Mrs. Grey's affection for her brother was the deepest sentiment of her superficial nature, and for the time she was bowed down with sorrow; which, however, constantly found vent in words amd tears. She would rise from it soon, but not until the emergency had passed. She lived only in the sunshine; she lost herself when the clouds gathered. Assunta was the first to recover her calmness and presence of mind. Necessity made her strong; not so much for the sake of the sick man—that might come by and by—but for his sister, who clung to the young girl as to the last plank from the shipwreck of her bright, happy life. The physician was in constant attendance, and at the first he had proposed sending a nurse. But the faithful Giovanni had pleaded with so much earnestness to be allowed the privilege of attending his master that he was installed in the sick-room. And truly no better choice could have been made, for he combined the physical strength of the man with the gentleness of woman, and every service was rendered with the tenderness of that love which Mr. Carlisle had the rare power of inspiring and retaining in dependents. But only Assunta was able to quiet his wandering mind, and control the wild vagaries of delirium. It was a painful duty to strive to still the ringing of those bells, once so full of harmony, now " jangled, out of tune, and harsh." But, once recognizing where her duty lay, she would have performed it at any cost to herself.

Her good and devoted friend, F. du Pont, came to see her the second day of the illness, and brought sympathy and consolation in his very presence. She had so longed for him that his coming seemed an echo of her earnest wish—his words of comfort an answer to her prayers.

" Father," she said at length," you know all—the past and the present circumstances. May I not, in the p＿ nt necessity, and in spite of th＿ ast, forget all but the debt of gratitude I owe. and devote myself to my dear friend and guardian? You know," she added, as if there were pain in the remembrance, " it was Mr. Carlisle's care for me that exposed him to the fever. I would nurse him as a sister, if I might."

" My dear child," replied the priest, " I do not see how you could do less. From my knowledge of Mrs. Grey, I should consider her entirely unfit for the services of a sick-room. It seems, therefore, your plain duty to perform this act of charity. I think, my child, that the possible near-ness of death will calm all merely human emotion. Give that obedient little heart of yours into God's keeping, and then go to your duty as in his sight, and I am not afraid. The world will probably look upon what it may consider a breach of propriety with much less leniency than the angels. But human respect, always bad enough as a motive, is never so wholly bad as when it destroys the purity of our intention, and consequently the merit of our charity, at a time when, bending beneath the burden of some heavy trial, we are the more closely surrounded by God's love and protection. Follow the pillar of the cloud, my child. It is leading you away from the world."

" Father," said Assunta, and her voice trembled, while tears filled her eyes, " do you think he will die? Indeed, it is not for my own sake that I plead for his life. He is not prepared to go. Will you not pray for him, father? Oh! how gladly would I give my life as the price of his soul, and trust myself to the mercy of God!"

" And it is to that mercy you must trust him, my poor child. Do you, then, think that his soul is dearer to you than to Him who died to save it? You must have more confidence. But I have not yet told you the condition I must impose upon your position as nurse. It is implicit obedience to the physician, and a faithful use of all the precautions he recommends. While charity does sometimes demand the risk or even the sacrifice of life, we have no right to take the matter into our own hands. I do not apprehend any danger for you, if you will follow the good doctor's directions. I will try to see him on my way home. Do you promise?"

"Yes, father," said Assunta, with a faint smile; "you leave me no alternative."

"But I have not yet put a limit to your obedience. You are excited and worn out this afternoon, and I will give you a prescription. It is a lovely day, almost spring-like; and you are now, this very moment, to go down into the garden for half an hour—and the time must be measured by your watch, and not by your feelings. Take your rosary with you, and as you walk up and down the orange avenue let no more serious thoughts enter your mind than the sweet companionship of the Blessed Mother may suggest. You will come back stronger, I promise you."

"You are so kind, father," said Assunta gratefully. "If you knew what a blessing you bring with you, you would take compassion on me, and come soon again."

"I shall come very soon, my child; and meanwhile I shall pray for you, and for all, most fervently. But, come, we will walk together as far as the garden. And summoning the priest who had accompanied him, and who had been looking at the books in the library during this conversation, they were about to descend the stairs, when Mrs. Grey came forward to meet them.

"O F. du Pont!" she exclaimed impetuously, "will you not come and look at my poor brother, and tell me what you think of him? They say priests know so much." And then she burst into tears.

F. Joseph tried to soothe her with hopeful words, and, when they reached the door of the darkened chamber, she was again calm. The good priest's face expressed the sympathy he felt as they entered softly, and stood where they would not attract the attention of those restless eyes. Mr. Carlisle was wakeful and watchful, but comparatively quiet. It was pitiful to see with what rapid strides the fever was undermining that manly strength, and hurrying on towards the terrible moment of suspense when life and death confront each other in momentary combat. With an earnest prayer to God, the priest again raised the heavy damask curtain, and softly retired, followed by Mrs. Grey.

"Will he recover?" was her eager question.

"Dear madam," replied he, "I think there is much room for hope, though I cannot deny that he is a very sick man. For your encouragement, I can tell you that I have seen many patients recover in such cases when it seemed little short of miraculous. It will be many days yet before you must think of giving up good hope. And remember that all your strength will be needed."

"Oh!" said Mrs. Grey impulsively, "I could not live if it were not for Assunta. She is an angel."

"Yes, she is a good child," said the priest kindly; "and she is now going to obey some orders that I have given her, that she may return to you more angelic than ever. Dear madam, you have my deepest sympathy. I wish that I could serve you otherwise than by words."

The two priests bade Assunta good-by at the garden gate. F. Joseph's heart was full of pity for the young girl, whose act of sacrifice in surrendering human happiness for conscience' sake had been followed by so severe a trial. But, remembering the blessed mission of suffering to a soul like hers, he prayed—not that her chalice might be less bitter, but that strength might be given her to accept it as from the hand of a loving Father.

And so Assunta, putting aside every thought of self, took her place in the sick-room. She had a double motive in hanging her picture of St. Catherine, from which she was never separated, at the foot of the bed. It was a favorite with Mr. Carlisle, and often in his delirium his eyes would rest upon it, in almost conscious recognition; while to Assunta it was a talisman—a constant reminder of her mother, and of those dying words which now seemed stamped in burning letters on her heart and brain.

Mrs. Grey often visited the room; but she controlled her own agitation so little, and was so unreasonable in the number of her suggestions, that she generally left the patient worse than she found him. Assunta recognized her right to come and go as she pleased, but she could not regret her absence when her presence was almost invariably productive of evil consequences.

The first Sunday, Assunta thought she might venture to assist at Mass at the nearest church; it would be strength to her body as well as her soul. She was not absent from the house an hour, yet she was met on her return by Clara, in a state of great excitement.

"Assunta, we have had a dreadful time," she said. "Severn woke up just after you left, and literally screamed for help, because, he said, a great black cross had fallen on you, and you would be crushed to death unless some one would assist him to raise it. In his efforts, he was almost out of bed. I reasoned with him, and told him it was all nonsense; that there was no cross,

and that you had gone to church. But the more I talked and explained, the worse he got; until I was perfectly disheartened, and came to meet you." And with the ready tears streaming down her pretty face, she did look the very picture of discouragement.

"Poor Clara," said Assunta, gently embracing her, "it is hard for you to bear all this, you are so little accustomed to sickness. But you ought not to contradict Mr. Carlisle, for it is all real to him, and opposition only excites him. I can never soothe him except by agreeing with him."

"But where does he get such strange ideas?" asked the sobbing Clara.

"Where do our dreams come from?" said Assunta. "I think, however, that this fancy can be traced to the night when we visited the Colosseum, and sat for a long time on the steps of the cross in the centre. You know it is a black one," she added, smiling, to reassure her friend. "And now, Clara, I really think you ought to order the close carriage, and take a drive this morning. It would do you good, and you will not be needed at all for the next two or three hours."

Mrs. Grey's face brightened perceptibly. It was the very thing for which she was longing, but she would not propose it herself for fear it would seem heartless. To *seem*, and not to *be*, was her motto.

"But would not people think it very strange," she asked, "and Severn so sick?"

"I do not believe that people will know or think anything about it," answered Assunta patiently. "You can take Amalie with you for company, and drive out on the Campagna." And having lightened one load, she turned towards her guardian's room.

"Are you not coming to breakfast?" said Mrs. Grey.

"Presently." And Assunta hastened to the bedside. Giovanni had been entirely unable to control the panic which seemed to have taken possession of Mr. Carlisle. He continued his cries for assistance, and the suffering he evidently endured showed how real the fancy was to him.

"Dear friend," said the young girl, pushing back the hair from his burning forehead, "look at me. Do you not see that I am safe?"

Mr. Carlisle turned towards her, and, in sudden revulsion of feeling, burst into a wild laugh.

"I knew," he said, "that, if they would only come and help me, I should succeed. But it was very heavy; it has made me very tired."

"Yes, you have had hard work, and it was very kind in you to undertake it for me. But now you must rest. It would make me very unhappy if I thought that my safety had caused any injury to you."

And while she was talking, Assunta had motioned to Giovanni to bring the soothing medicine the doctor had left, and she succeeded in administering it to her patient, almost without his knowledge, so engrossed was he in his present vagary.

"But there was a cross?" he asked.

"Yes," she answered, in a meaning tone, "a very heavy one; but it did not crush me."

"Who lifted it?" he asked eagerly.

"A powerful hand raised its weight from my shoulders, and I have the promise of His help always, if I should ever be in trouble again, and only will cry to Him."

"Well, whoever he is," said Mr. Carlisle, "he did not hurry much when I called—and now I am so tired. And Clara said there was no cross; that I was mistaken. I am *never* mistaken," he answered, in something of his old, proud voice. "She ought to know that."

Assunta did not answer, but she sat patiently soothing her guardian into quiet at least, if not sleep. Once he looked at her, and said, "My precious child is safe;" but, as she smiled, he laughed aloud, and then shut his eyes again.

An hour she remained beside the bed, and then she crept softly from the room, to take what little breakfast she could find an appetite for, and to assist Mrs. Grey in preparing for her drive.

With such constant demands upon her sympathy and strength, it is not strange that Assunta's courage sometimes failed. But, when the physician assured her that her guardian's life was, humanly speaking, in her hands, she determined that no thought or care for herself should interfere with the performance of her duty.

Mrs. Grey's drive having proved an excellent tonic, she was tempted to repeat it often—always with a protest and with some misgivings of conscience, which were, however, set aside without difficulty.

It was a singular coincidence that Mr. Sinclair should so often be found riding on horseback in the same direction. A few words only would be exchanged—of enquiry for the sufferer, of sympathy for his sister. But somehow, as the days went by, the tone in which the words of sympathy were expressed grew more tender, and conveyed the impression of something held back out of respect and by an effort. The manner, too—which showed so little, and yet seemed to repress so much—began to have the effect of heightening the color in Mrs. Grey's pretty face, and softening a little the innocent piquancy of her youthful ways. It was no wonder that, loving the brightness and sunshine of life, and regarding with a sort of dread the hush and solemnity which pervade the house of sickness, and which may at any moment become the house of mourning, she should have allowed her anxiety for her brother to diminish a little under the influence of the new thought and feeling which were gaining possession now, in the absence of all other excitement. And yet she loved her brother as much as such hearts can love—as deeply as any love can penetrate in which there is no spirit of sacrifice—love's foundation and its crown. If the illness had lasted but a day, or at the most two, she could have devoted herself with apparent unselfishness and tender assiduity to the duties of nursing. But, as day after day went on without much perceptible change in Mr. Carlisle, her first emotion subsided into a sort of graceful perplexity at finding herself out of her element. And by the time the second week was drawing towards its close—with the new influence of Mr. Sinclair's sympathy seconding the demands of her own nature—she began to act like any other sunflower, when it "turns to the god that it loves." And yet she continued to be very regular in her visits to the sick-room, and very affectionate to Assunta; but it may be greatly doubted whether she lost many hours' sleep. Surely it would be most unjust to judge Clara Grey and Assunta Howard by the same standard. Undine, before and after the possession of

a human soul, could hardly have been more dissimilar.

It was the fifteenth day of Mr. Carlisle's illness when Assunta was summoned from his bedside by Mrs. Grey, who desired to see her for a few moments in her own room. As the young girl entered, she found her sitting before a bright wood-fire; on her lap was an exquisite bouquet fresh from fairy-land, or—what is almost the same thing—an Italian garden. In her hand she held a card, at which she was looking with a somewhat perturbed expression.

" Assunta, love," she exclaimed, " I want you to tell me what to do. See these lovely flowers that Mr. Sinclair has just sent me, with this card. Read it." And as she handed her the dainty card, whose perfume seemed to rival that of the flowers, the color mounted becomingly into her cheeks. There were only these words written :

" I have brought a close carriage, and hope to persuade you to drive a little while this afternoon. I will anxiously await your reply in the garden. Yours, S——."

" Well ?" questioned Clara, a little impatiently, for Assunta's face was very grave.

" Dear Clara," she replied. " I have no right to advise you and I certainly shall not question the propriety of anything you do. I was only thinking whether I had not better tell you that I see a change in your brother this afternoon, and I fear it is for the worse. I am longing for the doctor's visit."

" Do you really think he is worse ?" exclaimed Clara. " He looks to me just the same. But perhaps I had better not go out. I had a little headache, and thought a drive might do me good. But, poor Severn! of course I ought not to leave him."

"You must not be influenced by what I say," said Assunta. "I may be entirely mistaken, and so I should not alarm you. God knows, I hope it may be so!"

"Then you think I might go for an hour or two, just to get a breath of air," said Mrs. Grey. "Mr. Sinclair will certainly think I have found it necessary to call a papal consistory, if I keep him much longer on the promenade."

Poor Assunta, worn out with her two weeks of watching and anxiety, looked for a moment with a sort of incredulous wonder at the incarnation of unconscious selfishness before her. For one moment she looked "upon this picture and on that"— the noble, devoted brother, sick unto death; and that man, the acquaintance of a few days, now walking impatiently up and down the orange avenue. The flush of indignation changed her pale cheeks to scarlet, and an almost pharisaical thanksgiving to God that she was not like *some* women swept across her heart, while a most unwonted sarcasm trembled on her lips. She instantly checked the unworthy feeling and its expression; but she was so unstrung by care and fatigue that she could not so easily control her emotion, and, before the object of unusual indignation had time to wonder at the delay of her reply, she had thrown herself upon the sofa, and was sobbing violently. Mrs. Grey was really alarmed, so much so that she dropped both card and flowers upon the floor, and forgot entirely her waiting cavalier, as she knelt beside the excited girl, and put her arms about her.

"Assunta dear, what is the matter? Are you ill? Oh! what have I done?" she exclaimed.

"My poor guardian—my dear, kind friend, he is dying! May God have mercy on him and on me!" were the words that escaped Assunta's lips between the sobs.

A shudder passed through Mrs. Grey at this unexpected putting into words of the one thought she had so carefully kept from her mind; and her own tears began to flow. Just at this moment the physician's step sounded in the hall, and she went hastily to summon him. He took in the whole scene at a glance, and, seating himself at once upon the sofa beside Assunta, he put his hand gently and soothingly upon her head, as a father might have done.

"Poor child!" said he kindly, "I have been expecting this."

The action expressing sympathy just when she needed it so much caused her tears to flow afresh, but less tumultuously than before. The remains of Mrs. Grey's lunch were standing on a side-table, and the good doctor poured out a glass of wine, which Assunta took obediently. Then, making an effort at self-control, she said:

"Please do not waste a moment on me. Do go to Mr. Carlisle; he seems very ill. I have been weak and foolish, but I will control myself better next time."

"I have just left Mr. Carlisle's room," replied the doctor. "I will not deceive you. He is, as you say, very ill; but I hope we may save him yet. You must call up all your courage, for you will be much needed to-night."

He knew by the effect that he had touched the right chord, so he continued: "And now, Miss Howard, I am going to ask of you the favor to send one of your servants to my house, to notify my wife that I shall not return to-night. I will not leave you until the crisis is passed—successfully, I hope," he added with a smile.

Assunta went at once to give the desired order, relieved and grateful that they would have the support of the physician's presence and skill; and yet the very fact of his remaining discouraged the hope he had tried to inspire. When she had gone, he turned to address a few comforting words to Mrs. Grey, when, suddenly recollecting himself, he said:

"By the way, Mrs. Grey, I forgot to tell you that I met Mr. Sinclair down-stairs, and he begged me to inquire if you had received a message from him. Can I be of service in taking him your reply?"

"O poor man! I quite forgot him," exclaimed the easily diverted Clara, as she stooped to pick up the neglected flowers. "Thank you for your kind offer, but I had better run down myself, and apologize for my apparent rudeness." And, hastily wiping her eyes, she threw a shawl over her shoulders and a becoming white *rigolette* about her head, and with a graceful bow of apology she left the room.

"Extraordinary woman!" thought the doctor. "One would suppose that a dying brother would be an excuse, even to that puppy Sinclair. I wish he had had to wait longer—it wouldn't have hurt him a bit—he has never had half enough of it to do. And what the devil is he coming here for now, anyhow?" he added to his former charitable reflections, as he went to join Assunta in her faithful vigil beside the unconscious and apparently dying man.

Mr. Sinclair met Mrs. Grey at the foot of the stairs with an assump-

tion of interest and anxiety which successfully concealed his inward impatience. But truly it would have been difficult to resist that appealing face, with its traces of recent tears and the flush caused by excited feeling.

As a general thing, with all due deference to poetic opinion, "love is (*not*) loveliest when embalmed in tears." But Mrs. Grey was an exception to many rules. Her emotion was usually of the April-shower sort, gentle, refreshing, even beautifying. Very little she knew of the storm of suffering which desolates the heart, and whose ravages leave a lasting impression upon the features. Such emotions also sometimes, but rarely, leave a beauty behind them; but it is a beauty not of this world, the beauty of holiness; not of Mrs. Grey's kind, for it never would have touched Mr. Sinclair as hers did now.

"My dear Mrs. Grey," he said, taking her hand in both his, "how grieved I am to see you showing so plainly the results of care and watching! Privileged as he must be who is the recipient of such angelic ministrations, I must yet protest—as a friend, I trust I have a right to do so—against such over-exertion on your part. You will be ill yourself; and then who or what will console me?"

Mr. Sinclair knew this was a fiction. He knew well enough that Mrs. Grey had never looked fresher or prettier in her life. But the *rôle* he had assigned to himself was the dangerously tender one of sympathy; and where a sufficient occasion for displaying his part was not supplied, he must needs invent one.

Clara was not altogether deceived, for, as she put her lace-bordered handkerchief to her eyes, from which the tears began again to flow, she replied:

"You are mistaken, Mr. Sinclair. I am quite well, and not at all fatigued; while dear Assunta is thin and pale, and thoroughly worn out with all she has done. I can never be grateful enough to her."

Had the lady raised her eyes, she might have been astonished at the expression of contempt which curled Mr. Sinclair's somewhat hard mouth, as he rejoined:

"Yes; I quite understand Miss Howard's *motive* in her devotion to her guardian, and it is not strange that she should be pale. How do you suppose I should look and feel if the dearest friend I have in the world were at this moment lying in her brother's place?"

Mrs. Grey might have received a new light about the young girl had she not been rendered obtuse to the first part of this speech by the very pointed allusion to herself afterwards, that was accompanied by a searching look, which she would not see, for she still kept her handkerchief before her eyes. Mr. Sinclair placed her disengaged hand upon his arm, and gently drew her towards the garden. Had she been able to look down into the heart of the man who walked so protectingly beside her, she would doubtless have been surprised to find a disappointment lurking in the place where she had begun to feel her image was enshrined. She would have seen that Assunta's face had occupied a niche in the inner sanctuary of the heart of this man of the world, before which he would have been content to bow; that pique at her entire indifference to his pretensions, and the reserve behind which she always retreated in his

presence, had led him to transfer his attentions to the older lady and the smaller fortune; and that his jealous observation had brought to his notice, what was apparent to no one else, the relations between Assunta and her guardian.

All this would not have been very flattering to Mrs. Grey, so it was perhaps as well that the gift of clairvoyance was not hers; though it is a sad thought for men and angels how few hearts there are that would bear to have thrown on them the clear light of unveiled truth. The day is to come when the secrets of all hearts are to be revealed. But Mr. Sinclair, even if he knew this startling fact, would not have considered it worth while to anticipate that dread hour by revealing to the lovely lady at his side any of those uncomfortable circumstances which would inevitably stand in the way of the consummation of his present wish. So he bravely undertook the noble enterprise of deceiving a trusting heart into believing in a love which did not exist, but which it was not so very difficult to imagine just at that moment, with the little hand resting confidingly on his arm, and the tearful eyes raised to meet his.

In a broken voice, Mrs. Grey said: "Mr. Sinclair, I came down myself to thank you for the beautiful flowers you sent me, and to excuse myself from driving with you this afternoon. Poor Severn is worse, they think. Oh! if he should not recover, what will become of me?" And as she spoke, she burst into renewed weeping, and threw herself upon a seat beneath a group of orange-trees, whose perfume stole upon the senses with a subtle yet bewildering influence. Mr. Sinclair sat down beside her, saying gently:

"I hope, dear Mrs. Grey, it is not so serious as that. I am confident that you have been needlessly alarmed."

The world will, no doubt, pardon him—seeing that Mammon was his chosen master—if the thought was not altogether unpleasing that, should Mr. Carlisle die now, before Assunta could have a claim upon him, it would make an almost princely addition to the dowry of his sister. Nor on this account were his words less tender as he added :

"But, even so, do you not know of one heart waiting, longing to devote itself to you, and only with difficulty restrained from placing itself at your feet by the iron fetters of propriety? Tell me, Clara, may I break these odious chains, and say what is in my heart?"

"Mr. Sinclair, you must not speak such words to me now, and my poor brother so ill. Indeed, I cannot stay to hear you. Thank you very much for your kind sympathy, but I must leave you now."

"Without one word of hope? Do I deserve this?" And truly the pathos he put into his voice was calculated to melt a heart of stone; and Clara's was much more impressible. She paused beside him, and, allowing him still to retain in his the hand he had taken, continued :

"I think you take an unfair advantage of my lonely position. I cannot give you a favorable answer this afternoon, for I am so bewildered. I begin to think that I ought not to have come down at all; but I wanted to tell you how much I appreciated the bouquet."

"I hope you read its meaning," said Mr. Sinclair, rising. "And do you not see a happy omen in your present position, under a bower of orange blossoms? It needs but

little imagination to lower them until they encircle the head of the most lovely of brides. Will you accept this as a pledge of that bright future which I have dared to picture to myself?" And as he spoke he put up his hand to break off a cluster of the white blossoms and dark-green leaves, when Giovanni appeared at the gate.

"Signora," he said, "will you please to come up-stairs? The Signorina is very anxious to see you."

"I am coming," she replied. "Pardon me, Mr. Sinclair, and forget what has been said." And she walked towards the house.

"Do you refuse the pledge?" he asked, placing the flowers in her hand, after raising them to his lips.

"Really," answered Clara, almost petulantly, "I am so perplexed, I do not know what to say. Yes, I will take the flowers, if that will please you." Saying which, she began to ascend the stairs.

"And I take hope with me," said Mr. Sinclair, in a tender tone. But as he turned to go he mentally cursed Giovanni for the interruption; "for," thought he, "in one minute more I would have had her promise, and who knows but now that brother of hers may recover and interfere?"

Assunta met Mrs. Grey just outside the door of Mr. Carlisle's room, and drew her into the library, where she sat down beside her on the sofa, and, putting her arm affectionately about her, began to speak to her with a calmness which, under the circumstances, could only come from the presence of God.

"I thought, dear Clara, that I had better ask you to come here, while I talk to you a little about your brother, and what the doctor says. We must both of us try to prepare." Here her voice broke, and Mrs. Grey interrupted her with,

"Tell me, Assunta, quickly, is he worse?"

"I fear so, dear," replied Assunta; "but we must help each other to keep up what courage and hope we may. It is a common sorrow, Clara, for he has been more than a brother to me."

"But, Assunta, I do not understand. You are so calm, and yet you say such dreadful things. Does the doctor think he will die?" And once again she shuddered at that word, to her so fearful and so incomprehensible.

"I dare not deceive you, dear—I dare not deceive myself. The crisis has come, and he seems to be sinking fast. O Clara, pray for him!"

"I cannot pray; I do not know how. I have never prayed in my life. But let me go to him—my poor, dear Severn!" And Mrs. Grey was rushing from the room, when Assunta begged her to wait one moment, while she besought her to be calm. Life hung upon a thread, which the least agitation might snap in a moment. She could not give up that one last hope. Mrs. Grey of course promised; but the instant she approached the bed, and saw the change that a few hours had made, she shrieked aloud; and Assunta, in answer to the doctor's look of despair, summoned her maid, and she was carried to her own room in violent hysterics, the orange blossoms still in her hand. Truly they seemed an omen of death rather than of a bridal. The doctor followed to administer an opiate, and then Assunta and himself again took up their watch by Mr. Carlisle. Hour after hour passed.

Everything that skill could suggest was done. Once only Assunta left the room for a moment to inquire for Mrs. Grey, and, finding that she was sleeping under the influence of the anodyne, she instantly returned. She dared not trust herself to think how different was this death from that other she remembered. She could not have borne to entertain for one moment the thought that this soul was going forth without prayer, without sacrament, to meet its God. She did everything the doctor wished, quietly and calmly. The hours did not seem long, for she had almost lost her sense of time, so near the confines of eternity. She did not even *feel* now—she only *waited*.

It was nearly twelve when the doctor said in a low voice:

"We can do nothing more now; we must leave the rest to nature."

"And to God," whispered Assunta, as she sank on her knees beside the bed; and, taking in both hers her guardian's thin, outstretched hand, she bowed her head, and from the very depths of her soul went up a prayer for his life—if it might be—followed by a fervent but agonized act of resignation to the sweet will of God.

She was so absorbed that she did not notice a sudden brightening of the doctor's face as he bent over his patient. But in a moment more she felt a motion, and the slightest possible pressure of her hand. She raised her head, and her eyes met those of her guardian, while a faint smile—one of his own peculiar, winning smiles—told her that he was conscious of her presence. At last, rousing himself a little more, he said:

"*Petite*, no matter where I am, it is so sweet to have you here." And, with an expression of entire content, he closed his eyes again, and fell into a refreshing sleep.

"Thank God!" murmured Assunta, and her head dropped upon her folded hands.

The doctor came to her, and whispered the joyful words, "He will live!" but, receiving no answer, he tried to lift the young girl from her knees, and found that she had fainted. Poor child! like Mary, the Blessed Mother of Sorrows, she had *stood* beneath her cross until it was lightened of its burden. She had nerved herself to bear her sorrow; she had not counted on the strength which would be needed for the reaction of joy.

"Better so," said the doctor, as he placed her upon the couch. "She would never have taken rest in any other way."

IV

CONVALESCENCE.

"I HAVE almost made up my mind to go back to bed again, and play possum. Truly, I find but little encouragement in my tremendous efforts to get well, in the marked neglect which I am suffering from the feminine portion of my family. Clara is making herself ridiculous by returning to the days of her first folly, against which I protest to unheeding ears, and of which I wash my hands. Come here, Assunta; leave that everlasting writing of yours, and enliven the ' winter of my discontent ' by the 'glorious summer' of your presence, of mind as well as of body."

Mr. Carlisle certainly looked very unlike the neglected personage he described himself to be. He was sitting in a luxurious chair near the open window; and he had but to raise his eyes to feast them upon the ever-changing, never-tiring beauties of the Alban hills, while the soft spring air was laden with the fragrance of many gardens. Beside him were books, flowers, and cigars—everything, in short, which could charm away the tediousness of a prolonged convalescence. And it must be said, to his credit, that he bore the monotony very well *for a man*—which, it is to be feared, is after all damning his patience with very faint praise.

Assunta raised her eyes from her letter, and, smiling, said:

" Ingratitude, thy name is Severn Carlisle ! I wish Clara were here to give you the benefit of one of her very womanly disquisitions on man. You would be so effectually silenced that I should have a hope of finishing my letter in time for the steamer."

" Never mind the letter," said Mr. Carlisle. " Come here, child; I am pining to have you near me."

Assunta laughed, as she replied :

" Would it not do just as well if I should give you the opera-glass, and let you amuse yourself by making believe being me to you ?"

" Pshaw ! Assunta, I want you. Put away your writing. You know very well that it is two days before the steamer leaves, and you will have plenty of time." And Mr. Carlisle drew a chair beside his own.

Assunta did know all about it ; but, now that the invalid was so much better, she was trying to withdraw a little from any special attentions. She felt that, under the circumstances, it would not be right to make herself necessary to his comfort; she did not realize how necessary he thought her to his very life. However, though she would skirmish with and contradict him, she had never yet been able sufficiently to forget how near he had been to death to actually oppose him. Besides, she had not thought him looking quite as strong this morning; so she put the unfinished letter back in the desk, and, taking her work-basket, sat down beside her guardian, and tried to divert him from herself by pointing out the wonderful loveliness of the view. His face did have a weary expression, which his quondam nurse did not fail to perceive. She at once poured out a glass of wine, and, handing it to him, said:

"Tell me the truth, my friend; you do not feel very well to-day?"

"I do not feel quite as strong as Samson," he replied; "but you forget, Dalila, how you and the barber have shorn off the few locks the fever left me. Of course my strength went too."

"Well, fortunately," said Assunta, "there are no gates of Gaza which require immediate removal, and no Philistines to be overcome."

"I am not so sure of that," said Mr. Carlisle, putting down the wine-glass. "There are some things harder to overcome than Philistines, and some citadels so strong as to bid defiance to Samson, even in the full glory of his wavy curls. What chance is there, then, for him now, cruel Dalila?"

Assunta wilfully misunderstood him, and, taking her work from her pretty basket, she answered, laughing:

"Well, one thing is very certain: your illness has not left you in the least subdued. Clara and I must begin a course of discipline, or by the time your brown curls have attained their usual length you will have become a regular tyrant."

"Give me your work, *petite*," said Mr. Carlisle, gently disengaging it from her hand. "I want this morning all to myself. And please do not mention Clara again. I cannot hear her name without thinking of that miserable Sinclair business. It is well for him that I am as I am, until I have had time to cool. I am not very patient, and I have

an irresistible longing to give him a horse-whipping. It is a singular psychological fact that Clara has been gifted with every womanly attraction but common sense. But I believe that even you Catholics allow to benighted heretics the plea of invincible ignorance as an escape from condemnation; so we must not be too severe in our judgment of my foolish sister."

"Hardly a parallel case," said Assunta, smiling.

"I grant it," replied her guardian; "for in my illustration the acceptance of the plea, so you hold, renders happiness possible to the heretic, to whom a 'little knowledge' would have been so 'dangerous a thing' as to lose him even a chance among the elect; whereas Clara's invincible ignorance of the world, of human nature, and in particular of the nature of George Sinclair, serves only to explain her folly, but does not prevent the inevitable evil consequences of such a marriage. But enough of the subject. Will you not read to me a little while? Get Mrs. Browning, and let us have 'Lady Geraldine,' if you will so far compassionate a man as to make him forget that he is at sword's points with himself and all the world, the exception being his fair consoler. Thank you, *petite*," he continued, as Assunta brought the book. "There is plenty of trash and an incomprehensible expression or two in the poem; but, as a whole, I like it, and the end, the vision, would redeem it, were it ten times as bad. Well, I too have had a vision! Do you know, Assunta, that the only thing I can recall of those weeks of illness is your dear form flitting in and out of the darkness? But—may I dare say it?—the vision had in it a certain tenderness I do not find in the reality. I could almost believe in your doctrine of guardian angels, having myself experienced what their ministry might be."

"I am afraid," interrupted Assunta, "that your doctrine would hardly stand, if it has no other basis than such very human evidence. Shall I begin?"

"No, wait a minute longer," said Mr. Carlisle. "'Lady Geraldine' will keep. I wish to put a question to your sense of justice. When I was sick, and almost unconscious, and entirely unappreciative, there was a person—so the doctor tells me—who lavished attentions upon me, counted nothing too great a sacrifice to be wasted upon me. But now that I am myself again, and longing to prove myself the most grateful of men, on the principle that 'gratitude is a lively sense of favors *to come*,' that person suddenly retires into the solitude of her own original indifference (to misquote somewhat grandiloquently), and leaves me wondering on what hidden rock my bark struck when I thought the sea all smooth and shining, shivering my reanimated hopes to atoms. But," he added, turning abruptly towards her, and taking in his the hand which rested on the table beside him, "you saved my life. Bless you, child, and remember that the life you have saved is yours, now and always."

The color had rushed painfully into Assunta's face, but her guardian instantly released her hand, and she answered quietly:

"It really troubles me, Mr. Carlisle, that you should attach so much importance to a mere service of duty and common humanity. I did no more than any friend so situated would have had a right to claim at my hands. Your thanks

have far outweighed your indebtedness."

"Duty again!" exclaimed Mr. Carlisle bitterly. "I wish you had let me die. I want no *duty* service from you; and you shall be gratified, for I do *not* thank you for my life on those conditions. You spare no opportunity to let me understand that I am no more to you than all the rest of the world. Be it so." And he impatiently snatched the *Galignani* from the table, and settled himself as if to read.

Assunta's temper was always roused by the unjust remarks her guardian sometimes made, and she would probably have answered with a spirit which would have belied the angel had she not happened to glance at the paper, and seen that it was upside down; and then at Mr. Carlisle's pale and troubled features, to which even the crimson facings of his rich dressing-gown hardly lent the faintest glow. The same sentiment of common humanity which had prompted those days of care and nights of watching now checked the reproach she would have uttered. She turned over the leaves of Mrs. Browning, until her eye lighted upon that exquisite valediction, "God be with thee, my beloved." This she read through to herself; and then, laying the book upon the table, she said with the tone and manner of a subdued child:

"May I finish my letter, please?"

Mr. Carlisle scarcely raised his eyes, as he replied:

"Certainly, Assunta. I have no wish to detain you."

It was with a very womanly dignity that Assunta left her seat; but, instead of returning to her writing-desk, she went to the piano. For nearly an hour she played, now passages from different sonatas, and then selections from the grander music of the church. Without seeming to notice, she saw that the paper at last fell from her guardian's hand; and understanding, as she did, every change in his expressive face, she knew from the smoothing of the brow and the restful look of the eyes that peace was restored by the charm she wrought. When she was sure that the evil spirit had been quite exorcised by the power of music, she rose from the piano, and rang the bell. When Giovanni appeared, she said:

"I think that Mrs. Grey will not return until quite late, as she has gone to Tivoli; so you may serve dinner here for me as well as for Mr. Carlisle. If any one calls, I do not receive this afternoon."

"Very well, signorina," replied Giovanni. "I will bring in the small table from the library." And he left the room.

"It will be much pleasanter than for each of us to dine separately in solitary state," said Assunta, going towards her guardian, and speaking as if there had been no cloud between them; "though I know that dining in the drawing-room must, of necessity, be exceptional."

"It was a very bright thought of yours," answered Mr. Carlisle, "and a very appetizing one to me, I can assure you. Will you read 'Lady Geraldine' now? There will be just time before dinner."

Without a word Assunta took the book, and began to read. She had nothing of the dramatic in her style, but her voice was sweet, her enunciation very clear and distinct, and she showed a thorough apprehension of the author's meaning; so her reading always gave pleasure, and Mr. Carlisle had come to depend upon it daily. The vision to which he had referred was robbed,

perhaps fortunately, of some of its sentiment, by Giovanni's table preparations; and his presence prevented all but very general comment.

When they were once more by themselves—Giovanni having left them to linger over the fruit and wine—Mr. Carlisle said:

"By the way, Assunta, you have not told me yet what your friend Miss Percival had to say for herself in her last letter. You know I am always interested in her; though I fear it is an interest which partakes largely of the nature of jealousy."

"Well," replied Assunta, "she tells me that she is going to be married."

"Sensible girl! What more?"

"She regrets very much that her brother, whom she dearly loves, will not return from his year's exile in time for the ceremony."

"So much the better," exclaimed Mr. Carlisle with unusual energy. "I hope he may lose himself in the deserts of Arabia, or wander off to further India, and there remain."

Assunta laughed. "Truly, my guardian is most charitable! I should not be surprised if he did, one of these days, follow in the footsteps of S. Francis Xavier. But what has he done to merit sentence of banishment from you?"

"You know I am a student of human nature," rejoined her guardian, "and I have always observed that where a young girl has a brother and a friend, she cannot conceive of any other destiny for the two objects of her affection than to make of them one united object in the holy bonds of matrimony; and, in order to bring about the desired consummation, she devotes herself to intrigue in a manner and with a zeal truly feminine. Mary Percival has a brother and a friend.; ergo, may her brother be—induced to become an Oriental; that is all."

"In this case," replied the young girl with a merry laugh, "your observations are quite at fault. I am truly grieved to be compelled to spoil such a pretty romance. But, seriously, Mary has a far higher choice for her brother than her most unworthy friend. She has but one desire and prayer for him, and that is that he may enter the holy priesthood. I believe she will not be disappointed. Did you ever see Mr. Percival?"

"No, I have never had the pleasure," replied Mr. Carlisle.

"I wish you might know him," said Assunta enthusiastically. "I am sure you would like him. He is not what would generally be considered handsome, but I think his face beautiful, it is so very spiritual. It is the beauty of a remarkable soul, which literally shines in his eyes. He has taken the highest honors at college, and, if his health is only re-established, I think his sister's very laudable ambition will be more than gratified."

"He certainly has a most ardent admirer. I did not know you could be so enthusiastic about any member of the *genus homo*," said Mr. Carlisle. Assunta was not to be daunted by the perceptible sneer, and she at once added:

"I can hardly be said to admire him, but rather the power of grace in him. I have so great a reverence for Augustine Percival that I could not imagine it possible for any human affection to turn him from what I firmly believe to be his great vocation. So my guardian may see him return to the West with equanimity, and may perhaps

even be induced to look with favor upon another part of the letter."

"And what is that?" asked Mr. Carlisle.

"Mary invites me very urgently to pass next winter with her in Baltimore. Her husband-elect is a naval officer, and his leave of absence expires in October. She wishes me as a substitute, you understand."

"Is it your wish to go, my child?" said her guardian, looking at her earnestly.

"I never like to make any definite plan so long beforehand; but it seemed to me a very suitable arrangement. You remember," added Assunta, "that Clara will probably be married before then."

"I do not wish Clara to be mentioned; she has nothing to do with it," said Mr. Carlisle imperiously; and then he added more gently, "May I ask, *petite*, what answer you have given her?"

"None, as yet; you remember you interrupted my letter. But I think I will tell her that my guardian is such an ogre that I dare not reply to her invitation until after August. Will that do?"

"Tell her what you will," said Mr. Carlisle; "only, for heaven's sake, say no more to me upon the subject. I am not Augustine Percival, and consequently not elevated above the power of human feeling."

Poor Assunta! she too was not above human feeling, and sometimes it was very hard for her to keep her heart from being rebellious; but she had learned to put God before every earthly consideration, and to find her strength in his presence. But it required constant watchfulness and untiring patience to conquer herself. Therefore she could not but feel great compassion for her friend, who must bear his disappointment with no help outside of his own strong nature. She rose from the table, and moved it a little to one side, in order that she might arrange the cushions for her guardian, who looked unusually weary to-night.

"Are you angry with me, Mr. Carlisle?" said she softly, as he sank back in his chair.

"Angry, *petite?*" he repeated, looking steadily in her face. "Yes, I am angry, but not with you, or with anything you have said to-night, but rather with that accursed barrier. Go, child, ring for Giovanni, or I shall say what you will not like to hear." As she turned away, he caught her hand, saying:

"One moment. I have been very rude, and yet I would die for you! There, I will not say another word. Please ring for Giovanni, since I am compelled to be so ungallant as to request the favor of you; and then let us talk a little about the Sienna plans. I must try and put myself into a good-humor before Clara comes; for she will have something to say about her handsome Sinclair, and then I would not give much for my temper."

The table having been removed, and the wood which had been laid ready in the fire-place kindled into a blaze—for the evenings were still cool enough to admit of its cheery influence—the two, whose lives seemed so united, and yet were, in reality, so far apart, drew towards the fire. The heavy curtains, which had been put aside to admit the warm, genial air and sunshine of mid-day, were now closely drawn, in order to shut out the chilling dampness of evening. A hanging lamp cast a soft, mellow light

through its porcelain shade upon an exquisite basket of roses and carnations adorning the centre of the table, which was covered elsewhere with books, arranged with studied negligence, and numberless little suggestions of refinement and feminine occupation. Everything seemed favorable to a most harmonious conversation, except that inevitable something which, like a malicious sprite, awakens us from our dreams just when they are brightest; breaks the spell of our illusions at the moment when we are clinging to them most persistently; ruthlessly crosses, with its fatal track, our promised pleasures; and unfeelingly interrupts us in some hour of complete rest and satisfaction. Ah! we may fret in our impatience, and wonder at the fatality which seems to pursue us. It is no mischief-loving Puck, no evil-minded genie, but a good angel, who thus thwarts us. This is no time to dream and cherish illusions which can but deceive. It is no time for repose. To detach ourselves from all these things which would make this world a satisfaction to us is the labor we must all perform, more or less generously and heroically, if we would one day enjoy the reality of the one dream that never fades—the vision of the Apocalypse; the one repose that never palls—the rest that remaineth for the people of God. Welcome, then, those misnamed "juggling fiends" that "keep the word of promise to our ear, and break it to our hope." Welcome the many disappointments, trifling in themselves, the daily crossings of our will and pleasure, which seem so petty; they perform a great mission if they succeed in loosening ever so little the cords which bind down to earth the souls that were meant for heaven. Thrice welcome whatever helps to turn the sweetness of this world to bitterness!

Poor Mrs. Grey! it had never occurred to her that she had a mission, still less such an one as we have now assigned to her. For it was her voice which caused Mr. Carlisle to sigh so profoundly that Assunta could not but smile, in spite of the regretful feeling in her own heart. It was better—and she knew it—that the softening influence of the hour should be thus rudely interrupted; but nature will not be crushed without an occasional protest. The expression of annoyance still lingered on Mr. Carlisle's face when Clara entered the room, exclaiming:

"Come, *caro mio,* they have had the livelong day to themselves, and must have talked out by this time, even if they had the whole encyclopædia in their brains." And as Mr. Sinclair followed with an apologetic bow, she continued:

"This ridiculous man has conscientious objections to interrupting your *tête-à-tête.* I am sure, Severn, if Assunta is not tired to death of you by this time, she ought to be, particularly if you have been as solemn all day as you look now. I would much rather spend the whole day in church—and that is the most gloomy thing I can think of—than be condemned to the company of a man in a mood. Make a note of that, George.

"I think, Clara," said her brother, somewhat coldly, "that Mr. Sinclair was judging others by himself, and in doing so he judged kindly in my regard and gallantly in yours; but this is not always the true criterion. Mr. Sinclair, I beg you will be seated, and excuse me if I do not rise. I am still obliged to claim the invalid's cloak of charity. No doubt a cup of tea will be acceptable after your long drive; and it will soon be served."

The eyes of the two men met. They had measured each other before now, and understood each other well; and each knew that he was most cordially disliked by the other. Their ceremonious politeness was all the more marked on that account. Assunta's tact came to the rescue, and made a diversion. As she assisted Mrs. Grey in removing her shawl and hat, she said:

"And how have you enjoyed the day, Clara? You must be very tired!"

"Oh! I am nearly dead with fatigue," replied the lady, looking very bright and very much alive for a moribund; "but we have had a delicious time. You should have seen George trying to support his dignity on a donkey which he could easily have assisted in walking, as his feet touched the ground on both sides; and which started with a spasmodic jerk every two or three minutes when the donkey boy brought down a small club on its back. I laughed so much at Mr Sinclair's gravity and the ludicrous figure he cut that I narrowly escaped falling off my own donkey down a precipice."

"'Now, what a thing it is to be an ass,'" quoted Mr. Carlisle. "My lovely sister visits a spot whose present beauty is hardly surpassed by the richness of its classic associations; where romance lurks, scarcely hidden, in the memory of Zenobia: where the olives that cover the hill sides have a primeval look; and, like a very Titania under the love-spell, she wakes from her dream of the past, and, behold! her vision is—a donkey!—no, I beg pardon—*two* donkeys; one that nearly lost its burden; and the other that its burden nearly lost!"

"How foolish you are, Severn!" said Clara, pouting very becomingly, while the others laughed heartily. "Besides, you need not expect me to get up any sentiment about Zenobia. The mistake of her life was that she did not die at the proper time, instead of retiring to a country town—of all places in the world—living a comfortable life, and dying a commonplace death in her bed, for all I know. It was just stupid in her!"

Her brother smiled. "I think you are right, Clara. Zenobia should never have survived her chains and the Roman triumph, if she had wished to leave a perfect picture of herself to posterity. However, I doubt if we have the right to exact the sacrifice of her merely to gratify our ideas of romantic propriety. By living she only proved herself less heroine, more woman. But, Clara, what *did* you see?—besides the donkeys, I mean."

Mr. Carlisle felt so keenly the antagonism of Mr. Sinclair's presence, that he must either leave the room or find some vent; and therefore his sister was compelled to be safety-valve, and submit to his teasing mood. Perhaps she was not altogether an innocent victim, since she it was who had somewhat wilfully introduced the discordant element into the family.

"We saw ruins and waterfalls, of course," she replied to the last question—a little petulance in her tone, which soon, however, disappeared. "But the most enjoyable thing of the whole day was the dinner. I usually cannot see any pleasure in eating out of doors, but to-day we were obliged to do so, for the hotel was not at all inviting; and then it is the proper thing to

do to have the table spread in the portico of the Temple of Vesta. Gagiati had put up a delicious dinner at Mr. Sinclair's order, so we were not dependent upon country fries and macaroni. Just as we were sitting down Lady Gertrude came up with her mother and lover, and we joined forces. I assure you we were not silent. I never enjoyed a meal more in my life."

"O Tivoli! ancient Tibur, how art thou fallen! Donkeys and dinner!" exclaimed Mr. Carlisle. "Well, fair Titania, did you supply your gentle animal with the honey-bag of the 'red-hipped humble-bee,' or was his appetite more plebeian, so that 'a peck of provender' was more acceptable?"

"Assunta, do you allow your patient to talk so much?" said Mrs. Grey, her amiability still proof against attack. "If he excites his imagination in this way, he can hardly hope to sleep without a powerful anodyne."

"My patient, as you call him," replied Assunta, smiling, "is not quite so submissive, I find, as when obedience was a necessity, and not a virtue. Still, if he would allow me a very humble suggestion, I would remind him that he has not been quite as well to-day, and that it is some time past his usual hour for retiring."

There was no irritation in Mr. Carlisle's face as he looked at Assunta with one of his rare smiles. The very tones of her voice seemed to give him a feeling of rest. "A very broad hint on the part of my tyrant," he replied, "which I will be wise enough to take, in its present form, lest it should become more emphatic. Good-night, Mr. Sinclair. I feel that there is the less need of an apology for excusing myself, as I leave you in good hands

Clara, when Giovanni has served the tea, please send him to me."

In leaving the room Mr. Carlisle dropped his cigar-case, which Assunta perceived, and hastened with it to the library, where she knew she should find him awaiting Giovanni.

"*Petite,*" he exclaimed, as she entered, "kill that man for me, and make me everlastingly your debtor."

"I am sure," she answered, laughing, "you have had it all your own way to-night. I began to think he must have taken a vow of silence."

"Still waters!" said her guardian. "He can afford to be silent; he is biding his time."

"Are you not the least bit unjust and uncharitable?" asked Assunta. "But never mind, you shall not have a lecture to-night, for you look very weary. Promise me that you will take the medicine I send you."

"I will take it, if you bring it yourself."

"But I cannot do that. I have your enemy to entertain, you know."

"And much joy do I wish you," said Mr. Carlisle. "I intend to study up affinities and repulsions psychologically; and then I shall perhaps be able to understand why one person, without any assignable cause, should act as a perpetual blister—genuine Spanish flies—and another, a certain dear little friend of mine for instance, should be ever a soothing balm."

"Cold cream!" suggested Assunta, "since you will use such pharmaceutical comparisons. And now, if I have shocked your sense of refinement sufficiently, I must say good-night."

"Good-night, dear child," returned her guardian cordially, but his next thought was a bitter one, and an almost prophetic feeling of

loneliness came over him, as he watched the smoke curling up from his cigar.

As soon as the incubus of Mr. Carlisle's presence was removed, Mr. Sinclair threw off the silence which was so unnatural to him, and became at once the attentive, gallant man of the world. Even Assunta, had she met him then for the first time, would not have received that impression of insincerity which had repelled her formerly. She could hardly wonder to-night that Clara Grey, who never looked below the surface, or cared, so long as peace reigned on the outside, what elements of disturbance might be working in the depths, should have suffered her heart to confide itself to the keeping of one apparently so devoted. She had never before imagined that they were so well suited to each other; and as Mr. Sinclair, after an hour, arose to take his leave, she was surprised into most unusual cordiality, as she bade him good-night. But, unfortunately for the impression he had been at such pains to produce, the glamour of fascination disappeared with his retreating footsteps; so that even while Mr. Sinclair was congratulating himself upon his success, Assunta found herself wondering at the almost painful revulsion of feeling which followed his departure.

Mrs. Grey's bright face indicated no such change. She was perfectly satisfied with her lover, and no less so with herself. She checked a movement of Assunta's to retire by saying:

"Do you mind waiting a little longer, dear? I want so much to have a quiet chat. Come, let us draw our chairs up to the fire, the blaze is so cheering."

"You do not look as if you need-

ed any help from outside influences," said Assunta, and there was
a shade of sadness in her tone.
" But I am all ready for a talk."

A cloud—a light summer one—
overspread Mrs. Grey's clear sky
and shadowed her face, as she said,
after a pause : "Assunta, why does
Severn dislike George so much ?"

Assunta was too truthful to deny
the fact, so she simply said :

"We cannot always control our
feelings, Clara ; but, as a general
thing, I do not find Mr. Carlisle
unreasonable."

" He certainly is very unreasonable in this case," returned Mrs.
Grey quickly, "and I am sorry
it is so, for I love Severn very
much. Still, I shall not allow an
unfounded prejudice to stand in
the way of my happiness. Assunta, I have promised Mr. Sinclair
that I will marry him in September,
when we shall be in Paris, on our
way to America."

" I supposed," said Assunta, "that
it would come soon, and I hope,
dear Clara, that you will be very,
very happy." Doubt was in her
mind, but she had not the heart to
let it appear in her manner.

" And," Mrs. Grey continued, " I
want you to understand, dear, that
with us you will always have a
home at your disposal, where you
will be welcomed as a sister.
George wished me to tell you that
this is his desire as well as mine."

" You are both too kind," replied
Assunta, touched by this thoughtfulness of her at a time when selfishness is regarded as a special
privilege. " My arrangements can
easily be made afterwards ; but I
do very much appreciate your kindness."

" Nonsense !" said Mrs. Grey,
" you belong to us ; and the difficulty will probably be that we

shall not be able to keep such an
attractive bit of property."

" You are setting me the example," said Assunta, laughing.

" Ah ! yes," returned Mrs. Grey ;
" but then, there is only one
George Sinclair, you know, as a
temptation."

Assunta fancied she could hear
Mr. Carlisle exclaim, " God be
praised !" to that natural expression of womanly pride, and she
herself wondered if it would be
possible for her to fall under such
a delusion.

But Mrs. Grey had not yet reached the point of the conversation ·
what had been said was only pre-
liminary. The truth was, she
dreaded her brother's reception of
the news, and she wished to avoid
being present at the first outbreak.

"You have so much influence
with Severn," she said at last, " I
wish you would tell him about it,
and try to make him feel differently
towards George. I am sure you
can. We are going to the Villa
Doria to-morrow, and this will give
you an opportunity. I hope the
storm will be over before we return," she added, laughing ; " at
any rate, the lightning will not
strike you."

It was like Mrs. Grey to make
this request—so like her that
Assunta did not think it either
strange or selfish. She promised
to break the news, which she knew
would be unwelcome. But she
could not conscientiously promise
to use an influence in overcoming
a prejudice she entirely shared.
An affectionate good-night was exchanged, and then Assunta retired
to her room. It was not often that
she indulged herself in a revery—
in those waking dreams which are
so unprofitable, and from which
one is usually aroused with the

spiritual tone lowered, and the heart discontented and dissatisfied. But this had been a trying day; and now, as she reviewed it, and came at last to its close, she found herself envying her friend the joy which seemed so complete, and wondering why her lot should be so different. Happiness had come to Mrs. Grey as to a natural resting-place; while she, to whom a bright vision of it had been presented, must thrust it from her as if it were a curse and not a blessing. And here she paused, and better thoughts came to replace the unworthy ones. This lot which she was envying—was it not all of the earth, earthy? Would she change, if she could? Had she not in her blessed faith a treasure which she would not give for all the human happiness this world has power to bestow? And here was the key to the difference at which she had for the moment wondered. Much, very much, had been given to her; was it strange that much should be required? Had she, then, made her sacrifice only to play the Indian giver towards her God, and wish back the offering he had accepted at her hands? No, she would not be so ungenerous. In the light of faith the brightness which had illuminated the life of her friend grew dim and faded, while the shadow of what had seemed so heavy a cross resting upon her own no longer darkened her soul. And soon, kneeling before her crucifix, she could fervently thank the dear Lord that he had granted her the privilege of suffering something for his love; and she prayed for strength to take up her cross *daily*, and bear it with courage and generosity.

V.

SIENNA.

IT was on a beautiful evening in June, just when spring was merging into summer, that Mr. Carlisle's family arrived in Sienna, and found a truly delightful home awaiting them, thanks to Giovanni's energy and thoughtful skill. The soft but somewhat enervating air of Rome had failed to restore Mr. Carlisle's strength; and the physician imperatively ordered that panacea which seems, in the opinion of the faculty, to be the last resource when other prescriptions have failed—complete change. An almost unaccountable attraction had drawn their thoughts towards Sienna, and Giovanni had been despatched to Tuscany with *carte blanche* as to preparations. He had proved himself entirely worthy of confidence; and the praises bestowed upon him by all the family, as they inspected the result of his efforts, were not unmerited. He had succeeded in engaging, for the season, a pleasant, airy villa about a mile beyond the Florentine gate of that quaint, proud city, and no expense had been spared to render it comfortable and home-like. A small grove in front of the house and a flower garden on one side promised many a pleasant hour during those days when shade and beauty afford relief and divert the mind from the power of the midsummer sun. The *loggia* in the rear of the house, where Mr. Carlisle, his sister, and ward were now standing, commanded a most extensive and beautiful view. Directly beneath them the land sloped down into a graceful valley covered with vineyards. Beyond was a long stretch of *campagna* ; and in the far distance, like a giant sentinel, rose Radicofani, on the summit of which still lingered the glory of a sunset whose gorgeousness had already departed. There is much in first impressions—more, perhaps, than we are willing to acknowledge—and it may well be doubted whether any after-sunshine would have secured for Sienna the favor it now enjoyed had Radicofani appeared for the first time before the little group assembled on the balcony, rising weird-like from out a veil of mist and cloud.

Mrs. Grey actually sighed, as, instantly spanning with a loving, womanly thought the distance which separated her from the lover she had regretfully left in Leghorn, she turned to her companions, saying : "Oh! I wish George were here. I think Sienna is lovely. There! I have seen the new moon over my left shoulder, and now I am sure he will not come this month."

Mrs. Grey was evidently very much in love. Mr. Sinclair's presence and absence formed the light and shade of her life's picture ; and a picture it was whose colors were too glaring, its contrasts too striking, and it lacked deep feeling in its tone. After a pause she continued : "But then I have always noticed that George does not like views." And removing her pretty travelling-hat, she went away to superintend Amalie's unpacking.

"He certainly did not like *my* views," said Mr. Carlisle in a low voice to Assunta, "when I expressed them to him rather freely the other day. But neither did I like his ; so we were quits there."

But the attention of the traveller was soon entirely engrossed in securing the rest needful after so fatiguing a journey ; and it was some days before Mr. Carlisle was sufficiently strong to explore the city, whose walls and towers could be seen, in all their mediæval picturesqueness, from the *loggia.*

At last, however, the change recommended began to tell upon the invalid, and each day added its portion of renewed strength, until Mr. Carlisle threatened every possible and impossible herculean labor, by way of proving that he was, as he said, "ready for anything."

The ladies had insisted upon postponing any sight-seeing until all could enjoy it together, though Clara protested that complete stagnation was evidently her fate. One could not find much excitement in a grove and a mountain after the first hour of novelty. Still, as long as the mail brought her a daily letter from Mr. Sinclair, and took in return the dainty, perfumed envelope containing so many pretty, loving nothings, she did not appear to be hopelessly inconsolable.

Assunta had, without scruple, made one exception to the generous resolution of waiting. But it was because she knew that the expedition she wished particularly to make alone would afford no pleasure to the others, while their presence might be the occasion of much pain to herself. Of course the interest Sienna had for her was its association with S. Catherine ; and she longed to see the spot consecrated by the heroic sanctity of one whose humility was as profound as her influence on the world was powerful. She took the opportunity on Sunday, after she and Marie had assisted at Mass in a little suburban church, to visit the house of the dyer whose honor and privilege it was to be the father of a woman the life and character of whom might well be studied by the women of to-day. S. Catherine possessed all that the most ambitious of her sex in the present day could desire—an immense public influence. How did she gain it? Only by seeking to lose herself in the obscurity of an ignoble origin; in labors and privations for the sake of a love whose consuming fire many waters of tribulation could not quench; and in that truly hidden life in which God delights to work his wonders. The only right she claimed was that of loving, and consequently of suffering, more than others. The only insignia of rank she coveted was a crown of thorns, and it was granted to her. by her Eternal Lover, who could refuse her nothing. Her power was in God's exaltation of the humble, in his use of the weak things of the world to confound the mighty. Well might those hands, which·were privileged to bear in them the marks of the Lord Jesus—the sacred stigmata—be made instrumental in leading back to Rome its exiled pontiff-king. Self-annihilation was the secret of the influence of those glorious women of the ages of faith who have since been placed upon the altars of the church. O restless, self-seeking women of to-day! striving for a power which will curse and not bless you, where is the sweet perfume of your humility? Where are the fruits of mortification? Where the aureola of sanctity ⸳ Where are those grand works for God, offspring of a faith that believes all and a love that dares all? For these are the virtues in a S. Catherine or a S. Teresa which all can imitate. Or, if these standards are too high for modern souls, where are the homely qualities of those women commended by S. Paul, who adorn themselves with modesty, learn in silence, are faithful in all things, having a care of the house? Thank God, the hand of the Lord is not shortened, and holy mother church cherishes many a hidden gem of sanctity which will one day adorn the bride at the coming of her divine Spouse! Yet these are but the exceptions, unknown in the midst of the vast, ever-moving multitude seeking the open arena of life, and desiring a part in its contests, animated by hopes as false as they are human, placing that almost insuperable barrier of pride between their souls and the Sacred Heart of our divine Lord. S. James has given us this simple rule of a holy life: "To visit the fatherless and widows in their tribulation, and to keep ourselves unspotted from the world"—in two words, charity and purity. May the ever Blessed Mother of God and her glorious servant S. Catherine intercede for the women of the church, that they may never covet those empty baubles for which the women of the world are now spending their lives!

Assunta, simple child of the faith, thought nothing of all this, as she passed reverently over the threshold of the house, whose rooms, retaining still something of their original appearance, are now converted into chapels. The sacristan, perceiving in the young girl an earnestness of piety to which he was not accustomed in most of the strangers who visited this holy spot, showed to her without solicitation, the crucifix before which S. Catherine was kneel·. ing when she received the stigmata. With kind attention the good man placed a *prie-dieu* before the precious object of veneration and, then retiring, gave Assunta an opportunity to satisfy her devotion. Making a place for Marie beside her, she was soon absorbed in prayer. Here, where the very atmosphere was filled with a spirit of love and sacrifice, where the crucifix before her spoke so eloquently of the closeness of the union between the faithful soul and its suffering Lord, how easy it seemed to make aspirations and resolutions which would of necessity lose something of their heat when exposed to the chilling air of the world's indifference! How far off now was Mr. Carlisle's affection, of whose influence she never ceased to feel something; how near the divine love of the Sacred Heart, that one sole object of S. Catherine's desire and adoration! It had been the last request of Father Du Pont, when he gave Assunta his good-by and blessing, that, while in Sienna, she would often visit this holy house. He judged rightly that the evident presence of the supernatural would help to counteract the spirit of worldliness which surrounded her in her daily life. She herself already felt that it was good for her to be there; and though, when she returned home, the sensible fervor of the moment died away, the effects remained in reanimated strength. " Courage, my child, and perseverance; God is with you," were the last words she had heard from the good priest's lips; and they kept singing on in her soul a sweet, low harmony, like the music of seashells, soothing her in many an anxious hour.

When once Mr. Carlisle was able to go out without danger of fatigue, Mrs. Grey could no longer complain of stagnation. The cathedral, the academy, and the numberless places of interest within the city walls, the drives, the walks through the shady lanes near the villa, twilight strolls through the vineyards, and excursions into the surrounding country, filled up the time through all those pleasant weeks. Before they could realize it Assunta's birthday, her day of freedom, was at hand. A week before the eventful occasion Mr. Sinclair had arrived in Sienna, making Mrs. Grey superlatively happy. The joy he imparted to the others must be expressed in something less than the positive degree.

The sun rose brightly on the 15th of August. Nature responded to the joyous Benedicite, and " all the works of the Lord" seemed to "magnify him for ever " for the great things he had done in giving to heaven a Queen, to earth an Advocate. Nor was man silent. The grave city of Sienna put off its wonted dignity, and, by the unfurling of its gay flags, the spreading of tapestries, and the ringing of bells, testified its share in the common rejoicing of Christendom. It was the Feast of the Assumption, and Assunta Howard's twenty-first birthday. Was it strange that the young girl should have arisen with a heavy heart but little in sympathy with the glad sights and sounds that greeted her in these first waking moments ? Surely, to those who understand the workings of the human heart it was most natural. On this day ended the relations between herself and her guardian. However hard the tie which bound her had made her duty towards him, it was harder still to nature to sever the bond. She was free now to go where she would; and it would soon be right for her to separate from him who was no longer her guardian, and was not satisfied to be only her friend. She had not realized before how much happiness she had experienced in the relationship which existed no longer; how she had rested content in the very face of danger, because the peril had in it so much more of pleasure than of pain. How sweet had been the intercourse which duty had sanctioned, and which duty must now interrupt! The feeling was all wrong, and she knew it, and she would not fail to struggle against it. Her will was resolute, but it was evident that she was not to conquer in life's battle by throwing aside her arms and withdrawing from the contest. The bearing of the cross must be daily, and not only day after day, but year after year. Only to-day she seemed to feel its weight more, and she sank a little beneath it. Was it her guardian angel that whispered courage to her soul, or was it the Blessed Mother, to whose loving protection she had· been specially confided, who reminded her that our dear Lord fell three times beneath the overwhelming burden of his cross, and bade her be comforted? Yes, it was the feast of that dear Mother, and no mere human feeling should prevent her joining in the church's exultation and corresponding to her salutation in the Introit: "Gaudeamus omnes in Domino."

Assunta had ordered the carriage to be in readiness to take her to San Domenico for early Mass, and Marie's knock at the door informed her that it was waiting. She had before visited the church, but only in the way of sight-seeing. She had then been struck with its many points of interest; she had no idea until this morning how devotional it was. After Mass, at which she had received, in the Holy Communion, strength and peace, she remained a long time before the chapel containing those most beautiful frescos, by Razzi, of incidents in the life of the great saint of Sienna. The finest of all, S. Catherine in Ecstasy, is a treasure both of art and devotion. Apparently fainting, supported by two of her nuns, the countenance of the saint has that indescribable expression of peace which we see in those whose conversation is in heaven. But, more than this, the evident absence of all sensation indicates that the soul is rapt into an ineffable union with its divine Lord, and has passed, for the moment, beyond the confines of earth. Seemingly dead, and yet alive, the frail body, with its beautiful, calm face, rests upon its knees in the arms of the two Sisters, who, with all the tranquillity of the cloister, yet form a contrast to her who is so wholly dead to the world.

Assunta gazed upon the picture until it seemed to impart rest to her own soul; and yet the impression was very different from that she always received in looking at the other S. Catherine whom angels are bearing to her sepulture. Marie at last interrupted her, and, reminding her that she was the important personage at the villa on that day, suggested that she should return to breakfast. And Assunta determined that no cloud should disturb the serenity of the occasion, which all intended should be joyous.

Mr. Carlisle met her at the door on her return, and assisted her to alight. Then he took her hand in both his, and his eyes spoke volumes, as he said:

"Let me look at you, child, and see how you bear your honors

You are more of a heroine than I thought; for even at this distance we have heard the bells and have seen the flags. What an important little body you are! No one thought it worth while to ring me into my majority."

"It is because you did not come into the world under the same auspices," replied Assunta.

"Auspice Maria—that is the secret, then." And Mr. Carlisle lowered his voice as he added: "Consider me a Mariolater from this time, my devotion deriving an ever-increasing fervor from the doctrine of the Assumption. Well, you are free, and I suppose I am expected to congratulate you. How do you enjoy the sensation of liberty?"

"I do not think that I am yet enough accustomed to the use of my wings to feel the difference between what I was yesterday and what I am to-day. But in one point I am unchanged. I have an excellent appetite for my breakfast."

Assunta was determined to ward off all approach to sentiment.

"And here is Clara, wondering, no doubt, if I have been left behind in Sienna."

Mrs. Grey came out into the garden, looking very lovely in her white morning dress, and followed by Mr. Sinclair.

"Severn, you are the most selfish man I ever saw," exclaimed the impetuous little lady. "Do you flatter yourself that you have the monopoly of Assunta, and that no one else is privileged to wish her *cento di questi giorni*, as Giovanni says?—though I am sure I should not like to live a hundred years. My beauty would be gone by that time." And she looked archly at her lover standing beside her.

"I fancy that even relentless time

would 'write no wrinkles on thine antique brow,' reluctant to spoil anything so fair," said Mr. Sinclair in his most gallant tone; then extending his hand to Assunta, he continued:

"Miss Howard, allow me to congratulate you, and to wish that your life may be as cloudless as is this wonderful sky. The day is like yourself—exquisitely beautiful."

The color mounted into Assunta's cheeks, but it was with displeasure at such uncalled-for flattery. Mr. Carlisle turned away, and walked into the house; while his sister, with that amiability which often atoned for her want of tact, exclaimed:

"Bravo! George, you have said quite enough for us both; so I will only ditto your speech, and add to it my birthday kiss. Now, dear, let us go to breakfast. Severn is already impatient."

The table had been placed in a large hall running the whole length of the house; and as the three were about to enter, Assunta paused on the threshold, in astonishment and delight at the magical transformation. The walls were literally garlanded with flowers, and fresh greens were festooned from the ceiling, while in the centre of the breakfast-table was a basket of the rarest exotics. Not only Sienna, but Florence, had been commissioned to furnish its choicest flowers for the occasion. Assunta's eyes filled with tears, and for a moment she could not speak. Mr. Carlisle, perceiving her emotion, offered her his arm, and led her towards a side-table, saying:

"And here are our trifling birthday gifts, which you must not despise because they fall so far short of expressing all that we feel for you."

There was a beautifully-framed proof engraving of Titian's masterpiece, the Assumption, from Mr. Carlisle. Clara had chosen as her gift a set of pearls, "because they looked so like the darling," she said. Mr. Sinclair's offering was a bouquet of rare and exquisite flowers. He had all the penetration of an experienced man of the world, and understood well that Miss Howard would prefer not to accept from him anything less perishable. Assunta put her hand in Clara's, as she said :

"I never can thank you, it is all so beautiful." And then she paused, until Clara exclaimed :

"Why, Assunta love, what a solemn birthday face ! To be sure, the flight of time is a serious thing. I begin to feel it myself, and shall very soon dispense with birthdays altogether—such disagreeable reminders as they are."

"What is it, *petite ?*" asked Mr. Carlisle. "You know that to-day you have only to command us, and we will prove your most obedient subjects."

"Oh ! it was nothing of any consequence ; only a thought that you would consider very foolish crossed my mind. I am sure my solemnity was quite unintentional."

"Well, a penny for that thought, twice told."

Assunta, perceiving that Mr. Sinclair was out of hearing, explained :

"All this for my poor worthless self and nothing for Her whom God has delighted to honor. I think I was feeling a little jealous for my dear Mother. I did not want my feast to be better than hers."

"Is that all ?" said Mr. Carlisle. "To hear is to obey." And without another word he quickly removed from the table everything but the picture, and, taking flowers and candles from the mantel-piece, he improvised a really artistic shrine. Giovanni, who was serving breakfast, lighted the candles, and surveyed the effect with satisfaction.

"Thank you," said Assunta, and she would not even remember that the love was wanting which would give value to the offering. "I shall hardly dare think a wish to-day, the consequence is so magical."

"And now, Severn," said his sister, "if you have finished your popery, you had better call Assunta's attention to my ever-increasing appetite. Giovanni, too, will not like to have his efforts to honor the occasion slighted by a want of appreciation."

Mr. Carlisle offered the young girl his arm, and led her to the table, saying :

"This is my first attempt at Mariolatry. Quite a success, is it not ?"

"If it were only an outward sign of inward grace," said Clara, laughing, "exterior piety would be quite becoming to you, Severn. You really have an artistic taste. But you are too absent-minded to-day ! Can you not see that we are starving ?"

Assunta was so accustomed to hear sacred things spoken of lightly, and often irreverently, that she had learned to make a little solitude in her heart, into which she could retire from the strife, or even the thoughtlessness, of tongues, and many a short act of reparation was there performed for those who were unconscious of offence.

"I wonder," said Mrs. Grey, as after breakfast the party were standing on the *loggia*—"I wonder if Giovanni has succeeded in finding a good balcony for the races to-morrow. I would not miss seeing them for the world. I dote on horses."

"I very much doubt," replied her brother, "if the horses will excite the least admiration, judging frcm the specimens Sienna has tnus far produced. But the races will be interesting, because they are entirely unique. I believe that Giovanni has been very successful in securing a balcony, and he intends to have it surpass all others in decoration; so I hope that the ladies will do their part, not to disgrace his efforts. He will expect the jewels to be set in a manner worthy of the casket which contains them."

"Never fear, Severn! Do you think a lady ever failed to look her best on such an occasion? An open balcony and a crowd—surely, she needs no other occasion for vanity."

George Sinclair removed his cigar to remark carelessly:

"And so the admiration of *one* is, after all, insufficient to satisfy you?"

"No, it is not, you dear, lazy, old fellow, and you know it. It is only because I like your taste to be appreciated that I want others to admire me. I do not think there is a more delicious sensation than to feel that you are pretty to begin with, and then dressed so as to show every point to the best advantage, and to know that every eye is fixed upon you. One can be so innocently unconscious of it all the time."

"Clara, I am ashamed of you," exclaimed her brother. "You are a perfect mirror of your sex; only, unfortunately, it is the weaknesses that you reflect to the life, and none of the virtues."

"Hush, impertinence!" replied Clara, laughing merrily. "One cannot always be a well awfully deep and reflecting only the stars. Come, George, what will be most becoming to me for to-morrow?"

If it had been a few months after marriage, instead of before, this devoted lover would probably have replied, "A fool's cap and bells, for all I care!" As it was, he concealed his inward irritation, and no one would have doubted his sincerity as he said: "You cannot fail to be charming in anything; and I will not choose or suggest, because I would like to enjoy the pleasure of a surprise."

Mr. Sinclair was sometimes fascinated by Clara's piquancy and brightness; but she did not suit all moods, and to-day Assunta's quiet dignity and the antagonism that Mr. Carlisle always excited more or less, produced an interior disturbance of which a wife would surely have received the full benefit. It is strange that an entirely worldly man will often, from a selfish motive, show a power of self-control which Christians find it difficult to practise, even for the love of God. Alas! that the devil should receive many a sacrifice, many an offering of suffering and heroism, which, the intention being changed, would produce a saint.

Mrs. Grey had not penetration enough to see below the surface, and she was entirely satisfied with her lover, whom she considered the best and handsomest man in the world, not even excepting her brother. She could rush fearlessly against a mood which would have kept a more appreciative nature at a distance; and here, perhaps, she had an advantage.

She was now about to answer Mr. Sinclair's very gratifying speech when an interruption came in the shape of Giovanni with a note for herself, which she read hastily, and then said: "Severn, it is from Lady Gertrude. They were passing through Sienna, and have remained over a day expressly to see your humble servant. They wish me to dine with them this evening, accompanied by my *preux chevalier*— her own expression, George. But I do not know about leaving Assunta alone on her birthday, even for Lady Gertrude."

"Oh! I hope you will not disappoint your friends on my account," said Assunta. "I have already had my celebration this morning, and it is quite proper that I should devote this evening to reflections upon my coming responsibilities."

"Besides," said Mr. Carlisle, "I beg to inform you that Assunta will not be left alone. I flatter myself that I count for one, at least; and I will endeavor to act as your substitute, Clara, in most effectually preventing those contemplated reflections. Responsibility and golden hair are an association of ideas quite incongruous, in my opinion."

"I see," said Clara, "that the balance is in Lady Gertrude's favor. What do you say, *caro*?"

"If you mean me," said George Sinclair in a slightly unamiable tone, "I am always at your service."

"You bear!" replied the irrepressible Clara, "I will not allow you to go if you are cross. Well, Giovanni, come to my room in ten minutes for the answer; and remember to order the carriage for half-past five."

"Truly," said Mr. Carlisle, turning to Assunta after his sister had left the *loggia*, "I think I never saw so sunshiny a person as Clara. It is always high noon with her."

While Assunta assented cordially, Mr. Sinclair said to himself:

"Too much sunshine makes an unpleasant glare, and noon is always the most disagreeable part of the day. I confess to liking a little of the shadow of repose."

He was careful, however, to keep his thoughts to himself. If the lover could feel imperfections so keenly, it argued but poorly for the blindness of love on the part of the husband. And yet this blindness, false and unworthy as it is, seems to be the only chance of peace for worldly husbands and wives, the only protection against the evil tendencies of uncontrolled human nature. All Clara's sunshine might fail to make even a silver lining to the cloud rising in the distant future.

The sun shone brightly enough, however, when Mrs. Grey and Mr. Sinclair took their seats in the barouche to drive into Sienna; and the lady, who so much delighted in the delicious sensation of undisguised admiration, must have been more than satisfied this afternoon. Many eyes followed the handsome pair, as they passed rapidly towards the hotel. Clara knew that she was looking uncommonly well, and she was very proud of her companion's distinguished air and manner; so, altogether, she enjoyed quite a little triumph.

Assunta and Mr. Carlisle dined alone; and, as they rose from the table just at sunset, Mr. Carlisle proposed a walk down into the vineyards.

"It will soil that pretty white dress of yours, I know; but the air is so refreshing, and I want you to occupy for a while the new rustic seat I have had placed near the brook, in that lovely spot we discovered the other day. Take a shawl with you, *petite*, for it will be cooler as soon as the sun sets."

They strolled along slowly down through the narrow paths which separated the vines heavy with the fast-ripening fruit, pausing now and then, as some new beauty in the distant view or in their immediate surroundings excited their attention. At last, at the bottom of the valley, close beside a brook, and beneath a clump of trees, they came upon one of those fairy spots where nature seems to have arranged herself expressly to attract an artist's eye.

"Giovanni is truly invaluable," said Mr. Carlisle. "I had only to give him a suggestion, and see how well he has carried out my ideas. This is the very luxury of comfort." And seating himself, he lighted a cigar, advised Assunta to put on her shawl, and was evidently prepared for a pleasant hour.

As they sat there, almost in silence, the Angelus sounded from a distant convent tower; and, as if in answer to its summons, Assunta began to sing in a sweet, low voice Schubert's Ave Maria. Mr. Carlisle did not say a word until it was finished; then he begged for just one more, and, knowing how much he liked the simple Scotch songs, she sang "Robin Adair."

"Assunta, your voice grows sweeter every day. It is perfect rest to me to hear you sing." Then, after a pause, he threw away his cigar, and turned towards her a very earnest face.

"*Petite*, listen to me patiently a moment. I am a very proud man, as you know, and one who is not apt to sue, even where he greatly desires. It seems "—and the peculiar smile broke over his face— "that you have exercised some magic power, and with a touch of

your finger have thrown down the barrier of pride against which an army might beat in vain. My child, you know what I am going to say, because I have not changed since that moonlight night in the Colosseum, except, indeed, that the feeling I then expressed has strengthened and deepened every day. I made you a promise that night. I confess that it has been poorly enough redeemed; still, you must judge me by my self-conquests rather than by my failures. But to-day releases me; and having ceased to be your guardian, I cannot give you up. I need not repeat to you what I have already said. You know that you are dearer to me than the life you have saved. I only ask, as before, the right to devote that life to you. May I ?"

"I had hoped, Mr. Carlisle, that you would consider my former answer as final," said Assunta; but, though her words were cold, her voice trembled. "I, too, am unchanged since that night you speak of. I am compelled to be so."

"Assunta, you are such a child; do you, then, think it nothing to have won the love of a man who has reached middle life and has never loved before ?"

"Mr. Carlisle," said the young girl sadly, "if I thought it nothing, I should not feel the pain it costs me to repeat to you, that it cannot be. I am so unworthy of your love; you must not think I do not value it. Your friendship has been more to me than I dare tell you, lest you should misunderstand me."

"Your heart pleads for me, child."

"Then I must not listen to it; for the voice of God in my soul pleads more loudly."

"Assunta," said Mr. Carlisle, "I

think you did not understand me before—you do not understand me now. Do you suppose I should interfere in your religion? No more than I have ever done. You do not know me, child."

"I think I know you better than you know yourself, presumptuous as this sounds," said Assunta, forcing a smile. "I am sure that, were I to marry you, you would not be satisfied to hold a place in my heart second even to God. But," she added, as the old expression of bitterness crossed her guardian's face, "all this is useless. Let me put a question to you, and answer me candidly. Suppose I had made a promise to you, who love me—made it, we will grant, out of love for you—and afterwards, yielding to my own weakness, I should break that promise. Would you feel that I had done rightly— that I was to be trusted?"

"Certainly not, child. You ask strange questions."

"Well, I have, out of love for our dear Lord, made him a promise which I believed his love required of me. He is a jealous Lover, Mr. Carlisle. I dare to say this reverently. Suppose, for the sake of a human affection—for your sake—I should fail to keep my promise; would you not have reason to doubt my fidelity to you, when I could be unfaithful to my God?"

"My child, I do not comprehend such reasoning. You either do not, cannot love me, or else you have suffered religious fanaticism to get the better of your judgment. I hoped that the plea of love would be sufficient to win my cause; but it is not all. Look your future fairly in the face, Assunta. What are you going to do? You are young; I need not add, beautiful.

Surely, you understand that without me you are unprotected. Have you any plans, or have you already become so independent that you prefer not to make me your confidant? My pride is gone indeed when I put my suit in another form. I ask only your hand. Let me have the right to protect you in the world you know so little. I will wait to win your heart."

"Mr. Carlisle," interrupted Assunta with more emotion than he had ever seen in her before, "you are cruel in your persistence. You wilfully misunderstand me. It seems to give you pleasure to make this trial as hard for me as possible. I have told you before that I can never marry you; let that be enough." And bursting into tears, she rose hastily from her seat.

Her guardian was so taken by surprise that for an instant he sat motionless; then he followed the excited girl, and joined her before she had proceeded far along the vineyard path.

"Take my arm, *petite,*" he said gently, and they walked some distance in silence. At last Assunta said with regained composure:

"Mr. Carlisle, you asked me about my plans, and you have a right to know. I have thought much of the future, as you may believe. My desire is to return to Baltimore with Clara after her marriage, and pass the winter with Mary Percival Further than this I need not look."

There was no immediate answer. After a pause Mr. Carlisle said:

"You are your own mistress now. I shall of course place no obstacle in the way of your carrying out any wish or design which will conduce to your welfare. As for myself, the time may come when I shall cease to regret that I am in no wise necessary to your happiness. Meanwhile, it shall be as you say. Good heavens! to think that a mere girl should have the power to move me so," he went on, as if speaking to himself.

And apparently his thoughts were so full of Assunta that he forgot her actual presence, for they reached the house in silence, and then Mr. Carlisle proceeded at once to his own room; and so ended the birthday.

The Sienna races are a thoroughly unique spectacle—almost childish, like many features of the Roman Carnival, to the over-cultivated and consequently over-fastidious taste of this age. They take one back to the days when men were more simple, when hearts did not grow old and faith was strong. These childlike traits produced a race of men who were but "children of a larger growth," and, like children, amused with even a small amount of pomp and show, heroes as they were. And a strange contrast were the races of that 16th of August to the usual occupations of the Siennese. Mr. Carlisle's carriage passed beneath innumerable flags, and between gayly-tapestried windows, as it drove to the amphitheatre-shaped piazza, the centre of which was already filled, while every seat placed against the houses which bounded the square was occupied. The bright colors worn by the peasant women, with their large Tuscan hats and the more subdued dress of the men, produced an effect at once very peculiar and very picturesque. A little cheer from the bystanders greeted Mr. Carlisle's party, as they appeared upon the balcony; for no other decorations in all that vast piazza were so fine as those in

which Giovanni had shown so much skill, and surely no other ladies were as beautiful. There was no appearance of heartache or disappointment on any of the four faces which now looked out upon the crowd. We all, sooner or later, learn to wear a mask before the world, and the interior life of each one of us is often a sealed book to our nearest friends.

"Clara," said Assunta, as they seated themselves after their survey, "you seem to know more about the races than the rest of us. Please to enlighten my ignorance."

"I heard about them at the hotel last night," replied Mrs. Grey; "so you will find me very learned. Sienna is divided into seventeen wards; but only ten take part in the race, and these are decided by lot. The victor receives a prize and a sort of diminutive triumph, while the losers may think themselves lucky if they only get a scolding from their respective wards. The oracle has spoken, and further than this she is not informed."

"The rest we shall now see for ourselves," said Mr. Sinclair, "for I hear the music which I suppose accompanies the procession." And, as he spoke, the band entered the piazza from a side street. Then followed, in turn, the representatives of the different wards, each representation consisting of two flags—the colors of the ward—a number of pages, the race-horse led by an esquire, and the man who was afterwards to ride the racer, on horseback as a knight. The flag-bearers, as well as all in each division, wore exactly the colors of the flag of the ward, in costumes of the olden time ; and, as these flags were of entirely different combinations of colors, and most of them very brilliant, the procession would have been very effective without its peculiar charm. The flag-bearers were men of grace and skill, and from the moment of entering the square the flags were in continual motion—waved above their heads, flung into the air, passed under their arms and legs, and all without once touching the ground. It was a very poetical combination of color and motion, and Mrs. Grey impulsively clapped her hands with delight—a performance which her dignified lover evidently looked upon as childish. After this part of the procession came a large chariot drawn by four horses, with postilions, and bearing the ten different flags tastefully arranged. This was the model of the old Siennese battle-car, which bore the standard, and was in consequence the scene of the thickest of the fight. Upon it, in time of battle, stood a priest, invoking by his prayers protection and success. There also was the trumpeter, in readiness to give signals. A truly mediæval picture was this chariot, with associations which carried one back hundreds of years into the past. A band of music closed the procession, which, after passing around the piazza, entered the court-yard of the Palazzo Pubblico. Here the knights exchanged their helmets and plumes for jockey-caps, and mounted their racers. As they emerged from beneath the archway, and proceeded slowly towards the starting-place, across which a rope was drawn, Mr. Carlisle exclaimed, with a laugh in which there was more sarcasm than merriment:

"Are you a judge of horses, Clara? If so, you, who yesterday announced your jockey proclivities, must be greatly disappointed; for truly a set of sorrier-looking steeds I never beheld. The prize ought to be given to the one that comes

in last; for, where all are so slow, there would really be no little exercise of skill in moving more slowly than a coach-horse going up-hill, and yet moving at all."

"I think, Severn," replied his sister, "that your temper was not improved by the fever. It is very disagreeable in you to inform me that the horses are not Arabian chargers, for I never should have been the wiser."

"Most men are disagreeable," he retorted.

"George, you hear that, and do not resent it?" said Mrs. Grey indignantly.

"I leave that for you to do when you can, from experience of the contrary, deny the charge. But the horses are starting on their three times round." And Mr. Sinclair leaned over the balcony with an air of interest.

"Why do the men carry those short sticks in their hands?" asked Assunta.

"I believe," said Mr. Sinclair—for Mr. Carlisle became strangely inattentive—"that the riders are allowed by rule to do all the damage they can with the sticks, which are short, so as to limit somewhat their power; for their aim is to knock each other off the horses."

"The barbarians!" exclaimed Clara. "Oh! look, see how many are falling back on the third round. It rests with the two now. I bet on the sorrel."

"And he has won, Clara," said Assunta.

The whole piazza was now in motion. Shouts greeted the victor, and the defeated retired into obscurity.

"The modern Olympics are finished," said Mr. Carlisle. "Shall we go?"

As they drove towards home in

the red glow of the setting sun, Mr. Carlisle said abruptly :

"Clara, when did you tell me that you and Sinclair intend to make each other miserable?"

"I will not answer such a question, Severn. You are a perfect dog in the manger. You will not marry yourself or let any one else."

"If you wish to know," said Mr. Sinclair, "when your sister intends to make me the happiest of men, she has permitted me to hope that the end of September will be the term of my most impatient waiting."

"Then," continued Mr. Carlisle in the same abrupt tone, "we had better be on our way to Paris. We might start day after to-morrow, I think."

Mrs. Grey gave a little scream.

"Severn, you must be out of your mind. I thought you wished never to leave Sienna."

"I am weary to death of it; but that is not all. I have business matters to arrange, and the preparation of your *trousseau* will no doubt occupy weeks."

"But it will be so warm in Paris," persisted Mrs. Grey.

"Do people whose hearts are filled with love and their minds with coming matrimony think of weather, then? I thought such sublunary interests were left to those whose hearts were still unthawed. However, there are fans and ices enough in Paris to cool you off. I will write to-night to engage rooms." And then Mr. Carlisle relapsed into silence and abstraction.

Assunta understood well enough the cause of this change in the plans; but she was powerless to act, and could only submit. It, indeed, made little difference to her.

"George," said Clara to her lover, as they were strolling down the avenue in the moonlight, "can you imagine what is the matter with Severn? I never saw him in such a mood."

"Disappointed in love, I should judge from appearances," he replied indifferently.

"Nonsense! He does not know the meaning of the word," was the not very intelligent reply of the lady.

VI.

WOMAN'S INFLUENCE.

"AND so I have you all to myself once more; no interference from cruel guardians on your side, and none from unreasonable husbands on mine. Joking apart, Assunta darling, I think God has been very good to me to give me such a compensation for Harry's long absence. Every trial seems to have a blessing in its train, by way of a set-off. And you are just the very dearest of blessings." And Mary Lee moved her chair a little nearer to her friend, by way of showing her appreciation. Assunta looked up from her work with a bright smile, as she replied :

"You are not in the least changed from the dear Mary Percival of convent days—and happy days they were, too—while I feel twenty years older than I did the day I bade you good-by at the garden gate. But now you are mistaken. I am the one blessed, not blessing. For think what it is to me—a waif—to find awaiting me so kind a welcome and so pleasant a temporary home. God only knows what would have become of me without you."

"Oh !" said Mary, "my only fear was that, with so many claimants for the honor, I should never succeed in carrying off the prize. I am sure, until it was decided, and I saw your trunks safely landed at my door, I looked upon Mrs. Sinclair as my deadly enemy."

"Clara is very kind—much more

so than I deserve," said Assunta, while an expression of seriousness passed over her face; "but I should not have liked to accept her hospitality now. I think the present arrangement is more for the happiness of all parties."

And the remembrance of a certain evening on board the steamer, when Mr. Sinclair, a married man, had dared to tell her, his wife's friend, that she had first possessed his heart, and that his love for her was still unchanged, made her shudder now involuntarily. He must indeed have strangely forgotten himself, when, after that, he added his entreaties to those of his unsuspecting wife that she would look upon their home as hers. Assunta felt as if the word love had indeed been profaned by the lips of George Sinclair. God is love ; but she knew that he would not hesitate to take even that most holy name in vain. Why then scruple to profane the attribute ? However, all this was a secret, known to herself alone.

"Mrs. Sinclair must have been a lovely bride," said Mary musingly. "But, Assunta, why did Mr. Carlisle return at once to Europe ? I should think he would be tired of travelling by this time, and would like to settle down for a while on his own place. I have heard it is so beautiful."

"The habit of travelling grows

upon one," replied Assunta. "He only returned to Maryland to attend to certain matters in regard to his sister's property and mine. It was his intention to spend some time longer in Europe and the East.' Then, to change the subject, she continued: "But, Mary dear, when does your brother enter the seminary?"

"I do not know," said Mrs. Lee. "I cannot understand Augustine at all. He seems just as good and earnest as ever, and yet something troubles him, I see it plainly. But he is unusually reserved with me; so that I feel a reluctance to question him. I wish you would ask him about the seminary. You can do it quite incidentally; and very likely he would tell you all about it."

"I certainly will," said Assunta. "He is your brother; so I almost feel as if he were mine too."

"I do not think," continued Mary, "that he is well. I am afraid his trip to the East may have done him more harm than good. He always protests that he is perfectly well, if I ask him; but I am sure he does not look so."

"I have thought so myself, and I think we must look upon his case as our next duty." And Assunta arose, as the clock struck eleven.

The opportunity to take the case in hand came much sooner than the fair conspirators had anticipated. The next afternoon, while Mrs. Lee had excused herself for a few hours, in order to pay the expected weekly visit to her mother-in-law, Mr. Percival joined Assunta, as she sat alone in the cosey library, finishing a garment for a poor child in whom she was already interested. Assunta noticed more than usual the paleness of the spiritual face she had always so much admired, and the weariness of its expression; but,

with true feminine tact, she made no comment; only, as he seated himself beside the table, she looked up with a smile of welcome, as his sister might have done.

"Hard at work, as usual. I hope I do not interrupt you, Miss Howard?" said Mr. Percival, with an answering smile.

"Oh! no indeed. I am delighted to see you this evening. We have not had a good long talk since I came; and yet we have so many topics of mutual interest."

Mr. Percival took from his pocket a little box, and, opening it, said:

"Miss Howard, I have ventured to bring you a souvenir of my travels, which I beg you will accept from Mary's brother, and because of the association."

He placed in her hand a heart-shaped locket, plain but heavy, in the centre of which glowed a large crimson ruby, and around it were engraved the words, "Cor cordium." Within, on one side, was a miniature painting of the Sacred Heart of Jesus; on the other side was set a tiny crucifix, carved from the olive-wood of Gethsemani by one of the monks of Jerusalem, and which had been laid upon the altar in the Chapel of the Holy Sepulchre.

"And I prayed for you in that sacred spot most fervently, you may be sure," said Mr. Percival.

Assunta's eyes were still fixed upon the beautiful treasure which she held in her hand. Tears were in them, as she raised them at last, saying:

"Words are poor thanks for such a gift as this. You know, Mr. Percival, how much I shall value it. Indeed, I feel most unworthy to possess anything so precious; yet I shall accept it, as you said, from the brother of my dearest friend, who is to me truly a sister in affection." And pressing her lips to the crystal which protected the crucifix, she carefully replaced the locket in its case.

"And so you did not forget those foolish, fanciful remarks I made by Shelley's grave. I had not dreamed they would have dwelt in your memory so long; still less did I imagine they would inspire so beautiful a design as this, which is, of course, your own." Then she added after a little pause: "There is one greater gift even than this that I shall ask of you one of these days. It is one of your first Masses, when, as a priest, you are privileged to offer the Holy Sacrifice."

"Miss Howard," exclaimed Mr. Percival, with deep emotion, "that is a subject of which I cannot even think without suffering."

"Forgive me," murmured Assunta, surprised beyond measure. "It was indeed unpardonable in me to pain you by speaking of that which is between yourself and God alone. My only excuse is that I thought the matter had long been settled."

Then followed a silence, so prolonged that Assunta began to wonder what kept that manly head bowed forward upon the table. Was it confusion, was it prayer, or had he perhaps fainted? At last he suddenly looked up, and fixed those fine, earnest eyes of his full upon Assunta's face; and even in that moment the thought struck her what pure, true eyes they were.

"Miss Howard, you are the last person on earth to whom I ought to speak on this subject, and I know not what impels me to do so now. Pray for me; for my salvation may depend upon it."

Assunta tried to be calm, as she said gently, while she breathed a silent prayer for guidance:

"You must think of me as almost a sister."

Mr. Percival went on:

"Even your image, true and beautiful and holy as it is, and pure as an angel's, should never have been allowed to come between me and the God to whose special service I was inclined. But believe me, Miss Howard, never for one moment have I cherished a hope that you might be to me other than you are; only, when I have striven to rise above all human feeling, and to give myself unreservedly to him who demanded the sacrifice, God help me! you seemed to fill his place in my soul. Forgive me and pity me! I am miserably weak."

After a moment he continued:

"Ah! Miss Howard, you know what I mean. It is only because of my own weakness that I have found the memory of you an obstacle to my advance towards the perfection to which I aspired."

"And to which you will still aspire." And Assunta's voice was low and sweet, as she for the first time broke silence. "I had not dreamed of this, Mr. Percival, but I hope you will never have occasion to regret the confidence you have reposed, not in the ideal which has for a moment passed as a cloud of temptation between your soul and its high calling, but in one who, though full of faults, may yet offer you her sympathy and her prayers."

"God bless you!" escaped from Mr. Percival's lips.

"I am too young and inexperienced," continued Assunta, "to give you counsel; besides, I am a woman; but, with my woman's intuition, I think I see how all this has come about. . . . May I go on?"

"I beg you will; it is the sort of soul-wound that needs probing."

Assunta smiled. "I do not think such severe treatment will be required—only an examination, perhaps, preparatory to healing. You met me in Rome—forgive me if I speak too freely of myself—surrounded by that atmosphere of beauty and poetry which steals into the soul, because it 'breathes from the very centre of Catholic faith and the glory of the church militant. But when you met me, I was with those whose hearts were not open to such influences; and it was very natural that you and I should feel drawn to each other by the attraction of a common faith and hope. Do you think I could have said those foolish words, which it seems you have remembered only too well"—and she glanced at the little case in her hand—"if I had not felt that you could sympathize with my thoughts, however poorly they were expressed? Believe me, it was a certain earnestness of faith in me, which your presence drew out into somewhat too free expression and which remained in your memory as an attraction; and the devil has ingeniously made use of that little opening to insinuate some subtle poison. But his power is at an end, thank God! He has, for me, overreached his mark. The very fact that you could speak of this to me proves that the danger is already passing. O my friend! think what a poor, miserable substitute is even the greatest human happiness for the life to which God calls you. Think of the reward! Heaven is the price! However, it is the Holy Spirit, not I, that should speak to your soul. Will you not give him the opportunity?

Will you not, perhaps, go into retreat? Or rather, please do not listen to me, but go to your director, and open your heart to him. I can only give you a few words of sympathy and encouragement. He can speak to you as the voice of God."

"You do not despise me, then, for having wavered?"

"Do not say that, Mr. Percival," exclaimed the young girl earnestly. "What saint is there that has not suffered temptation? Despise you? I envy you, rather. Think of the vocation God has given you! If it proves to be the mountain of sacrifice, and you ascend it with the cross upon your shoulders, will you not be all the better priest from your likeness to Him who was at once both priest and victim!"

"Miss Howard, pardon me, but you speak as if the lesson of Calvary were not new to you; as if you, too, knew what it is to suffer—not, as I have done, through your own weakness—God forbid! That I could never think."

"We each of us must bear some cross," said Assunta hastily; and then, to give a lighter turn to the conversation, she added: "I am sorry that I should have proved to be yours."

For the first time Augustine Percival smiled, as he said:

"But if, through you, I win my crown, you will not then regret it?"

"O that crown!" exclaimed Assunta; "let us both keep it ever in sight as an incentive. The way will not then seem so long or so hard. Mr. Percival, will you see your director to-night?"

"I will go to him now. It is what I have neglected only too long. God bless you, Miss Howard! But dare I now, after all that has passed, ask you to retain my trifling gift, that you may not forget to pray for me?"

"I shall prize it most highly," said Assunta. "But I shall not need to be reminded to commend you very often to the Sacred Heart of our divine Lord, where you will find strength and consolation. I am sure the least I can do for you is to pray for you, having been the occasion of your suffering."

"And of something more than that," said Mr. Percival.

"And I shall still hope for the other greater gift," said Assunta in pleading tones.

"Miss Howard," replied Mr. Percival, almost with solemnity, "if I, unworthy as I am, should ever be permitted to offer the Holy Sacrifice, my first Mass shall be for you, God willing. But I dare not yet look forward with hope to such a possibility. Once more, God bless you! Pray for me." And in a moment more he had left the house.

Assunta attended Mass daily at the cathedral. The next morning, as she was leaving the church, Mr. Percival joined her; but, without saying a word, he placed a note in her hand, and at the corner he turned, and took his way in the opposite direction. In her own room the young girl read these words:

"To-day I start for Frederick, where I shall make a retreat with the good Jesuit fathers. In solitude and prayer I hope that God may make known to me his will. Pray, that I may have light to see and grace to follow the inspirations of the Holy Spirit. The words you spoke last night are known to the loving Heart of Jesus. He will reward you. I can say no more now. Your brother in Christ, A. P"

"Thank God!" exclaimed Assunta.

After breakfast, Mary came to her, as she stood for a moment by the window, and, putting her arm about her affectionately, said:

"Darling, we need not make any more plans to entrap poor Augustine into a confession, for I do believe he is all right. He came here for a few minutes early this morning to say good-by, as he was going to Frederick. Of course that must mean a retreat; and a retreat is, of course, the first step towards the seminary."

"I am very, *very* glad," said Assunta, smiling. "Women are not always as bright as they think they are, you see."

Three weeks from that day Augustine Percival sailed for Europe to enter upon his theological course in Rome. And two faithful hearts daily begged for him of Almighty God grace and fortitude with that happy confidence which seems almost a presage of answered prayer.

And five years passed away—long and often weary in the passing, but short and with abundant blessings in the retrospect—five uneventful years, and yet leaving a lasting impress upon the individual soul. Assunta's home was still with her friend, Mary Lee—an arrangement to which she most gratefully consented, on condition that she might, from her ample income, contribute her share towards the ease and comfort of the family. It thus became a mutual benefit, as well as pleasure; for Capt. Lee's pay as a naval officer was small and their only dependence. Assunta had won the hearts of all, even down to Mary's two little ones, who came bringing plenty of love with them, as well as adding much to the care and solicitude of the young mother and her younger friend.

They saw but little of Mrs. Sinclair during those years. She had become a thorough woman of the world—a leader of fashion in her own circle. She had lost much of the simplicity and *naïveté* of character and manner which had made her charming in the old Roman days. Her laugh had not the genuine ring which her own light heart used to give it. She was still beautiful—very beautiful as queen of the ball-room. But Mary Lee always insisted that she had the unmistakable look of one who has an interior closet somewhere which might reveal a skeleton; and Assunta thought—but her thoughts she kept to herself—that it was not very difficult to divine what that skeleton might be. She understood her, and pitied her from her heart; and she loved her, too, with the old affection. But their life-paths, once seemingly parallel, had now diverged so widely that she felt she could not help her. The consolation Clara sought was very different from anything her brother's ward could supply.

And that brother, Mr. Carlisle—did Assunta never think of him? Daily, before God, she remembered him; but it was not for her peace to allow him a place in her memory at other times. They were entire strangers now, and she had long since given up the hope of any return to the old friendship. He had dropped out of her life, and God alone could fill the place left vacant by the surrender of this human love. She prayed for him, however, still, but as one might pray for the dead. Her days glided quietly by, each one bearing a record of deeds of love and kindness; while the consciousness of duty fulfilled gave her a peace that it is not in the power of mere human happiness to bestow. The blessings of the poor followed her,

and the blessing of God rested upon her soul.

Mary sometimes protested against this "waste of life," as she called it.

"My darling," she said one day, as she was rocking her baby to sleep in her arms, "you will be a nun yet."

"I fear not," replied Assunta. "I might have wished to enter religion, but it seems that God does not call me to that life."

"Then, Assunta, why don't you marry? It would break my heart to lose you, darling; but, truly, it grieves me to have you settle yourself down to our stupid life and ways, and you so young and rich and beautiful. It is contrary to nature and reason."

"Be patient with me, dear," said Assunta. "I do not believe that you want to be rid of me. Some time we shall know what it all means. I am sorry to disappoint my friends, but my life is just as I would have it."

"Well, you are a saint," said Mary with a sigh; "and as I am the gainer, I am the last one to complain. But I wish you had a dear little bother of your own like my Harry." And the maternal kiss had in it such a strength of maternal love that the baby-eyes opened wide again, and refused to shut.

Mary heard occasionally from her brother; and sometimes she heard *of* him in a way that filled her heart with joy. Austere, yet with wonderful sweetness, full of talent and a hard student, yet with touching humility, Augustine Percival, by a life of mortification and prayer, which his studies never interrupted, was preparing himself to do great things for God. A few words, uttered simply by a true-hearted Christian woman, had turned the scale for him; and God will receive so much the more glory. There will come a day which will reveal many such works, performed through the perhaps unconsciously-exercised influence of some noble woman, whose mission is none the less real because it is accomplished silently and out of the world's sight.

VII.

CREDO.

Five years had passed away, and their close found Mary Lee welcoming back to her home her long-absent brother, now a priest. Augustine Percival returned, the same, and yet changed. There was the same tender, earnest nature; but upon that nature grace had built up a superstructure of such strength and virtue that, in most respects, he was a different man—purified by suffering, sanctified by penance, and now consecrated by the sacrament of Holy Orders.

It was a happy circle that gathered around the blazing wood-fire on that cool October evening—so happy that they were almost subdued, and thought more than they talked. It was towards the end of the evening that Father Percival said quite incidentally:

"Mr. Carlisle returned in the steamer with me. I suppose he will soon pay his respects to the ladies."

Assunta did not start. Why should she? Had the name of one long since dead been mentioned, it might have caused an emotion of tenderness; but that would have been all. Mr. Carlisle was dead to her, and every memory of him had long been buried. So, though her face became a shade paler, she went on with her work, and her hand did not tremble.

"Is he well?" asked Mary, continuing the conversation, "and is he as fine-looking as he used to be?"

"He is just recovering from a very severe illness," replied her brother. "It has told upon him fearfully, so that you will find him much changed. Still, I hope his native air will restore him to health; and no doubt, Mary, his good looks will follow. He was already much better when I parted from him yesterday." And then Father Percival questioned Mary about her absent husband and her children, and listened with interest to the young mother's enthusiastic description of Harry's brilliancy and the little Assunta's sweetness.

The next evening, as Father Percival was giving the two ladies an account of his last days in Rome, Mr. Carlisle's name was announced, and immediately he himself entered the pleasant drawing-room. He was indeed much altered, for the traces of sickness and suffering were only too visible. There was another change, perceptible to one who had known him well. In his bearing there seemed to be less pride than of old, and more dignity; in his face the expression of bitterness had given place to one more contented, more peaceful. Suffering had evidently done a work in that proud spirit. But as Mr. Carlisle extended his hand to Assunta, who greeted him with the frank simplicity so peculiar to her, the same old smile lighted up his thin, pale face, and he truly seemed her guardian once more. Assunta was for the moment surprised to see the cordiality with which Mr. Carlisle took the hand of the young priest, and held it in both his, as if a brother's affection were in the pressure, and which was returned as warmly. A comfortable arm-chair was placed near the fire for the guest; and while he seated himself, as if fatigued, he said:

"Augustine, have you kept my secret?"

"Most faithfully. I did not even betray that I had one, as a woman might have done." And Father Percival glanced at his sister, who pretended indignation, but said nothing.

"Then," said Mr. Carlisle, "I must tell my own story. Assunta, come and sit by me." And he pointed to the vacant chair beside him, while Assunta obeyed at once, the words and manner were so like those of the old days.

"Forgive me," Mr. Carlisle went on, "if I call you to-night by the familiar name. I could not say Miss Howard, and tell you what I have to tell. And, Mrs. Lee, if I seem to address myself too exclusively to your friend, I beg you will pardon me, and believe that, if my story interests you, I am more than glad that you should know all. Assunta, put your hand here." And taking her hand in his, he laid it upon his brow. "In that Roman sickness it has often rested there, and has soothed and healed. Tell me, child, do you feel no difference now?"

Assunta looked at him wonderingly—still more so when she caught sight of a meaning smile on Father Percival's face.

"Mr. Carlisle, you puzzle me," she said.

Again that peculiar and beautiful smile, as he continued:

"The sign of the cross has been there; do you understand now, my child? No? Then, in one word, I will explain all. *Credo*—I believe! Not yet? Assunta, you have, I know, prayed for me. Your prayer has been answered. I am a Catholic, and, under God, I owe all to Augustine Percival."

Assunta could not speak. For a moment she looked in his face with those earnest blue eyes, as if to read there the confirmation of his words, and then she bowed her head upon her hands in silence. Mr. Carlisle was the first to break it.

"And so you are not sorry, *petite*, to welcome so old a sinner into the fold?"

"Sorry!" exclaimed Assunta at last. "Life will not be long enough to thank God for this happiness."

"You are so little changed, child, after all these years, that I must look at myself to realize how the time has gone. But shall I tell you how all this has come about? Three months ago I was as miserable an unbeliever as ever lived."

"Please tell us all," murmured Assunta.

"All the story of these five years would be long and wearisome. Life to me has been simply an endurance of existence, because I dared not end it. I have travelled a great deal. I have *stood*, not *kneeled*, in the Chapel of the Holy Sepulchre, and have wandered as a sight-seer through the holy places in Jerusalem. I have been in almost every part of Europe. Need I tell you that I have found satisfaction nowhere? And all this time I was drawn, by a sort of fascination, to read much on Catholic subjects; so I sneered and cavilled and argued, and read on.

"At last, about four months since, the same uneasy spirit which has made a very Wandering Jew of me for the last five years possessed me with the idea of returning home, and I started for Paris. I engaged my passage in the next steamer for New York; and, though feeling far from well, left for Havre. I reached the hotel, registered my name, and went to my room for the night. The steamer was to sail the next morning. I knew nothing more for three weeks. Fortunately, I had fallen into good hands, or I should never have been here. They said it was brain-fever, and my life was despaired of. Assunta, child, you need not look so pale. You see it is I myself who have lived to tell it."

Father Percival here rose, and, excusing himself on the ground of having his Office to say, left the room. As soon as he was gone Mr. Carlisle exclaimed:

"There is the noblest man that ever lived. No words can tell what he has been to me. It seems that, when I was beginning to give some hope of recovery, Father Percival arrived at the same hotel on his way to America. The landlord happened to mention the fact of the illness of a fellow-countryman, and showed the name upon his books. Father Percival at once gave up his passage, and remained to perform an act of charity which can only be rewarded in heaven."

"You remember, Assunta," said Mrs. Lee, "Augustine wrote that he was detained a few weeks by the illness of a friend."

"Yes," said Assunta; "but how little we dreamed who the friend was!"

"And a most ungrateful friend he was, too, at first," said Mr. Carlisle. "When he came to see me, and I learned his name, and that he had become a priest, it was nothing but weakness that prevented my driving him from the room. As

it was, I swore a little, I believe. However, with the tenderness of a woman he nursed me day and night; and even when I was better, there was still no word about religion, until one day I introduced the subject myself. Even then he said but little. I was too weak to have much pride, or that little would not perhaps have made the impression that it did. My pride has always been the obstacle, and it is not all gone yet, *petite*," he added, looking at Assunta, who smiled in answer.

"One night, from what cause I do not know, I had a relapse, and death seemed very near. Then Father Percival came to me as priest. I can hear now the solemn tones in which he said: 'Mr. Carlisle, I will not deceive you. I hope that you will recover, but you may not. Are you willing to die as you are now, unbaptized?' I answered, 'No.' 'Do you, then,' he said, 'believe the Catholic Church to be the infallible teacher of truth, and will you submit to her teaching?' Here I paused. The question was a difficult one; the word *submit* was a hard word. But death was very near, and at last, with desperate energy, I said: 'Yes; baptize me!' He then knelt beside me, and made for me an act of contrition—for I seemed to be sinking fast—and in a moment more I was baptized, a Catholic. He then left me instantly, and went for the parish priest, who came and administered Extreme Unction to—as they supposed—a dying man. But the sacrament did its work for life, and not for death. From the moment of receiving it the scale turned. Of course much that I have told you I have learned since from Augustine. I was conscious only of the one act—the *submission*.

"And how mean a specimen of a man I have since felt myself to have been—resisting God year after year with all the strength of human pride and that most powerful auxiliary of the devil—pride of intellect; and then, when life was at its last gasp, and everything had slipped from under me but that one foothold—then to say, 'Life is going; the world has already gone. I have lost everything else; now I, a sinner, will condescend to receive the portion of the saints—God and heaven!' Do you think, Assunta, that the angels would have had much cause for rejoicing over such an addition to their bright company?"

"That is a genuine drop of your old bitterness, Mr. Carlisle," replied Assunta, laughing, nevertheless, at his frankness.

"Oh! there is plenty of it left, *petite*. But to go on: when I found that I was to live, I was determined, before leaving for home, to make my profession of faith in the church, as a Christian should who is not ashamed of his colors. Augustine would do nothing official for me after the baptism, but he was ever the kindest friend, and I love him with a real David and Jonathan affection. Oh! child, how often have I thought of you and of how much you would have been amused to see me, Severn Carlisle, meekly receiving instruction in Catholic doctrine and practice from that simple French priest. Truly, I needed some one to identify me to myself. Well, to bring this long story to an end, the day before sailing I made my profession of faith and received Holy Communion in the quiet little parish church. And now I am here, the same proud, self-sufficient man as of old, I fear, but with a peace of soul that I have never known before."

"How good God is!" exclaimed Assunta.

"What does your sister say?" asked Mrs. Lee.

"My sister? I do not think she took in the idea. Her thoughts would have to travel miles before they would approach a religious sentiment. Poor Clara! I find her much changed. I spent two or three hours with her this afternoon. She was very gay, even brilliant—too much so, I thought, for real happiness. She did not imagine how transparent her mask was, and I would not destroy her illusion. I did not see Sinclair at all. But," exclaimed he, looking at his watch, and rising hastily, "it is eleven o'clock. I ordered the carriage for ten, and no doubt it has been waiting a long time. I owe you ladies many apologies for my thoughtlessness and egotism."

"Mr. Carlisle," began Assunta, placing her hand in his, as she bade him good-night; but the words would not come as readily as the tears.

Mrs. Lee had gone to summon her brother, so the two, so long parted, were left alone.

"My child," said Mr. Carlisle in a low voice, "I know all that you would say, all the sweet sympathy of that tender, unchanged heart. I have much to say to you, Assunta, but not to-night—not in the presence of others."

Then turning to Father Percival, who entered the room, "Augustine," he said, "I am going for a few days to my place in the country for rest, and also that I may see how much it has suffered from my long neglect. Come and see me there. It will do me good, heart and soul."

"I will try to arrange my plans so as to give myself that pleasure," replied the priest, as he assisted Mr. Carlisle into the carriage.

What strange contradictions there are in human nature! How little can we account for our varying moods and the motives which influence our actions! And how often we seem to get at cross-purposes with life, and only see how far we have been wrong when a merciful Providence, overruling all, unknots the tangled thread and straightens the crooked purpose!

Excepting the visit of a few hours paid by Father Percival to his friend, two months passed by, and nothing was heard of Mr. Carlisle. Those two months were to Assunta longer, more wearisome, than the five years that had preceded them. We may talk of hopes that are dead, and may honestly believe them buried deep down in the grave which duty has prepared and time has covered. But hope is the hardest thing in this world to kill; and thank God that it is so! Let but a gleam of sunshine, a breath of the warm upper air, into that sepulchre, and the hopes that have lain buried there for years will revive and come forth with renewed vigor. It is much more difficult to lay them to rest a second time.

Assunta had borne her trial nobly; but, as she sat alone on Christmas Eve, and her thoughts naturally dwelt upon that happy return, and then the unaccountable disappearance of Mr. Carlisle, her courage almost failed her, and her brave heart sank within her, as she thought how dreary the future looked. She had excused herself from joining the others at a little family party, and for an hour she had sat idle before the fire—a most un-wonted self-indulgence for one so conscientious as Assunta Howard.

A ring at the door and a voice in the hall made her start and tremble a little, as she had not done on that first evening of Father Percival's return. She had scarcely recovered herself when Mr. Carlisle entered the room.

"I have come to account for myself," were his first words. "I hoped that I should find you alone to-night."

"Mrs. Lee has gone to her mother's," was the reply.

"Yes, I knew it. Assunta, what have you thought of me? Still more, what will you think of me now? I have suffered much in these two months; perhaps it is ungenerous in me to say this to you. Assunta, never for one moment have I been unfaithful to the love I told you of so many years ago; but I had given up the hope of ever possessing yours. Even when the obstacle you know of had been removed, I thought that I could bear to see you happy, as I believed you were, in a life in which I had no share. I felt that it would not be right even to ask you to marry one so much older than yourself, with broken health and darkened spirits. And your fresh beauty, still so girlish, so all-unchanged, confirmed my purpose. Ah! child, time, that has silvered my hair, has not dimmed the golden aureola which crowns your dear head. But in the many lonely hours that I have passed since my return, my courage has grown faint. I have longed for your sweet presence in my home, until an answering voice has urged me to come to you. Assunta, once, beneath the shadow of the cross, in the moonlit Colosseum, I offered you my love, and you put God between us. Again I urged my suit, and again you erected the same impassable barrier. To-night I am so selfish that, even as I have described myself to be, I come to you a third time with a love which years have but strengthened. My darling, God no longer comes between us; can I ever hope to win that true, brave heart?"

With a child-like simplicity and a true womanliness Assunta put her hand in his, and said :

"Mr. Carlisle, it has long been yours. 'Unless he can love you *in God*,' my mother said. I believe that the condition is now fulfilled."

"And may God bless the love he sanctions!" said Mr. Carlisle solemnly. After a silence—for where hearts understand each other there is no need of many words—Assunta said in her own sweet tones :

"Do you regret now the decision of that night in Rome? Was I a true prophetess?"

"But we have lost so many years," said Mr. Carlisle.

"Yes, lost for time, but gained for eternity."

When Mrs. Lee returned, she greeted the guest with surprise, as well as pleasure; but both these emotions were lost in a still greater joy when Mr. Carlisle, drawing Assunta towards him, said :

"Mrs. Lee, this is my Christmas gift—a precious treasure, is it not, to be entrusted to one so undeserving?"

"Indeed it is a precious treasure," echoed Mary enthusiastically; "but, Mr. Carlisle, there is not a man in the world in whose possession I would like to see it so well as in yours."

' Bless you, Mrs. Lee, for your kind words! *Petite*, perhaps your taste is not so much in fault after all."

"And, Mary," said Assunta archly, "he may yet recover his good looks, you know."

"Yes," said Mr. Carlisle, "love and happiness are said to be great beautifiers. I have no objection to trying the experiment."

One bright morning, soon after Easter, there was a nuptial Mass at the cathedral, celebrated by Father Percival, and after the ceremony and a quiet. breakfast, Mr. and Mrs. Carlisle drove in their private carriage to the beautiful country. residence which was to be their future home.

Just at sunset, as they entered the long avenue which with many windings led towards the house, Mr. Carlisle said :

"My darling, we are at home. I have waited, like Jacob, almost seven years for my Rachel. I cannot say, as he did, that the days have seemed *few*, though I believe my love has been no less."

"And suppose," replied Assunta, with the happy confidence of a loving wife—"suppose your Rachel should turn out a Lia after all?"

"In that case," said her husband coolly, "I should insist that the description of that much-injured lady had done her great injustice. And I should consider myself a lucky fellow to have been cheated into the mistake, and be ready to wager my Lia against all the Rachels in the world. And now, my precious wife, welcome home!"

Ten years later. It is not always a pleasure to look in upon loved friends after a lapse of ten years. Sickness, sorrow, death, or disgrace may each do a mighty work in even fewer years, and, at the best, time itself brings about marked changes. But a glance at Carlisle Hall, on this tenth anniversary of that happy wedding-day, will only show that same happiness ripened into maturity. In a marriage like that of Severn and Assunta Carlisle, whatever life might bring of joy or sorrow would come to both alike, and nothing could divide them. Even death itself would but *seem* to part them, for their union was *in God.* In Assunta the added dignity of wifehood and motherhood had taken nothing from the charm of earlier years; and, if the beauty of the young girl had faded somewhat, the ever-growing grace and purity of soul more than supplied its want, even in her husband's eyes. And Mr. Carlisle? Noble by nature, and possessing the finest qualities of mind and heart, his soul was now developed to the full stature of its manhood. He was a proud man still, but with a pride which S Paul might have commended. He was so proud that he was never ashamed to kneel beside the poorest villager in the little church. In his pride he gloried in Jesus Christ, and him crucified. The beautiful church itself had been erected as a thank-offering, by Mr. Carlisle and his wife, in the factory village two miles from their home; and for some years Father Percival had been parish priest of the Church of the Assumption. And Carlisle Hall resounded with the merry voices of three children at the end of those ten years: Severn, the pride of his mother's heart; Augustine, Father Percival's godchild and special favorite, already destined for the priesthood by the wishes of the senior trio; and the baby, her father's darling, to whom he would give the name of Mary, and no other, "to show," he said, "how he had progressed in Mariolatry since his first lesson in Sienna."

Father Percival had been the only guest at this anniversary-dinner, except, indeed, the children, who must appear on this occasion, at no matter how great a risk of noise and accident. They had now returned to the nursery, but the others still lingered at the table.

"Father Augustine," said Assunta—for she had learned to follow the little ones in their name for the priest they loved so well— "I received a letter yesterday from dear old Father Joseph. He is just as happy in our marriage to-day as he was when he first heard of it, and he blesses it, and us, and the children so sweetly and kindly. How much I should like to see him again!"

"I suppose," said Father Percival, "he looks upon the marriage as a striking illustration of the wonderful ways and goodness of God, as it surely is. S. Ignatius ought to send Father Dupont here, to see for himself the result of his direction, and, I must add, of your generosity and faithfulness, Mrs. Carlisle."

"I am so sorry, Severn," said Assunta after a pause in the conversation, "that Clara would not come to us to-day. I think a glimpse of quiet country life might be a pleasant change for her."

"I fear," replied her husband sadly, "that poor Clara has much to suffer yet. It is my opinion that Sinclair has no intention of returning from Europe at all. But who could have made her believe, in those sunshiny days, that she would ever live to be a deserted wife? *Petite,* the subject is a very painful one. I am going to change it for one of which I am never weary. Augustine, it is not the custom, I believe, for a man to toast his wife on such an occasion, but I am going to be an exception to the rule to-day. Lord Lytton has in that grand work of his, *My Novel*, two types of women—the one who exalts, and the one who consoles. He probably had never seen the combination of the two types in one person. I now propose— and, my darling, you must drink and not blush—'Assunta Carlisle: blessed be the woman who both exalts and consoles!' And let me add that a happy man was I—unworthy—when, ten years ago, that woman became my wife."

NUMBER THIRTEEN.

AN EPISODE OF THE COMMUNE.

MLLE. DE LEMAQUE and her sister Mme. de Chanoir lived at No. 13 Rue Royale. They were the daughters of a military man whose fortune when he married consisted in his sword, nothing else; and of a noble Demoiselle de Cambatte, whose wedding portion, according to the good old French fashion, was precisely the same as her husband's, minus the sword. But over and above this joint capital the young people had a good stock of hope and courage, and an inexhaustible fund of love; they had therefore as good a chance of getting on as other young folk who start in life under the same pecuniary disadvantages. M. de Lemaque, moreover, had friends in high place who looked kindly on him, and promised him countenance and protection, and there was no reason, as far as he and his wife could see, why he should not in due time clutch that legendary baton which Napoleon declared every French soldier carries in his knapsack. Nor, indeed, looking at things from a retrospective point of view,

was there any reason, that we can see, why he should not have died a marshal of France, except that he died too soon. The young soldier was in a fair way of climbing to the topmost rung of the military ladder; but just as he had got his foot on the third rung, Death stepped down and met him, and he climbed no further. His wife followed him into the grave three years later. They left two daughters, Félicité and Aline, the only fruits of their short and happy union. The orphans were educated at the Legion of Honor, and then sent adrift on the wide, wide world, to battle with its winds and waves, to sink or swim as best they could. They swam. Perhaps I ought rather say they floated. The eldest, Félicité, was married from S. Denis to an old general, who, after a reasonably short time, had the delicacy to betake himself to a better world, leaving his gay wife a widow at the head of an income of £40 a year. Aline might have married under similar circumstances, but, after turning it over in her mind, she came to the conclusion that, all things considered, since it was a choice of evils, and that she must earn her bread in some way, she preferred earning it and eating it independently as a single woman. This gave rise to the only quarrel the sisters had had in their lives. Félicité resented the disgrace that Aline was going to put on the family name by degenerating into a giver of private lessons, when she might have secured forty pounds a year for ever by a few years' dutiful attendance on a brave man who had fought his country's battles.

"Well, if you can find me a warrior of ninety," said the younger sister, a month before she left S. Denis, " I'm not sure that he might not persuade me; but I never will capitulate under ninety ; I couldn't trust a man under that ; they live for ever when they marry between sixty and eighty, and there are no tyrants like them ; now, I would do my duty as a kind wife for a year or so, but I've no notion of taking a situation as nurse for fifteen or twenty years, and that's what one gets by marrying a young man of seventy or thereabouts."

Félicité urged her own case as a proof to the contrary. Général de Chanoir was only sixty-eight when she married him, and he retired at seventy. Aline maintained, however, that this was the one exception necessary to prove the rule to the present generation, and as no eligible *parti* of fourscore and ten presented itself before she left school, she held to her resolve, and started at once as a teacher.

The sisters took an apartment together, if two rooms, a cabinet de toilette, and a cooking-range in a dark passage, dignified by the name of kitchen, can be called an apartment, and for six years they lived very happily.

Mme. de Chanoir was small and fair, and very distinguished-looking. She had never known a day's illness in her life, but she was a hypochondriac. She believed herself afflicted with a spine disease, which necessitated reclining all day long on the sofa in a Louis Quinze dressing-gown and a Dubarry cap.

Aline was tall and dark, not exactly pretty, but indescribably piquant. Without being delicate, her health was far less robust than her sister's ; but she was blessed with indomitable spirits and a fund of energy that carried her through a variety of aches and pains, and often bore her successfully through her round of daily work when another would have given in.

The domestic establishment of the sisters consisted in a charwoman, who rejoiced in the name of Mme. Cléry. She was a type of a class almost extinct in Paris now ; a dainty little cook, clean as a sixpence, honest as the sun, orderly as a clock, a capital servant in every way. She came twice a day to No. 13, two hours in the morning and three hours in the afternoon, and the sisters paid her twenty francs a month. She might have struck for more wages, and rather than let her go they would have managed to raise them ; but Mme. Cléry was born before strikes came into fashion, it was quite impossible to say how long before ; her age was incalculable ; her youth belonged to that class of facts spoken of as beyond the memory of the oldest man in the district. Aline used to look at her sometimes, and wonder if she really could have been born, and if she meant to die like other people ; the crisp, wiry old woman looked the sort of person never to have either a beginning or an end ; they had had her now for eight years—at least Mme. de Chanoir had—and there was not the shadow of a change in her. Her gowns were like herself, they never wore out, neither did her caps — high Normandy caps, with flaps extended like a wind-mill in repose, stiff, white, and uncompromising. Everything about her was antiquated. She had a religious regard for antiquity in every shape, and a proportionate contempt for modernism; but, of all earthly things, what her soul loved most was an old name, and what it most despised a new one. She used to say that if she chose to cook the *rôtis* of a parvenu she might make double the money, and it was true; but she could not bend her spirit to it; she liked her dry bread and herbs better from a good family than a stalled ox from upstarts. She was as faithful as a dog to her two mistresses, and consequently lorded over them like a step-mother, perpetually bullying and scolding, and bewailing her own infatuation in staying with them while she might be turning a fatter pullet on her own spit at home than the miserable *coquille* at No. 13 ever held a fire to. Why had she not the sense to take the situation that M. X——, the *agent de change*, across the street, had offered her again and again? The *femme de ménage* was, in fact, as odious and exasperating as the most devoted old servant who ever nursed a family from the cradle to the grave. But let any one else dare so much as cast a disrespectful glance at either of her victims! She shook her fist at the *concierge's* wife one day for venturing to call Mme. de Chanoir Mme. de Chanoir *tout court*, instead of Mme. la Générale de Chanoir, to a flunky who came with a note, and she boxed the *concierge's* ears for speaking of Aline as "l'Institutrice." As Mme. la Générale's sofa was drawn across the window that looked

into the court, she happened to be an eye-witness to the two incidents, and heard every word that was said. This accidental disclosure of Mme. Cléry's regard for the family dignity before outsiders covered a multitude of sins in the eyes of both the sisters. Indeed, Mme. de Chanoir came at last, by force of habit, almost to enjoy being bullied by the old soul. "*Cela nous pose, ma chère,*" she would remark complacently, when the wind from the kitchen blew due north, and Aline threatened to mutiny.

Aline never could have endured it if she had been as constantly tried as her easy-going sister was; but, lucky for all parties, she went out immediately after breakfast, and seldom came in till late in the afternoon, when the old beldame was busy getting ready the dinner.

It was a momentous life they led, the two young women, but, on the whole, it was a happy one. Mme. de Chanoir, seeing how bravely her sister carried the burden she had taken up, grew reconciled to it in time. They had a pleasant little society, too; friends who had known them from their childhood, some rich and in good positions, others struggling like themselves in a narrow cage and under difficult circumstances; but one and all liked the sisters, and brought a little contingent of sunshine to their lives. As to Aline, she had sunshine enough in herself to light up the whole Rue Royale. Every lesson she gave, every incident of the day, no matter how trivial, fell across her path like a sunbeam; she had a knack of looking at things from a sunny focus that shot out rays on every object that came within its radius, and of extracting amusement or interest from the most commonplace things and people; even her own vexations she had turned into ridicule. Her position of governess was a fountain of fun to her. When another would have drawn gall from a snub, and smarted and been miserable under a slight, Aline de Lemaque saw a comic side to the circumstance, and would dress it up in a fashion that diverted herself and her friends for a week. Moreover, the young lady was something of a philosopher.

" You never find out human nature till you come to earn your own bread—I mean, women don't," she used to say to Mme. de Chanoir. " If I were the mother of a family of daughters, and wanted to teach them life, I'd make every one of them, no matter how big their *dots* were, begin by running after the *cachet.* Nobody who hasn't tried it would believe what a castle of truth it is to one—a mirror that shows up character to the life, a sort of moral photography. It is often as good as a play to me to watch the change that comes over people when, after talking to them, and making myself pass for a very agreeable person, I suddenly announce the fact that I give lessons. Their whole countenance changes, not that they look on me straightway with contempt. Oh I dear no. Many good Christians, people of the ' help yourself and God will help you ' sect, conceive, on the contrary, a great respect for me; but 1 become metamorphosed on the spot. I am not what they took me for, they took me for a lady, and all the time I was a governess I They did not think the less of me, but they can't help feeling that they have been taken in ; that, in fact, I'm an altogether different variety from themselves, and it is very odd they did not recognize it at first sight. But these are the least exciting experiences. The great fun is when I get hold of an out-and-out worldly individual, man or woman, but a woman is best, and let them go

on till they have thoroughly committed themselves, made themselves gushingly agreeable to me, perhaps gone the length of asking, in a significant manner, if I live in their neighborhood ; then comes the crisis. I smile my gladdest, and say, 'Monsieur, or Madame, I give lessons I *Changement de décoration à vue d'œil, ma chère.* It's just as if I *lancéd* an *obus* into the middle of the company, only it rebounds on me and hits nobody else ; the eyebrows of the company go up, the corners of its mouth go down, and it bows to me as I sit on the ruins of my respectability, shat tered to pieces by my own *obus.*"

" I can't understand how you can laugh at it. If I were in your place, I should have died of vexation and wounded pride long ago," said Mme. de Chanoir, one day, as Aline related in high glee an obus episode that she had had that morning ; " but I really believe you have no feeling."

" Well, whatever I have, I keep out of the reach of vulgar impertinence. I should be very sorry to make my feelings a target for insolence and bad breeding," replied Aline pertly. This was the simple truth. Her feelings were out of the reach of such petty shafts; they were cased in cheerfulness and common sense, and a nobler sort of pride than that in which Mme. de Chanoir considered her sister wanting. If, however, the obus was frequently fatal to Mlle. de Lemaque's social standing, on the other hand it occasionally did her good service ; but of this later. Its present character was that of an explosive bomb which she carried in her pocket, and *lancéd* with infinite gusto on every available opportunity.

On Saturday evening the sisters were " at home." These little soirées were the great event of their quiet lives. All the episodes and anecdotes of the week were treasured up for that evening, when the *intimes* came to see them and converse and sip a glass of cold *eau sucrée* in summer, and a cup of hot ditto in winter (but then it was called tea) by the light of a small lamp with a green shade. There was no attempt at entertainment or finery of any kind, except that Mme. Cléry, instead of going home as soon as the dinner things were washed up, stayed to open the door. It was a remnant of the sort of society that used to exist in French families some thirty years ago, when conversation was cultivated as the primary accomplishment of men and women, and when they met regularly to exercise themselves in the difficult and delightful art. It was not reserved to the well-born exclusively to talk well and brilliantly in those days, when the most coveted encomium that could be passed on any one was, " He talks well." All classes vied for it; every circle had its centre of conversation. The *fauteuil de l'aïeule* and the salon of the *femme d'esprit*, each had its audience, attended as assiduously, and perhaps enjoyed quite as much, as the vaudevilles and ambigus that have since drawn away the bourgeois from the one and the man of fashion from the other. Besides its usual habitués for conversation, every circle had one habitué who was looked upon as the friend of the family, and tacitly took precedence of all the others. The friend of the family at No. 13 was a certain professor of the Sorbonne named M. Dalibouze. He was somewhere on the sunny side of fifty, a bald, pompous little man who wore spectacles, took snuff, and laid down the law; very prosy and very estimable, a model professor. He had never married, but it was the dream of his life to marry. He had meditated on marriage for the last thirty years, and of course knew more about it than any man who had been married double that time. He was never so eloquent or so emphatic as when dilating on the joys and duties of domestic life; no matter how tired he was with study and scientific researches, how disappointed in the result of some cherished literary scheme, he brightened up the moment marriage came on the tapis. This hobby of the professor's was a great amusement to Mme. de Chanoir, who delighted to see him jump into the saddle and ride off at a canter while she lay languidly working at her tapestry, patting him on the back every now and then, by a word of encouragement, or signifying her assent merely by a smile or a nod. Sometimes she would take him to task seriously about putting his theories into practice and getting himself a wife, assuring him that it was quite wicked of him not to marry when he was so richly endowed with all the qualities necessary to make a model husband.

" Ah! madame, if I thought I were capable of making a young woman happy!" M. Dalibouze would exclaim with a sigh; "but at my age! No, I have let my chance go by."

" How, sir, at your age!" the générale would protest. " Why, it is the very flower of manhood, the moment of all others for a man to marry. You have outlived the delusions of youth and none of its vigor; you have crossed the Rubicon that separates folly from wisdom, and you have left nothing on the other side of the bridge but the silly chimera of boyhood. Believe me, the woman whom you would select would never wish to see you a day younger."

And M. Dalibouze would caress his chin, and observe thoughtfully: " Do you think so, madame?" Upon

which Mme. de Chanoir would pour
another vial of oil and honey on the
learned head of the professor, till the
wonder was that it did not turn on
his shoulders.

Aline had no sympathy with his
rhapsodies or his jeremiads; they
bored her to extinction, and sometimes it was all she could do not to
tell him so; but she disapproved
of his being made a joke of, and testified against it very decidedly when
Félicité, in a spirit of mischief, led
him up to a more than usually ridiculous culmination. It was not fair,
she said, to make a greater fool of
the good little man than he made of
himself, and instead of encouraging
him to talk such nonsense one ought
to laugh him out of it, and try and
cure him of his silly conceit.

" I don't see it at all in that light,"
Mme. de Chanoir would answer.
" In the first place, if I laughed at
him, or rather if I let him see that I
did, he would never forgive me, and,
as I have a great regard for him, I
should be sorry to lose his friendship;
and in the next place, it's a great
amusement to me to see him swallow my little doses of flattery so complacently, and I have no scruple in
dosing him, because nothing that I
or any one else could say could possibly add one grain to his self-con-
ceit, so one may as well turn it to
account for a little entertainment."

It was partly this system of flattery,
which Aline resented on principle, that
induced her occasionally to snub the
professor, and partly the fact that
she had reason to suspect his dreams
of married bliss centred upon herself.
In fact, she knew it. He had never
told her so outright, for the simple
reason that, whenever he drew near
that crisis, Aline cut him short in such
a peremptory manner that it cowed
him for weeks, but nevertheless she
knew in her heart of hearts that she

reigned supreme over M. Dalibouze's.
She would not have married him, no,
not if he could have crowned her queen
of the Sorbonne and the Collége de
France, but the fact of his being her
slave and aspiring to be her master
constituted a claim on her regard
which a true-hearted woman seldom
disowns.

Félicité would have favored his
suit if there had been the ghost of a
chance for him, but she knew there
was not.

Mme. Cléry looked coldly on it.
Needless to say, neither M. Dalibouze
nor his cruel-hearted lady-love had
ever made a confidante of the *femme
de ménage;* but she often remarked
to her mistresses when they ventured
an opinion on anything connected
with her special department, "Je ne
suis pas née d'hier," an assertion
which, strange to say, even the rebellious Aline had never attempted to
gainsay. Mme. Cléry was not, indeed,
born yesterday, moreover she was a
Frenchwoman, and a particularly
wide-awake one, and from the first
evening that she saw Aline sugaring
M. Dalibouze's tea, dropping in
lump after lump in that reckless way,
while the little man held his cup and
beamed at her through his spectacles
as if he meant to stand there for ever
simpering, " Merci encore !"—it occurred to Mme. Cléry when she saw
this that there was more in it than
tea-making. Of course it was natural and proper that a young woman,
especially an orphan, should think of
getting married, but it was right and
proper that her friends should think
of it too, and see that she married
the proper person. Now, on the face
of it, M. Dalibouze could not be the
proper person. Nevertheless, Mme.
Cléry waited till the suspicion that
M. Dalibouze had settled it in his
own mind that he was that man
took the shape of a conviction be-

fore she considered it her duty to interfere.

By interfering Mme. Cléry meant going *aux renseignements.* Nobody ever got true *renseignements,* especially when there was a marriage in question, except people like her; ladies and gentlemen never get behind the scenes with each other, or, if they do, they never tell what they see there. They are very sweet and smiling when they meet in the salon, and nobody guesses that madame has rated her *femme de chambre* for not putting the flowers in her hair exactly to her fancy, or that monsieur has flung a boot at his valet for giving him his shaving-water too hot or too cold. If you want the truth, you must get it by the back-stairs. This was Mme. Cléry's belief, and, acting upon it, she went to M. Dalibouze's *concierge* in the Rue Jean Beauvais to consult him confidentially about his *locataire.*

The first thing to be ascertained before entering on such secondary details as character, conduct, etc., was whether or not the professor was of a good enough family to be entertained at all as a husband for Mlle. de Lemaque. On this *sine qua non* question the *concierge* could unfortunately throw no light. The professor had a multitude of friends, all respectable people, many of them *décorés,* who drove to the door in spruce *coupés,* but of his family Pipelet knew nothing; of his personal respectability there was no doubt whatever; he was the kindest of men, a very pearl of tenants, always in before midnight, and gave forty francs to Pipelet on New Year's day, not to count sundry other little bonuses on minor *fêtes* during the year. But so long as her mind was in darkness on the main point, all this was no better than sounding brass in the ears of Mme. Cléry.

"Has he, or has he not, the *par-*

ticule ?" she demanded, cutting Pipelet short in the middle of his panegyric.

"The *particule ?"* repeated Pipelet. "What's that ?"

"The *particule nobiliaire,"* explained Mme. Cléry, with a touch of contempt. "There is some question of a marriage between him and one of my ladies; but, if M. Dalibouze hasn't got the *particule,* it's no use thinking of it."

"Madame," said Pipelet, assuming a meditative air—he was completely at sea as to what this essential piece of property might be, but did not like to own his ignorance—"I'm not a man to set up for knowing more of my tenant's business than I do, and M. Dalibouze has never opened himself to me about how or where his money was placed; but I could give you the name of his agent, if I thought it would not compromise me."

"I'm not a woman to compromise any one that showed me confidence," said Mme. Cléry, tightening her lips, and bobbing her flaps at Pipelet; "but you need not give me the name of his agent. What sort of a figure should I make at his agent's! Give me his own name. How does he spell it ?"

"Spell it !" echoed Pipelet.

"A big *D* or a little *d?"* said Mme. Cléry.

"Why, a big *D,* of course ! Who ever spelt their name with a little one ?" retorted Pipelet.

"Ah ! . . . " Mme. Cléry smiled a smile of serene pity on the benighted ignoramus, and then observed coolly: "I suspected it ! I'm not easy to deceive in that sort of things. I was not born yesterday. Good-morning, M. le Concierge." She moved towards the door.

"Stop !" cried Pipelet, seizing his berette as if a ray of light had shot through his skull—"stop! Now that I think of it, it's a little *d*. I have not a doubt but it's a little *d*. I noticed it only yesterday on a letter that came for monsieur, and I said to myself: 'Let us see!' I said. 'What a queer fancy for a man of distinction like M. le Professeur to spell his name with a little *d*!' Là! if I didn't say those words to myself no later than yesterday!"

Mme. Cléry was dubious. Unluckily there was no letter in M. Dalibouze's box at that moment, which would have settled the point at issue, so she had nothing for it but to go home, and turn it in her mind what was to be done next. After all, it was a great responsibility on her. The old soul considered herself in the light of a protector to the two young women, one a cripple on the broad of her back, and the other a light-hearted creature who believed everything and everybody. It was her place to look after them as far as she could. That afternoon, when Mme. Cléry went to No. 13, after her fruitless expedition to the Rue Jean Beauvais, she took a letter in to Mme. de Chanoir. She had never seen, or, at any rate, never noticed, the writing before, but as she handed the envelope to her mistress it flashed upon her that it was from M. Dalibouze, and that it bore on the subject of her morning's peregrination.

She seized a feather-broom that hung by the fireplace, and began vigorously threatening the clock and the candlesticks, as an excuse for staying in the room, and watching Mme. de Chanoir in the looking-glass while she read the letter. The old woman was an irascible enemy to dust; they were used to see her at the most inopportune times pounce on the feather-broom and begin whipping about her to the right and left, so Mme. de Chanoir took no notice

of this sudden castigation of the chimney-piece at four o'clock in the afternoon. She read her note, and then, tossing it into the basket beside her resumed her tapestry as if nothing had occurred to divert her thoughts from roses and Berlin wool.

"Mme. la Générale, pardon and excuse," said Mme. Cléry, deliberately hanging the feather-broom on its nail, and going up to the foot of the générale's sofa. "I have it on my mind to ask something of madame."

"Ask it, my good Mme. Cléry."

"Does Mme. la Générale think of marrying Mlle. Aline?"

Mme. de Chanoir opened her eyes, and stared for a moment in mild surprise at her charwoman, then a smile broke over her face, and she said:

"You are thinking that you would not like to come to me if I were alone?"

"I was not thinking of that, madame," replied Mme. Cléry, in a tone of ceremony that was not habitual, and which would have boded no good (Mme. Cléry was never so respectful as when she was going to be particularly disagreeable), except that she looked very meek, and, Félicité thought, rather affectionately at her as their eyes met.

"Well," said Mme. de Chanoir, "I suppose we must marry her some day; I ought, perhaps, to occupy myself about it more actively than I do; but there's time enough to think about it yet; mademoiselle is in no hurry."

"Dame!" said Mme. Cléry testily, "when a demoiselle has become an old maid, there is not so much time to lose! Pardon and excuse, Mme. la Générale, but I thought, I don't know why, that that letter had something to do with it?"

"This letter! What could have put that into your head?"

Mme. de Chanoir took up the note to see if the envelope had anything about it which warranted this romantic suspicion, but it was an ordinary envelope, with no trace of anything more peculiar than the post-mark.

" As I have told Mme. la Générale before," said Mme. Cléry, shaking her head significantly, " I was not born yesterday "—she emphasized the *not* as if Mme. de Chanoir had denied that fact and challenged her to swear to it on the Bible—" and I don't carry my eyes in my pocket ; and when a demoiselle heaps lumps of sugar into a gentleman's cup till it's as thick as honey for a spoon to stand in, and a shame to see the substance of the family wasted in such a way, and she never grudging it a bit, but looking as if it would be fun to her to turn the sugar-bowl upside down over it—I say, when I see that sort of thing, I'm not femme Cléry if there isn't something in it."

Félicité felt inclined to laugh, but she restrained herself, and observed interrogatively :

" Well, Mme. Cléry, suppose there is ?"

This extravagance of sugar on M. Dalibouze was an old grievance of Mme. Cléry's. In fact, it had been her only one against the professor, till she grew to look upon him as the possible husband of Mlle. Aline, and then the question of his having or not having the *particule* assumed such alarming importance in her mind that it magnified all minor defects, and she believed him capable of every misdemeanor under the sun.

" Mme. la Générale," she replied, " one does not marry every day ; one ought to think seriously about it ; Mlle. Aline has not experience ; she is *vive* and light-hearted ; she is a person to be taken in by outward appearances ; such things as learning, good principles, and *esprit* would blind her to serious shortcomings ; it is the duty of Mme. la Générale to prevent such a mistake in time."

" What sort of shortcomings are you afraid of in M. Dalibouze, Mme. Cléry ?" inquired Mme. de Chanoir, dropping her tapestry, and looking with awakened curiosity at the old woman.

" Let us begin with a first principle, Mme. la Générale," observed Mme. Cléry, demurely slapping the palm of her left hand. " Mlle. Aline is *née ;* the father and mother of mamzelle were both of an excellent family ; it is consequently of the first necessity that her husband should be so, too ; the first thing, therefore, to be considered in a suitor is his name. Now, has M. Dalibouze the *particule* or has he not ?"

It was a very great effort for Mme. de Chanoir to keep her countenance under this charge and deliver with which the old woman solemnly closed her speech, and then stood awaiting the effect on her listener ; still, such is the weakness of human nature, the générale in her inmost heart was flattered by it ; it was pleasant to be looked up to as belonging to a race above the common herd, to be recognized in spite of her poverty, even by a *femme de ménage*, as superior to the wealthy parvenus whose fathers and mothers were not of a good family.

" My good Mme. Cléry," she said after a moment's reflection, " you, like ourselves, were brought up with very different ideas from those that people hold nowadays. Nobody cares a straw to-day who a man's father was, or whether he had the *particule* or not ; all that they care about is that he should be well educated, and well conducted, and well off ; and, my dear, one must go with the times, one must give in to the force of public opinion around one. Customs change with the times. I would, of course, much rather have a brother-in-law of our own rank than one cleverer and richer who was not ; but what would you have ? One cannot have everything. It is not pleasant for me to see Mlle. de Lemaque earning her own bread, running about the streets like a milliner's apprentice at all hours of the day. I would overlook something to see her married to a kind, honorable man who would keep her in comfort and independence."

"*Bonté divine !*" exclaimed Mme. Cléry, with a look of deep distress and consternation, "madame would then actually marry mamzelle to a *bourgeois sans particule ?* For madame admits that M. Dalibouze has not the *particule*, that he spells his name with a big *D ?*"

"Alas ! he does," confessed the générale ; "but he comes, nevertheless, of a good old Normandy stock, Mme. Cléry ; his great-grandfather was *procureur du roi* under —"

"Tut ! tut !" interrupted Mme. Cléry ; "his great-grandfather may have been what he liked ; if he wasn't a gentleman, he has no business marrying his great grandson to a de Lemaque. No, madame ; I am a poor woman, but I know better than that. Mamzelle's father would turn in his grave if he saw her married to a man who spelt his name with a big *D.*"

The conversation was interrupted by a ring at the door. It was Aline. She came back earlier than usual, because one of her pupils was ill and had not been able to take her lesson. The young girl was flushed and excited, and flung herself into an armchair the moment she entered, and burst into tears. Mme. de Chanoir sat up in alarm, fearing she was ill, and suggested a cup of *tisane.*

"Oh ! 'tis nothing. I'm an idiot to mind it or let such impertinence vex me," she said, when the first outburst had passed off and relieved her.

"*Mon Dieu !* but what vexes mamzelle ?" inquired Mme. Cléry anxiously.

"A horrid man that followed me the length of the street, and made some impudent speech, and asked me where I lived," sobbed Aline.

"Is it possible !" exclaimed the old woman, aghast, and clasping her hands. "Well, mamzelle does astonish me ! I thought young men knew better nowadays than to go on with that sort of tricks ; fifty years ago they used to. I remember how I was followed and spoken to every time I went to church or to market ; it was a persecution ; but now I come and go and nobody minds me. To think of their daring to speak to mamzelle !"

"That's what one must expect when one walks about alone at your age, *ma pauvre* Aline," said the générale, rather sharply, with a significant look at Mme. Cléry which that good lady understood, and resented by compressing her lips and bobbing her flaps, as much as to say, "One has a principle or one has not"—principle being in this instance synonymous with *particule.*

Things remained *in statu quo* after this for some years. Mme. de Chanoir did not enlighten her sister on the subject of the conference with Mme. Cléry, but she worked as far as she could in favor of the luckless suitor who spelt his name with a capital *D.* It was of no use, however. Aline continued to snub him so pertinaciously and persistently that Mme. de Chanoir at last gave up his cause as hopeless, and the professor himself, when he saw this, his solitary stronghold, surrender, thought it best to raise the siege with a good grace, and make a friendly truce with the victor. He frankly withdrew from the field of suitors, and took up his position as a friend of the family. This once done, he accepted its responsibilities and prerogatives, and held himself on the *qui vive* to render any service in his power to Mme. de Chanoir; he kept her *concierge* in order, and brought bonbons and flowers to No. 13 on every possible occasion. He knew Aline was passionately fond of the latter, and he was careful to keep the flower stand that stood in the pier of the little salon freshly supplied with her favorite plants, and the vases filled with her favorite flowers. He never dared to offer her a present, but under cover of offering them to the générale he kept her informed about every new book which was likely to interest her. Finally, Frenchman-like, having abandoned the hope of marrying her himself, he set to work to find some more fortunate suitor. This was *par excellence* the duty of a friend of the family, and M. Dalibouze was fully alive to its importance. The disinterested zeal he displayed in the discharge of it would have been comical if the spirit of genuine self-sacrifice which animated him had not touched it with pathos. One by one every eligible *parti* in the range of his acquaintance was led up for inspection to No. 13. Mme. de Chanoir entered complacently into the presentations; they amused her, and she tried to persuade herself that, sooner or later, something would come of them; but she knew Aline too well ever to let her into the secret of the professor's matrimonial manœuvres. The result would have been to furnish Mlle. de Lemaque with an *obus* opportunity and nothing more.

But do what she would, the générale could never cheat Mme. Cléry. The old woman detected a *prétendant*

as a cat does a mouse. It was an instinct with her. There was no putting her off the scent. She never said a word to Mme. de Chanoir, but she had a most aggravating way of making her understand tacitly that she knew all about it—that, in fact, she was not born yesterday. This was her system, whenever M. Dalibouze brought a *parti* to tea in the evening. Mme. Cléry was seized next day with a furious dusting fit, and when the générale testified against the feathers that kept flying out of the broom, Mme. Cléry would observe, in a significant way:

"Mme. la Générale, that makes an impression when one sees a salon well dusted; that proves that the servant is capable—that she attends to her work. Madame does not think of those things, but strangers do."

It became at length a sort of cabalistic ceremony with the old woman; intelligible only to Mme. de Chanoir. If Aline came in when the fit was on her, and ventured to expostulate, and ask what she was doing with the duster at that time of day, Mme. Cléry would remark stiffly: "Mamzelle Aline, I am dusting." Aline came at last to believe that it was a modified phase of S. Vitus' dance, and that for want of anything better the old beldame vented her nerves on imaginary dust which she pursued in holes and corners with her feathery weapon.

This went on till Mlle. de Lemaque was six-and-twenty. She was still a bright, brave creature, working hard, accepting the privations and toil of her life in a spirit of sunshiny courage. But the sun was no longer always shining. There were days now when he drew behind a cloud—when toil pressed like a burden, and she beat her wings against it, and hated the cage that cooped her in; and she longed not so much for rest or happiness as for freedom—for a larger scope and higher aims, and wider, fuller sympathies. When these cloudy days came around, Aline felt the void of her life with an intensity that amounted at times to anguish; she felt it all the more keenly because she could not speak of it. Mme. de Chanoir would not have understood it. The sisters were sincerely attached to each other, but there was little sympathy of character between them, and on many points they were as little acquainted with each other as the neighbors on the next street. They knew this, and agreed sensibly to keep clear of certain subjects on which they could never meet except to disagree. The younger sister, therefore, when the sky was overcast, and when her spirits flagged, never tried to ·lean upon the older, but worked against the enemy in silence, denying herself the luxury of complaint. If her looks betrayed her, as was sometimes the case, and prompted Mme. de Chanoir to inquire if there was anything the matter beyond the never-ending annoyance of life in general, Aline's assurance that there was not was invariably followed by the remark: " *Ma sœur*, I wish you were married." To which Aline as invariably replied : " I am happier as I am, Félicité." It was true, or at any rate Mlle. de Lemaque thought it was. Under all her surface indifference she carried a true woman's heart. She had dreamt her dreams of happiness, of tender fireside joys, and the dream was so fair and beautiful that for years it filled her life like a reality, and when she discovered, or fancied she did, that it was all too beautiful to be anything but a dream, that the hero of her young imagination would never cross her path in the form of a mortal. husband, Aline accepted the discovery with a sigh, but without repining, and laid aside all

thought of marriage as a guest that was not for her. As to the marriages that she saw every day around her, she would no more have bound herself in one of them than she would have sold herself to an Eastern pasha. Marriage was a very different thing in her eyes from what it was in Mme. de Chanoir's. There was no point on which the sisters were more asunder than on this, and Aline understood it so well that she avoided touching on it except in jest. Whenever the subject was introduced, she drew a mask of frivolity over her real feelings to avoid bringing down the générale's ridicule on what she would stigmatize as preposterous sentimentality.

M. Dalibouze alone guessed something of this under-current of deep feeling in the young girl's character. With the subtle instinct of affection he penetrated the disguise in which she wrapped herself, but, with a delicacy that she scarcely gave him credit for, he never let her see that he did. Sometimes, indeed, when one of those fits of *tristesse* was upon her, and she was striving to dissemble it by increased cheerfulness towards everybody, and sauciness towards him, the professor would adapt the conversation to the tone of her thoughts with a skill and apropos that surprised her. Once in particular Aline was startled by the way in which he betrayed either a singularly close observation of her character, or a still more singular sympathy with its moods and sufferings. It was on a Saturday evening, the little circle was gathered round the fire, and the conversation fell upon poetry and the mission of poets amongst common men. Aline declared that it was the grandest of all missions; that, after the prophet and priest, the poet did more for the moral well-being, the spiritual redemption of his fellows than any other missionary, whether philosopher, artist, or patriot; he combined them all, in fact, if he wished it. If he was a patriot, he could serve his country better than a soldier, by singing her wrongs and her glories, and firing the souls of her sons, and making all mankind vibrate to the touch of pain, or joy, or passionate revenge, while he sat quietly by his own hearth; she quoted Moore and Krazinski, and other patriot bards who living had ruled their people, and sent down their name a legacy of glory to unborn generations, till warmed by her subject she grew almost eloquent, and broke off in an impulsive cry of admiration and envy: " Oh! what a glorious privilege to be a poet, to be even a man with the power of doing something, of living a noble life, instead of being a weak, good-for-nothing woman !"

The little ring of listeners heard her with pleasure, and thought she must have a very keen appreciation of the beauties of the poets to speak of them so well and so fervently. But M. Dalibouze saw more in it than this. He saw an under-tone of impatience, of disappointment, of longing to go and do likewise, to spread her wings and fly, to wield a wand that had power to make others spread their wings; there was a spirit's war-cry in it, a rebel's impotent cry against the narrow, inexorable bondage of her life.

" Yes," said the professor, " it is a grand mission, I grant you, but it is not such a rare one as you make it out, Mlle. Aline. There are more poets in the world than those who write poetry ; few of us have the gift of being poets in language, but we may all be poets in action if we will; we may live out our lives in poems."

" If we had the fashioning of our lives, no doubt we might," asserted Aline ironically ; " but they are most

of them so shabby that I defy Homer himself to manufacture an epic or an idyl out of them."

" You are mistaken. There is no life too shabby to be a poem," said M. Dalibouze; " it is true, we can't fashion our lives as you say, but we can color them, we can harmonize them ; but we must begin by believing this, and by getting · our elements under command ; we must sort them and arrange them, just as Mme. la Générale is doing with the shreds and silks for the tapestry, and then go on patiently working out the pattern leaf by leaf; by-and-by when the web gets tangled as it is sure to do with the best workers, instead of pulling angrily at it, or cutting it with the sharp scissors of revolt, we must call up a soft breeze from the land of souls where the spirit of the true poet dwells, and bid it blow over it, and then let us listen, and we shall hear the spirit-wind draw tones of music out of our tangled web, like the breeze sweeping the strings of an Æolian harp. It is our own fault, or perhaps oftener our own misfortune, if our lives look shabby to us; we consider them piecemeal instead of looking at them as a whole."

" But how can we look at them as a whole ?" said Aline. " We don't even know that they ever will develop into a whole. How many of us remain on the easel a sort of washed-in sketch to the end ? It seems to me we are pretty much like apples in an orchard ; some drop off in the flower, some when they are grown to little green balls, hard and sour and good for nothing; it is only a little of the tree that comes to maturity."

" And is there not abundance of poetry in every phase of the apple's life, no matter when it falls ? " said M. Dalibouze. " How many poems has the blight of the starry blossom given birth to ? And the little green

ball, who will count the odes that the
school-boy has sung to it, not in
good hexameters perhaps, but in
sound, heart poetry, full of zest and
the gusto of youth, when all bitters
are sweet ? O mon Dieu! when I
think of the days when a bright-green
apple was like honey in my mouth,
I could be a poet myself! No *paté
de foie gras* ever tasted half so sweet
as that forbidden fruit of my school-
days ! "

" Good for the forbidden fruit ! "
said Aline, amused at the professor's
sentiment over the reminiscence;
" but that is only one view of the
question : if the apples could speak,
they would give us another."

" Would they?" said M. Dalibouze.
" I'm not sure of that. If the apples
discuss the point at all, believe me,
they are agreed that whatever befalls
them is the very best thing that
could. We have no evidence of any
created thing, vegetable, mineral, or
animal, grumbling at its lot; that is
reserved to man, discontent is man's
prerogative, he quarrels with himself,
with his destiny, his neighbors, everything by turns. If we could but do
like the apples, blossom, and grow,
and fall, early or late, just as the
wind and the gardener wished, we
should be happy. Fancy an apple
quarrelling with the sun in spring for
not warming him as he does in August ! It would be no more preposterous than it is for men to quarrel with
their circumstances. The fruit of
our lives have their seasons like the
fruit of our gardens ; the winter and
snows and the sharp winds are just
as necessary to both as the fire of the
summer heat ; all growth is gradual,
and we must accept the process
through which we are brought to
maturity, just as the apples do. It is
not the same for all of us ; some are
ripened under the warm vibrating
sun, others resist it, and, like certain

winter fruit, require the cold twilight
days to mellow them. But it matters
little what the process is, it is sure to
be the right one if we wait for it and
accept it."

" I wonder what stage of it I am
in at the present moment," said
Aline. " I can't say the sun has had
much to do with it; the winds and
the rain have been the busiest
agents in my garden so far."

" Patience, mademoiselle !" said M.
Dalibouze. " The sun will come in
his own good time."

" You answer for that ? "

" I do."

Aline looked him straight in the
face as she put the question like a
challenge, and M. Dalibouze met the
saucy bright eyes with a grave glance
that had more of tenderness in it than
she had ever seen there before. It
flashed upon her for a moment that
the sun might come to her through a
less worthy medium than this kind,
faithful, honorable man, and that she
had been mayhap a fool to her own
happiness in shutting the gate on
him so contemptuously.

Perhaps the professor read the
thought on her face, for he said in a
penetrated tone, and fixing his eyes
upon her:

" The true sun of life is marriage."

It was an unfortunate remark.
Aline tossed back her head, and
burst out laughing. The spell that
had held her for an instant was
broken.

" A day will come when some
one will tell you so, and you will not
laugh, Mlle. Aline," said M. Dalibouze humbly, and hiding his dis-
comfiture under a smile.

This was the only time within the
last two years that he had betrayed
himself into any expression of latent
hope with regard to Mlle. de Lemaque,
and it had no sooner escaped him
than he regretted it. The following

Saturday, by way of atonement, he brought up a most desirable *parti* for inspection, and next day Mme. Cléry was seized with the inevitable dusting fit. Nothing, however, came of it.

Things went on without any noticeable change at No. 13 till September, 1870, when Paris was declared in a state of siege. The sisters were not among those lucky ones who wavered for a time between going and staying, between the desire to put themselves in safe-keeping, and the temptation of living through the *blocus* and boasting of it for the rest of their days. There was no choice for them but to stay. Aline, as usual, made the best of it; she must stay, so she settled it in her mind that she liked to stay; that it would be a wonderful experience to live through the most exciting episode that could have broken up the stagnant monotony of their lives, and that, in fact, it was rather an enjoyable prospect than the reverse.

Mme. Cléry was commissioned to lay in as ample a store of provisions as their purse would allow. The good woman did the best she could with her means, and the little group encouraged each other to face the coming events like patriotic citizens, cheerfully and bravely. Of the magnitude of those events, or their own probable share in their national calamities, they had a very vague notion.

"The situation," M. Dalibouze assured them, "was critical, but by no means desperate. On the contrary, France, instead of being at the mercy of her enemies, was now on the eve of crushing them, of obtaining one of those astonishing victories which make ordinary history pale. It was the incommensurable superiority of the French arms that had brought her to this pass; that had driven Prussia mad with rage and envy, and roused her to defiance. Infatuated Prussia! she would mourn over her folly once and for ever. She would find that Paris was not alone the Greece of civilization and the arts and sciences, but that she was the most impregnable fortress that ever defied the batteries of a foe. Europe had deserted Paris, after betraying France to her enemies; now the day of reckoning was at hand; Europe would reap the fruits of her base jealousy, and witness the triumph of the capital of the world!"

This was M. Dalibouze's firm opinion, and he gave it in public and private to any one who cared to hear it. When Mme. de Chanoir asked if he meant to remain in Paris through the siege, the professor was so shocked by the implied affront to his patriotism that he had to control himself before he could trust himself to answer her.

"*Comment*, Mme. la Générale! You think so meanly of me as to suppose I would abandon my country at such a crisis! Is it a time to fly when the enemy is at our gates, and when the nation expects every man to stand forth and defend her, and scatter those miserable eaters of sauerkraut to the winds!"

And straightway acting up to this noble patriotic credo, M. Dalibouze had himself measured for a National Guard uniform. No sooner had he endorsed it than he rushed off to Nadar's and had himself photographed. He counted the hours till the proofs came home, and then, bursting with satisfaction, he set out to No. 13.

"It is unbecoming," he said, shrugging his shoulders as he presented his carte de visite to the générale, "*mais que voulez-vous?* A man must sacrifice everything to his country; what is personal appearance that it could weigh in the balance against duty! Bah! I could get myself up as a punchinello, and perch all day on the top of Mont Valérien, if it could scare away one of those despicable brigands from the walls of the capital!"

"You are wrong in saying it is unbecoming, M. Dalibouze," protested the générale, attentively scanning the portrait, where the military costume was set off by a semi-heroic military *pose*, "I think the dress suits you admirably."

"You are too indulgent, madame," said the professor. "You see your friends through the eyes of friendship; but, in truth, it was purely from an historical point of view that I made the little sacrifice of personal feeling; the portrait will be interesting as a souvenir some day when we, the actors in this great drama, have passed away."

But time went on, and the prophetic triumphs of M. Dalibouze were not realized; the eaters of sauerkraut held their ground, and provisions began to grow scarce at No. 13. The purse of the sisters, never a large one, was now seriously diminished, Aline's contribution to the common fund having ceased altogether with the beginning of the siege. Her old pupils had left, and there was no chance of finding any new ones at such a time as this. No one had money to spend on lessons, or leisure to learn; the study that absorbed everybody was how to realize food or fuel out of impossible elements. Every one was suffering, in a more or less degree, from the miseries imposed by the state of *blocus ;* but one would have fancied the presence of death in so many shapes, by fire without, by cold and famine within, would have detached them generally from life, and made them forgetful of the wants of the body and absorbed them in sublimer

cares. But it was not so. After the first shock of hearing the cannon at the gates close to them, they got used to it. Later, when the bombardment came, there was another momentary panic, but it calmed down, and they got used to that too. Shells could apparently fall all round without killing them. So they turned all their thoughts to the cherishing and comfort of their poor afflicted bodies. It must have been sad, and sometimes grimly comical, to watch the singular phases of human nature developed by the *blocus.* One of the oddest and most frequent was the change it wrought in people with regard to their food. People who had been ascetically indifferent to it before, and never thought of their meals till they sat down to table, grew monomaniac on the point, and could think and speak of nothing else. Meals were talked of, in fact, from what we can gather, more than politics, the Prussians, or the probable issue of the siege, or any of the gigantic problems that were being worked out both inside and outside the besieged city. Intelligent men and women discussed by the hour, with gravity and gusto, the best way of preparing cats and dogs, rats and mice, and all the abominations that necessity had substitued for food. Poor human nature was fermenting under the process like wine in the vat, and all its dregs came uppermost: selfishness, callousness to the sufferings of others, ingratitude, all the pitiable meanness of a man, boiled up to the surface and showed him a sorry figure to behold. But other nobler things came to the surface too. There were innumerable silent dramas, soul-poems going on in unlikely places, making no noise beyond their quiet sphere, but travelling high and sounding loud behind the curtain of gray sky that shrouded the winter sun of

Paris. The cannon shook her ramparts, and the shells flashed like lurid furies through the midnight darkness; but far above the din ana the darkness and the death-cries rose the low sweet music of many a brave heart's sacrifice; the stronger giving up his share to the weaker, the son hoarding his scanty rations against the day of still scantier supplies, when there would be scarcely food enough to support the weakened frame of an aged father or mother, talking big about the impossibility of surrender, and lightly about the price of resistance. There were mothers in Paris, too, and wherever mothers are there is sure to be found self-sacrifice in its loveliest, divinest form. How many of them toiled and sweated, aye, and begged, subduing all pride to love for the little ones, who ate their fill and knew nothing of the cruel tooth that was gnawing the bread-winner's vitals!

We who heard the thunder of the artillery and the blasting shout of the mitrailleuse, we did not hear these things, but other ears did, and not a note of the sweet music was lost, angels were hearkening for them, and as they rose above the dark discord, like crystal bells tolling in the storm wind, the white-winged messengers caught them on golden lyres and wafted them on to paradise.

THERE was music enough chiming at No. 13 to keep a choir of angels busy. Mme. de Chanoir, with the petulance of weakness, grumbled unceasingly, lamenting the miseries of her own position, altogether ignoring the fact that it was no worse, but in some ways better, than that of those around her, whinging and whining from morning till night, pouring out futile invectives against the Prussians, the Emperor, the Republic, General Trochu, and everybody and everything remotely conducive to her sufferings. She threatened to let herself die of hunger rather than touch horse-flesh, and for some days she so perseveringly held to her determination that Aline was terrified, and believed she would hold it to the end. The only thing that remained to the younger sister of any value was her mother's watch, a costly little gem, with the cipher set in brilliants; it had been her grandfather's wedding present to his daughter-in-law. Aline took it to the jeweller who had made it, and sold it for one hundred and fifty francs.

With this she bought a ham and a few other delicacies that tempted Mme. de Chanoir out of her suicidal abstinence; she ate heartily, neither asking nor guessing at what price the dainties had been bought; and Aline, only too glad to have had the sacrifice to make, said nothing of what it had cost her. Gradually everything went that could be sold or exchanged for food. Aline would have lived on the siege bread, and never repined, had she been alone, but it went to her heart to hear the never-ending complaints of Mme. de Chanoir, to see her childish indignation at the great public disasters which her egotism contracted into direct personal grievances. Fortunately for herself, Mlle. de Lemaque was not a constant witness of the irritating scene. From nine in the morning till late in the evening she was away at the Ambulance, active and helpful, and cheering many a heavy heart and aching head by her bright and gentle ministry, and forgetting her own sufferings in the effort to alleviate greater ones.

"If you only could come with me, Félicité, and see something of the miseries our poor soldiers are enduring, it would make your own seem light," she often said to Mme. de Chanoir, when, on coming home from her labor of love, she was met by the unreasonable grumbling of the invalid; "it is such a delight to feel one's self a comfort and a help to them. I don't know how I am ever to settle down to the make-believe work of teaching after this long spell of real work."

She enjoyed the work so much, in fact, that, if it had not been for the sufferings, real and imaginary, of her sister, this would have been the happiest time she had known since her school days. The make-believe work, as Aline called it, which had hitherto filled her time had never filled her heart. It was a means of living that kept her brains and her hands at work, nothing more; and it had often been a source of wonder to her in her busiest days to feel herself sometimes seized with *ennui*. That trivial, hackneyed word hardly, perhaps, expresses the void, the sort of hunger-pang, that more and more frequently of late years had made her soul ache and yearn, but now the light seemed to break upon her, and she understood why it had been so. The work itself was too superficial, too external. It had overrun her life without satisfying it; it had not penetrated the surface, and brought out the best and deepest resources of her mind and heart—it had only broken the crust, and left the soil below untilled. She had flitted like a butterfly from one study to another; history, and literature, and music had attracted her by turns; she had gone into them enthusiastically, mastered their difficulties, and appropriated their beauties; but after a time the spell waned, and she glided im-

perceptibly into the dry mechanism of the thing, and went on giving her lesson because it brought her so much a *cachet*. But this work of a Sister of Mercy was a different sort of life altogether. The enthusiasm, instead of waning, grew as she went on. At first, the prosaic details, the foul air, the physical fatigue and moral strain of the sick-nurse's life were unspeakably repugnant to her; her natural fastidiousness turned from them in disgust, and she would have thrown it all up after the first week but for sheer human respect; she persevered, however, and at the end of a fortnight she had grown interested in her patients; by degrees she got reconciled to the obnoxious duties their state demanded of her; and before a month had passed it had become a ministry of love, and her whole soul had thrown itself into the perfect performance of her duties. She was often tired and faint on leaving the Ambulance, but she always left it with regret, and the evident zest and gladness of heart with which she set out each morning became at last a grievance in the eyes of her sister. Mme. de Chanoir vented her discontent by harping all the time of breakfast on the hard-heartedness of some people who could look at wounds and all sorts of horrors without flinching; whereas the very sight of a drop of blood made her almost faint; but then she was so constituted as to feel other people's wounds as if they were her own; it was a great misfortune; she envied people who had hard hearts; it certainly enabled them to do more, while she could only weep and pity. Aline bore the querulous reproaches as cheerfully as if she had been blessed with one of those hearts of stone that Mme. de Chanoir so envied. She had the indulgence of a happy heart, and she had found the secret of making her life a poem. But the nurse's courage was greater than her strength. After the first three months, material privations, added to arduous attendance on the sick and wounded, began to tell; her health showed signs of rebellion. M. Dalibouze was the first to notice it. He came regularly on the Saturday evenings as of old; his age exempted him from the terrible outpost work on the ramparts; and he profited by the circumstance to keep up, as far as possible, his ordinary habits and enjoyments, "*afin de soutenir le morale,*" as he said. When he noticed this change in Aline, he immediately used his privilege of friend of the family to interfere; he begged her to modify her zeal for the poor sufferers at the Ambulance, and to consider how precious her life was to her sister and her friends.

Aline took the advice very kindly, but assured him that, far from wearing out her strength as he supposed, her work was the only thing that sustained it. The tone in which she said this convinced him it was the truth. It then occurred to him that her pallor and languid step must be caused by the unhealthy diet of the siege. Everybody suffered in a more or less degree; but, as it always happens, those who suffered most said least about it. The *gros rentier,* who fared sumptuously on kangaroo, and Chinese puppies, and elephant at a hundred francs a pound, talked loud about the miseries of starvation which he underwent for the sake of his country; but the *petit rentier,* whose modest meal had long since been replaced by a scanty ration of horse-flesh, and that only to be had by "making tail," as they call it, for hours at the butcher's shop—the *petit rentier* said very little. He was perishing slowly off the face of the earth; but, with the pride of poverty

strong in death, he gathered his rags around him, and made ready to die in silence.

It was on such people as Mme. de Chanoir and her sister that the siege pressed hardest; their *concierge* was far better off than they; she could claim her *bons,* and fight for her rations; and she had fifteen sous a day as the wife of a National Guard.

As to Mme. Cléry, she proved herself equal to the occasion. She had no National Guard to fall back upon, but she was sustained by the thought that she was suffering for her country; she, too, was a good patriot. Patriotism, however, has its limits of endurance, and hay bread was the border line that Mme. Cléry's patriotism refused to pass. When the good bread was rationed, she showed signs of mutiny; but when it degenerated into that hideous compound, of which we have all seen specimens, her indignation declared itself in open rage. "What is this?" she cried, when the first loaf was handed to her after three hours' waiting. "Are we cattle, to eat hay?" And, breaking the tawny, spongy lumps in two, she pulled out a long bit of the offensive weed, and held it up to the scorn of the *queue.*

As to Mme. de Chanoir, when she saw it she went into hysterics for the rest of the day. But Providence was mindful of No. 13. Just at this crisis, when Aline's altered looks aroused her sister from the selfish contemplation of her own ailments and wants, M. Dalibouze arrived early one morning soon after Mme. de Lemaque had started for the Ambulance, and announced that he had received the opportune present of a number of hams, tins of preserved meat, condensed milk, and an indefinite number of pots of jam. It was three times as much as he could consume before the siege was raised—for raised it infallibly would be, and, if he were not greatly mistaken, within forty-eight hours—so he begged Mme. la Générale to do him the favor of accepting the surplus.

Mme. de Chanoir, with infantine simplicity, believed this credible story, and did M. Dalibouze the favor he requested. So, thanks to his generous friend, the professor in turn became the benefactor of the two sisters, and had the delight of seeing Aline revive on the substantial fare that arrived so apropos. Well, it came at last, the end of the *blocus ;* not, indeed, as M. Dalibouze had prognosticated. But that was not his fault. He had not reckoned with treachery. He could not suspect what a brood of traitors the glorious capital of civilization was nourishing in her patriotic bosom. But wait a little! It would be made square yet. Europe would see France rise by-and-by, like the Phœnix from her ashes, and spread her wings, and take a flight that would astonish the world. As to the Prussians, those vile vandals, whose greasy moustaches were not fit to brush the boots of Paris, let them bide a while, and they shall see what they should see!

Thus did M. Dalibouze *resumer la situation,* while Paris on her knees waited humbly the terms that Prussia might dictate as the price of a loaf of bread for her starving patriots.

But the worst was to come yet. Hardly had the little *ménage* at No. 13 drawn a long breath of relief after the prolonged miseries and terrors of the siege, than that saturnalia, the like of which assuredly the world never saw before, and let us hope never will again, the Commune, began. Like a fiery flood it rose in Paris, and rose and rose till the red wave swept from end to end of the city, spreading desolation and terror everywhere, and making the respectable party of order long to call back the Prussians, and help them out of the mess. How it began, and grew, and ended we have heard till we know the miserable story by heart. I am not going to tell it here. The Commune is only the last episode in the history of No. 13.

There was work to do and plenty in binding the wounds and smoothing the pillows of dying men, and words to be spoken that dying ears are open to when spoken in Christian love. Aline de Lemaque's courage did not fail her in this last and fearful ordeal. She resumed her duties as Sister of Mercy, asked no questions as to the politics of the wounded men, but did the best she could for them. Mme. de Chanoir could not understand how her sister spent her time and service on Red-Republicans; the sooner the race died out, the better, and it was not the work of a Christian to preserve the lives of such snakes and fiends.

"There are dupes and victims as well as fiends among them," Aline assured her; "and those who are guilty are the most to be pitied." After a time, however, the dangers attendant on going into the streets became so great that Aline was forced to remain indoors. Barricades were thrown up in every direction, and madethe circulation a dangerous and almost impracticable feat to members of the party of order. The Rue Royale, which had been safe during the first siege, was now a threatened centre of accumulated danger. It was armed to the teeth. The Faubourg end of it was barred by a stone barricade that might have passed for a fortress—a wall of heavy masonry weighted with cannon, two black giants that lay couched like monster slugs peeping through a hedge. But after those terrible weeks there came at last the final tug, the troops came in, and Greek met Greek. Shell and shot rained on the city like hailstones. The great black slugs gave tongue, bellowing with unintermitting fury; all round them came responsive roars from barricades and batteries; it was the discord of hell broke upward through the earth, and echoing through the streets of Paris.

Aline de Lemaque and her sister sat in the little saloon at No. 13, listening to the war-dogs without, and straining their ears to catch every sound that shot up with any significant distinctness from the chaos of noise. Mme. Cléry was with them; she stayed altogether at No. 13 now, sleeping on the sofa at, night. It would have been impossible for her to come and go twice a day while the city was in this state of commotion. To-day the old woman could not keep quiet; she was constantly up and down to the *concierge's* lodge to pick up any stray report that came through the chinks of the *porte-cochère*. Once she went down and remained so long that the sisters were uneasy. An explosion had reverberated through the street, shaking the house from cellar to garret, and, like an electric shock, flinging both the sisters on their knees simultaneously. Mme. de Chanoir's spine had recovered itself within the last week as if by magic. She had abandoned her usual recumbent position, and came and went about the house like the rest of them. If the Commune did nothing else, it did this. We must give the devil his due.

" Félicité, I must go and see what it is. I hear groans close under the window; perhaps a shell has fallen in the court and killed her," said Aline. And, rising, she turned to go.

"Don't leave me! For the love of heaven, don't leave me alone, Aline!" implored her sister. " I'll die with terror if that comes again while I'm here by myself."

" Come with me, then," said Aline. And, taking her sister's hand, they went down together.

Mme. Cléry was not killed. This fact was made clear to them at once by the spectacle of the old woman standing in the *porte-cochère*, and shaking her fist vehemently at somebody or something at the further end of it. .

" Stay here," said Aline to Mme. de Chanoir, motioning her back into the house. " I will see what it is; and if you can do anything I'll call you."

It was the *concierge* that Mme. Cléry was apostrophizing. And this was why: a shell had burst, not in the yard, as the sisters fancied, but in the street just outside, and the explosion was followed by a shriek and a loud blow at the door, while something like a body fell heavily against it.

" *Cordon!*" cried Mme. Cléry; " it is some unfortunate hit by the shell."

" More likely a communist coming to pillage and burn. I'll *cordon* to none of 'em!" declared the *concierge*. " The door is locked ; if they want to get in, they may blow it open." But Mme. Cléry flew at her throat, and swore, if she didn't give up the key, she, Mme. Cléry, would know the reason why. The *concierge* groaned, and felt, in bitterness of spirit, what a difficult task the *cordon* was. But she opened the door ; under it lay two wounded men, both of them young; one was evidently dying; he had been mortally struck by a fragment of the shell that had burst over the thick oaken door and dealt death around and in front of it. The other was wounded, too, but much less seriously; he had been flung down by his companion, and the shock of the fall, more than his wound, had stunned him. Mme. Cléry dragged them in under the shelter of the *porte-cochère,* and proposed laying them on the floor of the lodge. But the *concierge* had no mind to take in a dead and a dying man, and vowed she would not have her lodge turned into a coffin. The dispute was waxing warm, Mme. Cléry threatening muscular argument, when Aline made her appearance. Her training in the Ambulance stood her in good stead now. •

" Poor fellow! He will give no more trouble to any one," she said, after feeling the pulse of the first, and laying her hand for a moment on his heart ; " bring a cloth, and cover his face ; he must lie here till he can be removed."

The *concierge* obeyed her. They composed the features, and laid the body under cover of the gateway.

Aline then examined the other. His arm was badly wounded. While she was still probing the wound, the man opened his eyes, stared round him for a moment with a speculative gaze of returning consciousness, made a spasmodic effort to rise, but fell back at once. " You are wounded— not severely, I hope," said Aline ; " but you must not attempt to move till we have dressed your arm."

She despatched Mme. Cléry for the box containing her ambulance appliances, lint, bandages, etc., and then, with an expertness that would have done credit to a medical student, she washed and dressed the shattered limb, while Mme. de Chanoir watched the operation in shuddering excitement through the glass door at the foot of the stairs. What to do next was the puzzle. The *concierge* resolutely refused to let him into her lodge ; there was no knowing who or what he was, and she was a lone woman, and had no mind to compromise herself by taking in bad characters. The poor fellow

was so much exhausted from loss of blood that he certainly could not help himself, and it would have been cruel to leave him down in the courtyard, where his unfortunate comrade was lying dead within sight of him. Aline saw there was nothing for it but to take him up to their own apartment. How to get him there was the difficulty. He looked about six feet long, and might have weighed any number of stone. She and Mme. Cléry could never succeed in carrying him. He had not spoken while she was dressing his arm, but lay so still with his eyes closed that they thought he had fainted.

" We must carry him," said Aline in a determined voice, and beckoned the *concierge* to come and help.

But before proceeding to the gigantic enterprise, Mme. Cléry poured out a tumbler of wine, which she had had the wit to bring down with the lint-box, and held it to the sufferer's lips, while Aline supported his head against her knee. He drank it with avidity, and the draught seemed to revive him instantaneously ; he sat up leaning on his right arm.

" We are going to carry you upstairs, *mon petit,*" said Mme. Cléry, patting him on the shoulder with the patronizing manner an amazon might have assumed towards a dwarf.

" *You* carry me !" said the young man, measuring the short, trim figure of the charwoman with a sceptical twinkle in his eyes : they were darkgray eyes, particularly clear, and piercing.

" Me and Mlle. Aline," said Mme. Cléry, in a tone that testified against the supercilious way in which her measure was being taken.

Aline was behind him. He turned to look at her with a jest on his lips, but, changing his mind apparently, he bowed ; then, with a resolute effort, he bent forward, and, before either she or Mme. Cléry could interfere, he was on his feet. It was well, however, they were both within reach of him, for he staggered, and must have fallen but for their prompt assistance.

" La !" said Mme. Cléry, " what it is to be proud ! Lean on Mlle. Aline and me, and try and get up-stairs without breaking your neck."

" It is the fortune of war," said the gentleman laughing, and accepting the shoulder that Aline turned towards him.

They accomplished the ascent in safety, and then, in spite of his assertion that he was all right now, Mme. de Chanoir insisted on their guest lying down on her sofa while the charwoman prepared some food for him. But safety, in truth, was nowhere. The fighting grew brisker from minute to minute. The troops were in possession of the neighboring streets ; they had taken the Federals in the rear, and were mowing them down like corn. The struggle could not last much longer, but it was desperate, and the loss of life, already appalling, must be still greater before it ended. The stranger who had introduced himself so unexpectedly to No. 13 had formed one of the party of order, he told his good Samaritans, who had gone unarmed, with a flag of truce, to the Federals in the Rue de la Paix ; he had seen the ghastly butchery that followed, and only escaped as if by miracle himself ; he had fought as a *mobile* against the Prussians, and received a sabre-cut in the head, which had kept him in the hospital for weeks ; he had, of course, refused to join the Federals, and it was at the risk of his life that he showed himself abroad in Paris ; just now he had been making an attempt to join the troops, when that shell burst, and stopped him in his

venturesome career. All day and all night the four inmates of the little *entresol* waited and watched in breathless anxiety for the close of the battle that was raging around them. It never flagged for an instant, and as it went on the noise grew louder and more bewildering, the tocsin rang from every belfry in the city, the drum beat to arms in every direction, the chassepots hissed, the cannon boomed, and yells and shrieks of fratricidal murder filled the air, mingling with the smell and smoke of blood and powder. It was a night that drove hundreds mad who lived through it. Yet the worst was still to come. Late the next afternoon, Aline, who was constantly at the window, peeping from behind the mattress stuffed into it to protect them from the shells, thought she discovered something in the atmosphere indicative of a change of some sort. She said nothing, but slipped out of the room, and ran up to a bull's-eye at the top of the house that served as a sort of observatory to those who had the courage of their curiosity, as the French put it, and ventured their heads for a moment to the mercy of the missiles flying amongst the chimney-pots. It was an awful sight that met her. A fire was raging close to the house. Where it began and ended it was impossible to say, but clearly it was of immense magnitude, and blazed with a fury that threatened to spread the flames far and wide. She stood rooted to the spot, literally paralyzed with horror. Were they to be burnt to death, after living through such miseries, and escaping death in so many shapes ? Yet how could they escape it ? There were barricades on every side of them ; if they were not shot down like dogs, which was the most likely event, they would never be allowed to pass. All this rushed through her mind as she gazed in blank despair out of the little bull's-eye, that embraced the whole area of the Rue Royale and the adjacent streets. As yet, there was a space between the fire and No. 13. Mercifully, there was no wind, and she saw by the swaying of the flames that they drew rather towards the Madeleine than in the direction of the Rue de Rivoli. Flight was a forlorn hope, but still they must try it. She turned abruptly from the window, and was crossing the room, when a loud crash made her heart leap. She looked back. The roof of another house, one nearer to No. 13, had fallen in, and the flames, leaping through like rattlesnakes out of a bag, sprang at the sky, writhing and hissing as they licked it with their long red tongues.

"O God, have pity on us!"

Aline fell on her knees for one moment, and then hurried down to the *salon.*

"We must leave this at once," she said, speaking calmly, but with white lips; "the street is on fire."

M. Varlay, *citoyen* Varlay, as he gave his name, started to his feet, and, pulling the mattress from the window, looked out. He saw the flames above the house-top.

"Let us go, with the help of God!" he exclaimed. "We must make for the Rue de Rivoli!"

Mme. de Chanoir and the charwoman, as soon as they caught sight of the fire, shrieked in chorus, and made a headlong rush at the stairs.

"You must be quiet, madame!" cried M. Varlay in a tone that arrested both the women; "if we lose our presence of mind, we had better stay where we are. Have you any valuables, papers or money, that you can take in your pocket?" he said, turning to Aline. She alone had not lost her head.

Yes; there were a few letters of her parents, and some trinkets, valuable only as souvenirs, which she had had the forethought to put together. She took them quickly, and the four went down the stairs. There was no one in the lodge. The *concierge* had taken refuge in her cellar, and her husband was supposed to be saving France somewhere else. Mme. Cléry pulled the string, and the little band sallied forth into the street. The air was so thick they could hardly see their way, except for the fiery forks of flame that shot up successively through the fog, illuminating dark spots with a momentary lurid brightness, while now and then the crash of a roof or a heavy beam was followed by a pillar of sparks that went rattling up into the sky like a fountain of rockets. The Babel of drums, and bells, and artillery added to the confusion of the scene as the fugitives hurried on singly under the shadow of the houses. They fared safely out of the Rue Royale and turned to the left. The Tuileries was enveloped in smoke, but the flames were nearly spent, only here and there a tongue of fire crept out of a crevice, licked the wall, twisted and twirled, and drew in again. A crowd was gathered under the portico of the Rue de Rivoli, watching the last throes of the conflagration, and discussing many questions in excited tones. Our travellers pushed on, and came unmolested to the corner of the Rue St. Florentine, where a sentry levelled his bayonet before them, and cried "Halt!" Mme. de Chanoir, who walked first, answered by a scream. *Citoyen* Varlay, laying his hand on her shoulder, drew her quickly behind him. "Stand here while I speak to him," he said, and he advanced to parley with the Federal, at the same time putting his hand into his pocket. They had not exchanged half a dozen words when the sentinel shouldered his chassepot, and said :

" Quick, then, pass along !"

Varlay stood for the women to pass first. Mme. de Chanoir and the charwoman rushed on, but no sooner had they stepped into the street than, clasping their hands, they fell upon their knees with a cry of agonized terror. The sight that met them was indeed enough to make a brave heart quail. To the left, extending right across the street, rose a barricade, a fortress rather, surmounted at either end by two warriors of the Commune, bending over a cannon as if in the very act of firing ; in the centre two amazon *pétroleuses* stood with chassepots slung *en baudelière* and red rags in their hands that they waved aloft proudly like women who felt that the eyes of Europe were upon them ; the intermediate space on either side of them was filled up with soldiers planted singly or in groups, and *posed* in the attitudes of men whom forty centuries look down upon. Just as Mme. de Chanoir and her *bonne* came in front of the terrible *mise-en-scène*, and before they could go backward or forward, the word *Fire !* rang out from the fortress, two matches flashed in the hands of the gunners, and the women dropped to the ground with a shriek that would have waked the dead.

" What's the matter now ?" cried the sentinel.

" They are going to fire !"

" Imbeciles ! No, they are going to be photographed !" *

And so they were. A photographic battery was set up against the railings opposite. Aline and *citoyen* Varlay seized the two half-fainting women by the arm, and dragged them across and out of the range of the formidable *tableau vivant.* Mean-

* Told to the writer as a fact.

while, the fire was gaining on No. 13. The house three doors down from it was *flambée.* It had been deserted the day before by all its occupants, save one family composed of a husband and wife, who had obstinately refused to believe in the danger till it was too late to evade it. They were friends of M. Dalibouze's and the professor turned in to see them this morning on his way to No. 13. " The situation was a difficult one," he said; "it were foolhardy to defy it, and the time was come when good citizens should save themselves." He convinced M. and Mme. X—— that this was the only reasonable thing to do. So casting a last look at their belongings, they sallied forth from their home accompanied by their servant, an *ex-sapeur,* too old for military service, but as hale and hearty as a youth of twenty. The professor had got in by a backway from the Faubourg St. Honoré, and thither he led his friends now ; but, though less than fifteen minutes had elapsed since he had entered, the passage was already blocked : part of the wall had fallen and stopped it up. There was nothing for it but to go boldly out by the front door, and trust to Providence. But they reckoned without the *pétroleuses.* Those zealous daughters of the Commune, braving the shot, and the shell, and the vengeful flames of their own creation, sped from door to door, pouring the terrible fluid into holes and corners, through the gratings of cellars, under the doors, through the chinks of the windows, everywhere, dancing, and singing, and laughing all the time like tigers in human shape — tigers gone mad with fire and blood. When the *sapeur* opened the door, he beheld a group of them on the *trottoir ;* one was rolling a barrel of petroleum on to the next house, another was steeping rags in a barrel already half empty, and handling them as fast as she could to others, who stuffed them into appropriate places, and set a light to them; every flame that rose was hailed by a shout of demoniacal exultation. The *sapeur* banged the door in their faces.

"We must set to work, and cut a hole through the wall," he said; "it's the last chance left us."

No sooner said than done. He knew where to lay his hands on a couple of crowbars and a pickaxe; the professor fired the contents of his chassepot at the wall, and then the three men went at it, and worked as men do when death is behind them and life before. It was an old house, built chiefly of stone and mortar, very little iron, and it yielded quickly to the hammering blows of the workmen. A breach was made—a small one, but big enough to let a man crawl through. M. X—— passed out first, and then helped out his wife. M. Dalibouze and the *sapeur* followed. They hurried through the next apartment. M. Dalibouze reloaded his gun; whiz! whiz! went the bullets; bang! bang! went the crowbars; down rattled the stones; another breach was made, and again they were saved. Three times they fought their way through the walls, while the fire like a lava torrent rolled after them, and then they found themselves at No. 13. M. Dalibouze's first thought was for the little apartment on the *entresol* at the other side. They made for it; but as they were crossing the court a blow, or rather a succession of blows, struck the great oak door; it opened like a nut, and fell in with a crash like thunder. The burglars beheld M. Dalibouze in his National Guard costume scudding across the yard, and greeted him with howls like a troop of jackals. Whiz! went the grape-shot. M. Dalibouze fell.

Mme. X—— and her husband had fallen back before the door gave way, and thus escaped observation. No one was left but the old *sapeur.*

"What sort of work is this?" he said, walking defiantly up to the men—there were five of them—"what do you mean by breaking into the houses of honest citizens?"

"You had better break out of this one if you don't want to grill," answered one of the ruffians; "we are going to fire it, *par ordre de le Commune.*"

The women had disappeared, and left their implements in the hands of the men.

"Oh! *par ordre de le Commune!*" echoed the *sapeur;* "then I've nothing to say; I hope they pay you well for the work?"

"Not over and above for such work as it is," said one of the incendiaries, rolling a barrel into the concierge's lodge.

"How much?"

"Ten francs apiece."

"Ten francs for burning a house down! Pshaw! you're fools for your pains!"

The *sapeur* shrugged his shoulders, and, turning on his heels, walked off. Suddenly, as if a bright thought struck him, he turned back, and faced them with his hands in his pockets.

"Suppose you got twenty for leaving it alone?"

"Twenty apiece?"

"Twenty apiece, every man of you!"

They stopped their work, and looked from one to another.

"*Ma foi,* I'd take it, and leave it alone!" said one.

"*Pardie!* we've had enough of it, and, as the *citoyen* says, it's beggarly pay for the work," said another.

"Done!" said the *sapeur.**

* This incident is authentic, and occurred at No. 13 Rue Royale

He pulled out a leathern purse from his breast-pocket, and counted out o :e hundred francs in five gold pieces to the five communists. "*Une poignée de main, citoyen !*" said the first spokesmen. The others followed suit, and the *sapeur*, after heartily wringing the five rascally hands, sent them on their way rejoicing to the cabaret round the corner. This is how No. 13 was saved. No. 11 was burnt to the ground, and then the fire stopped.

But to return to Aline and her friends. They got on well till they came to the Rue d'Alger, where they were caught in a panic, men, and women, and children struggling to get out of reach of the flames, and threatening to crush each other to death in their terror. Our friends got clear of it, but, on coming out of the *mêlée* at separate points, the sisters found they had lost each other. Mme. de Chanoir had held fast by Mme. Cléry, and was satisfied that Aline was safe under the wing of *citoyen* Varlay. But she was mistaken. He had indeed lifted her off the ground, holding her like a child above the heads of the crowd, and so saved her from being trampled under foot, most likely ; but when he set her down, and Aline turned to speak to him, he was gone. It would have been madness to attempt to look for him in the *mêlée*, so she determined to wait at the nearest point of shelter, and then when the crowd dispersed they would be sure to meet. She made for the door-way of a mourning house at the corner of the Rue St. Honoré. But she had not been many minutes there when she heard a hue and cry from the Tuileries end of the street, and a troop of men and women came flying along, driving some people before them, and firing at random as they went. The sensible thing for Aline to do was, of course, to flatten herself against the wall, and stay where she was, and of course she did not do it. She saw a flock of people running, and she started from her hiding-place, and turned and ran with them. They tore along the Rue St. Honoré till they came to the Rue Rohan; here the band broke up, and many disappeared at opposite points ; but one little group unluckily kept together, and, though diminished to a third its size at the starting point, it still held in view, and gave chase to the pursuers. Mlle. de Lemaque kept with this. On they flew like hares before the hounds, till, turning the corner of the Place du Palais Royal, they were stopped by two Federals, who levelled their chassepots and bade them stand. The fugitives turned, not like hares at bay to face the hunters and die, but to rush into an open shop, and fall on their knees, and cry, " Mercy !"

The Federals were after them in a second. Instead of shooting them right off, however, they set to discussing the propriety of taking them out and standing them in regulation order, with their backs to the wall, and doing the thing in a proper businesslike manner. While this parley was going on, Aline de Lemaque cast a glance round her, and saw that her fellow-victims were two young lads and half a dozen women, all of them of the lower class apparently ; most of them wore caps. The men who were making ready to shoot them without rhyme or reason, as if they were so many rats, were evidently of the very dregs of the Commune, and looked half-drunk with blood or wine, or both —it was hard to say—but there was no trace of manhood left upon the faces that gave a hope that mercy had still a lurking-place in their hearts. One of the women suddenly started to her feet. " What ! " she cried, " you call yourselves men, and you are going in cold blood to shoot unarmed women and boys? Shame on you for cowards! There is not a man amongst you!"

She snapped her fingers right into their faces with an impudence that was positively sublime. The cowards were taken aback. They looked at each other, and burst out laughing.

"*Sapristi!* She's right," exclaimed one of them; "they're not worth wasting our powder on!"

Like lightning, the women were on their feet, fraternizing with the men, embracing, shaking hands, and swearing fraternity in true communistic fashion. Mlle. de Lemaque alone stood aloof, a silent, terror-stricken spectator of the scene.

"What have we here? *Une canaille d'aristocrate*, I'll be bound! It's written on her face," said one of the ruffians, seizing her by the arm; "let us make away with her, comrades! It will be a good job for the Republic to rid it of one more of the lazy aristos that live by the *ouvrier's* meat." There was a lull in the kissing and hand-shaking, and they turned to stare at Aline. Her life hung by a thread. A timid word, a guilty look, and she was lost. But the soldier's blood rose up in her; she bethought her of her *abus*, and *lancéd* it.

"Lazy!" she cried; "I am a soldier's daughter; my father fought for France, and left his children nothing but his sword; I work for my bread as hard as any of you!"

The effect was galvanic; they gathered around her, shouting, "Bravo! Give us your hand, citoyenne!"

And Aline gave it, and, like the statesman who thanked God he had a country to sell, she blessed him that she had a hand to give.

—Blood ran like water in the sewers of Paris for a few days, and then the troops were masters of the field, and order was restored—restored so far as to enable honest men to sleep in their beds at night.

Mme. de Chanoir was back again in the little saloon at No. 13, and diligently reading the newspaper aloud to a gentleman who was lying on the sofa near her; the *générale's* spine complaint had been radically cured by the Commune, and she sat erect in a chair now like other people. The invalid's face and head were so elaborately bandaged that it was impossible to see what either were like, while his bodily proportions disappeared altogether under a voluminous travelling-rug. He listened for some time without comment to the political tirade which Mme. de Chanoir was reading to him, an invective against France, and her soldiers, and her generals, and the nation at large—a sweeping anathema, in fact, of everything and everybody, till he could bear it no longer, and, sitting bolt upright, he exclaimed:

"Madame, the man who wrote that article is a traitor. France is greater to-day in her unmerited misfortunes than she was in the apotheosis of her glory; she is more sublime in her widowed grief than her ignoble foe in his barbarous successes! She is, in fact, still France. The situation is compromised for a moment, but—"

"*Là, là, voyons!*" broke in Mme. Cléry, putting her head in at the door, and shaking the lid of a saucepan at the invalid. "How is the *tisane* to take effect if you will talk politics and put yourself into a rage about *la situation!* Mme. *la Générale*, make 'um keep still!"

The *générale* thus adjured laid down the newspaper, and gently insisted on M. Dalibouze's resuming his horizontal position on the couch. Aline was not there; she was off at her old work at the Ambulance again. The hospitals had been replenished to overflowing by the street-fighting of the last week of the Commune, *la dénouement de la situation*, as M. Dalibouze called it, and nurses were in great demand. *Citoyen* Varlay had not turned up since the night they had lost him in the crowd. The excitement and confusion which had reigned in the city ever since had made it difficult to set effective inquiries on foot, even if the sisters had been accurately informed regarding their quondam guest's identity and circumstances, which they were not. All they knew of him was his appearance, his name, and his wound. This was too vague to assist much in the search. Mme. de Chanoir was sincerely sorry for it; she had been attracted at once by the frank bearing and courteous manners of the young *citoyen;* but his cool courage, his forgetfulness of himself for others, and the stoical contempt for bodily pain which he had displayed on the occasion of their flight, had kindled sympathy into admiration, and she spoke of him now as a hero. She spoke of him constantly at first, loudly lamenting his loss; for lost she believed him. He had, no doubt, been overpowered by the crowd; his disabled arm deprived him of half his strength, and, exhausted as he was by previous pain, and the violent effort to protect Aline in the struggle, he had probably fainted and been suffocated or crushed to death. This was the conclusion Mme. de Chanoir arrived at; but when she mentioned it to Aline, the deadly paleness that suddenly overspread the young girl's features made her wish to recall her words, and from that out the name of the young soldier was never pronounced between the sisters.

Mme. Cléry had formed on her side an enthusiastic affection for him, and sincerely regretted his fate, but with a woman's instinct she guessed that the one who regretted it most said least about it. She never mentioned *citoyen* Varlay to Aline, but made up for the self-denial by pouring out his praises and her own grief into the sympathizing ear of the *générale.*

"What a pretty couple they would have made!" said the old woman one morning, wiping her eyes with the corner of her apron; "he was such a fine fellow, and so merry; he only wanted the *particule* to make him perfect; but, after all, who knows? He may not have been as good as he looked. One can never trust those *parvenus.*"

A month passed. Mme. de Chanoir was alone one afternoon, when Mme. Cléry rushed into the room in a state of breathless excitement, her eyes literally dancing out of her head.

"Madame! madame! I guessed it! I was sure of it! I'm not that woman not to know a gentleman when I see him. I told madame he was! Let madame never say but I did!"

And having explained herself thus coherently between laughing and crying, she held out a card to her mistress.

Mme. de Chanoir read aloud:

LE BARON DE VARLAY,
Avocat à la Cour de Cassation.

Another month elapsed, and the great door of the Madeleine was opened for a double marriage. The first bridegroom was a tall, slight man, on whose face and figure the word *distingué* was unmistakably stamped. The second was a plump, dapper little man, who, as he walked up the carpeted aisle of the church, seemed hardly to touch the ground, so elastic was his step; his countenance beamed, he was radiant, and it is hardly a figure of speech to say that he was buoyant with satisfaction. If he could have given utterance to his feelings, he would have said that "the situation was perfect, and absolutely nothing more could be desired."

Mme. Cléry was present in her monumental cap, trimmed with Valenciennes lace brand-new for the occasion, and a chintz gown with a peacock pattern on a pea-green ground that would have lighted up a room without candles. She, too, looked the very personification of content. The first couple was all her heart could wish, and more than her wildest ambition had ever dreamed of for her favorite Aline. The second she had grown philosophically reconciled to. The marriage had one drawback, a grievous one, but the charwoman consoled herself with the reflection that Mme. de Chanoir might condone the *bourgeoisie* of her new name, by signing herself:

FELICITE DALIBOUZE,
Née de Lemaque.

CHATEAU REGNIER.

A CHRISTMAS STORY

OF THE

TWELFTH CENTURY.

I.

A PROUD man was the Baron Regnier. In the old days of Charlemagne, the Château Regnier had risen, a modest mansion on the pleasant banks of the Garonne. That great monarch died; his empire fell to pieces; the lords became each one an independent sovereign in his own castle, making perpetual war on each other, and electing kings who could enforce neither respect nor obedience. Then the Château Regnier was enlarged and fortified, its retainers and vassals became numerous, and, as was the method of growing rich in those times, large parties of horsemen would sally from its gates, as suited their pleasure or necessities, to plunder neighboring lords or defenceless travellers.

The Barons Regnier were brave men; never was there a brilliant or dangerous expedition wherein some scion of the house did not distinguish himself. When the first preaching of the Crusades stirred the soul of Europe, there was bustle of preparation and burnishing of weapons at the château; even in the motley company of Peter the Hermit went one of the younger sons of the family, who did his part of plundering in Hungary and Dalmatia, and perished on the shores of the Bosphorus; and in the more orderly expedition that followed, the reigning baron himself led a brave array under the banner of Raymond of Toulouse.

The return of the crusaders brought more refined tastes into France, though not more peaceable manners. The Château Regnier was enriched and beautified; troubadours gathered there; feasts were continually spread; still plunder and anarchy were the order of the day till the reign of Louis le Gros. That energetic king devoted his life to establishing law and order in France. Then the house of Regnier, having plundered all that it conveniently could, took part with the king to prevent all further plundering, so it grew strong in its possessions.

With such a line of ancestry to look back on, no wonder that the Baron Regnier was proud. He himself in his youth had shared in the disasters of a crusade. After his return home, he had married a beautiful wife, whom he tenderly loved; but his happiness had been of short duration; in three years after their union she died, leaving him an image of herself—a frail and lovely little being, the last flower on the rugged stem of that great house.

A lovely land is the south of France. Two thousand years ago

the old geographer of Pontus* called it the Beautiful, and its soft *langue d'or* is the very language of love. It was on the shores of the Garonne, in the twelfth century, that the troubadours sang their sweetest songs. Among them was found Pierre Rogiers, who wearied once of the cloister, and so wandered out into the world—to the court of the beautiful Ermengarde of Narbonne, to the palaces of Aragon, at last to the shores of the Garonne, and, finding everywhere only vanity of vanities, once more entered the gates of the monastery and lay down to die.

Here, too, lived Bernard de Ventadour, who loved and celebrated in his songs more than one royal princess. Here he dwelt in courtly splendor, till he too grew weary of all things earthly, and yearned for the quiet of the cloister, and, wrapping the monk's robe around him, he too died in peace.

No wonder if Clemence Regnier, growing up a beautiful girl in the midst of these influences, should yield her soul to the soft promptings of affection. She was the favorite companion of her father; no wish of hers was ungratified; her sweetness of temper endeared her to all around her. She was sought in marriage by many rich nobles of Toulouse; she refused them all, and gave her preference to the younger son of a neighboring baron—a penniless and landless knight.

When the old baron first discovered their mutual attachment, he was at first incredulous, then amazed, then angry. He persistently and peremptorily refused his consent. The De Regniers had for so long married, as they had done everything else, only to augment their power and wealth, that a marriage where

* Καλὴ δὲ καὶ ἡ τῶν Αὐαχίων.—*Strabo.*

love and happiness only were considered, was an absurd idea to the baron.

" This comes of all these *jongleurs* and their trashy songs !" he exclaimed ; " they have got nothing to do but wander about the world and turn girls' and boys' heads with their songs. I'll have no more of them here !"

So the baron turned all poets and musicians out of his château, but he could not turn love and romance out; the young heart of Clemence was their impregnable citadel, and there they held their ground against all the baron's assaults.

Four years went by; Clemence was pining away with grief, for she loved her father and she loved her lover; at last, her love for the latter prevailed, and, trusting to win the old baron's forgiveness afterwards, Clemence fled from the château with the young Count de Regnault.

Baron de Regnier was a man who, when moderately irritated, gave vent to his wrath in angry words, but when deeply wounded he was silent ; and here both his pride and his affection had been wounded most deeply.

He signified to the guests at the castle that they might depart; he closed the grand halls, keeping near him a few old servants; dismissed his chaplain, whom he suspected, though falsely, of having married the runaway couple, and who had been their messenger to him, begging for his forgiveness and permission to come to him; closed his chapel doors; and shut himself up, gloomy and alone, in a suite of rooms in a wing of the château.

Many loving and penitent messages came to him from Clemence. At first he took no notice of them : at last, to one he returned an answer —" He would never see her again."

II.

The summer came and the winter, and many a summer and winter passed, and the dreariest domain in all France was the once merry Château Regnier. Year after year the old man brooded alone. If friendship or chance brought guests to the château, they were received with stately formality, which forbade their stay ; rarely did a stranger pass a night within its walls. The retainers kept their Christmas holidays as best they might; no great hall was opened and lighted, no feast was spread. They wondered how long the baron would live such a life, and what would become of the château should he die, for he had no heir to take it.

Ten years passed : the old man began to grow tired at last of his solitude; he listened to the voice of conscience—it reproached him with ten long years of neglected duties. The first thing he did was to open the doors of his chapel. He sent for artisans and ordered it to be repaired and refitted, then he sent a messenger to the Bishop of Toulouse, asking him to send a chaplain to the Château Regnier.

The church was in those days what the world is now—the great republic of the world ; but at that time she was the *only* republic, the one impregnable citadel where, through all the centuries that we call the middle ages, the liberties and the equality of men held their ground against hereditary right and feudal despotism. In the monastery the prior was often of lowly birth, while among the humbler brethren whom he ruled might be found men of patrician, even of royal lineage. Virtue and talent were the only rank acknowledged ; the noble knelt and confessed his sins, and received abolution from the hand of the serf. Thus, beside the princely-born Bernard we see the name of Fulbert, the illustrious Bishop of Chartres, raised to the episcopal throne from poverty and obscurity—as he himself says, "*sicut de stercore pauper*"; and the life-long friend and minister of Louis the Sixth, Suger, the abbot of St. Denis, and regent of France, was the son of a bourgeois of St. Omer.

So it happened that when the baron sent to the Bishop of Toulouse for a chaplain, a young priest, who was the son of a vassal of Château Regnier, threw himself at the prelate's feet, and begged that he might be sent. The bishop looked on him with surprise and displeasure.

"Monseigneur," said the priest, "you reproach me in your heart for what appears to you my presumption and boldness in making this request. I have a most earnest reason, for the love of God, in asking this; for a very brief time do I ask to remain chaplain at the Château Regnier, but I do most earnestly ask it." So he was sent.

The young Père Rudal had been in his childhood a favorite with the baron. It was the baron who had first taken notice of the bright boy, and who had sent him away to the great schools of Lyons to be educated; and now, when he saw his former favorite return to him, the old man's heart warmed again, and opened to the young priest.

It was with strange emotions that the Père Rudal stood once more in the home of his childhood. When a careless boy there, with no very practical plans for life, he had loved, with a boy's romantic love, the beautiful Clemence. He was something of a dreamer and poet; she had been the queen of his reveries. He was the child of a vassal, and she of noble birth. This thought saddened

him, and many were the ditties wherein he bewailed, in true troubadour fashion, this mournful fact; but that he was a boy of twelve when she was a girl of seventeen did not at the time occur to him.

After he had gone to the university he heard of her departure from her father's castle, and the old man's unforgiving anger against her. The thought of her grief kept the remembrance of her in his heart, and now —though he could laugh at those old dreams of romance—he could love her with a nobler love. He knew the baron's former predilection for himself, and he prayed daily to heaven that he might once more see her restored to her father's halls.

At the château now he was the baron's constant companion. He led the old man little by little to interest himself once more in the duties of life—in plans for ameliorating the condition of some of the poor vassals —in some improvements in the château. Before two years had passed the old man seemed to love him like a son. Yet often a cloud passing over the weary face, a deep sigh, a sudden indifference to all earthly things, betrayed the lifelong grief of the baron's heart, and the thought still kept of her whom that heart so truly loved but would not pardon.

It was drawing near to the Christmas season, when one day Père Rudal said to the Baron:

"My lord, more than a year have I been with you, and although you have heaped many favors upon me, I have never yet solicited one; now I am going to ask one."

"My dear friend and companion," replied the baron, "whatever is in my power, you know you have only to ask."

"In the old days," continued the priest, "this château of yours saw many a gay feast, especially at the

Christmas-tide; then there were nobles and ladies here; now it has grown gloomy and silent. What I ask is, that this Christmas you will give an entertainment, but one of a novel kind; let the halls be opened and a banquet spread, and invite all your poor neighbors, your vassals, your retainers, their wives and children; let none be omitted: do this for the love of that little Child who was so poor and outcast for love of us. I myself will superintend the whole, and pledge myself for the good conduct and happiness of all; and moreover, you yourself will accompany and remain among your guests, at least for a little while. I know I am making a bold request in asking this, but I am sure you will not refuse it, and I promise you will not repent of it."

The baron acceded to the request. Had he been asked to entertain grand company at his castle, in his present mood he would have refused at once and haughtily; but he was too generous to refuse anything asked in the name of the poor; besides, he felt in his heart the truth of what the young priest had said to him: "There is no solace for grief like that of solacing the sorrows of others; and no happiness like that of adding to their happiness."

III.

Christmas Day came; and, after the Grand Mass was over, the great hall of the château was opened, and tables were spread with abundance of good cheer; there were presents for the little children too; and there were *jongleurs* who, instead of the customary love ditties, sang old Christmas carols in the soft Provençal dialect. Amidst the hilarity there was, what by no means was common in those

days, order and decorum. This was due in part to the restraint and awe inspired by the old château—opened for the first time in so many years; but more to the presence in their midst of the baron and the priest, who passed from one group to another with a kind word to each.

After a while the priest laid his hand on the baron's arm:

"Let us retire to yonder oriel window—there we may sit in quiet and contemplate this merry scene."

The baron gladly escaped from the crowd, but, as he seated himself, a sigh of weariness escaped him, and a cloud gathered on his brow.

"How happy you have made all these good people," said the priest. "The merriment of children has something contagious in it, has it not?"

"What have I to do with the merriment of other people's children—I, a poor childless old man?"

The baron spoke bitterly; for the first time in his life had he made an allusion to his griefs.

"But see these three pretty little children coming towards us," the priest continued; "we did not see them as we passed through the hall." And he beckoned them nearer—a little girl about eight years old, a little boy some two or three years younger, and the smallest just able to walk: beautiful children they were, but dressed in the ordinary dress of peasant children.

"Do not refuse to kiss these pretty little ones for the love of the little Child who was born to-day," pleaded the priest, as he raised one on his own knee. "Now, my lord, if it were the poorest vassal in your domains, would he not be a happy man whom these pretty ones should call grandpapa?"

The baron's face assumed a look of displeasure. "I want no more of this; entertain your guests as you please, but spare me my presence here any further. I am glad if I can do anything towards making others happy, but happiness for myself is gone in this world."

"O my lord!" said the Père Rudal, "why is your happiness gone? Because you have cast it away. When your daughter, your Clemence, threw herself and her little ones at your feet, and prayed you, for the love of the little Child born in Bethlehem, to take *her* little ones to your heart, why did you coldly turn away and refuse her?"

The baron turned to him with unfeigned surprise. "What do you mean?" said he. "I have never seen her since, and her children never."

"But you see them now."

"O father!" said a well-known voice, and his own daughter Clemence was kneeling in the midst of her little ones at his feet.

The old man sank back in his seat—his daughter's arm was thrown around his neck—her head was resting on his heart—and after an instant's struggle between love, the divine instinct, and pride, the human fault, his arm was clasped closely about her. Père Rudal lifted up the youngest child, and placed it on the baron's knee, and then quietly stole away.

A merry place was the Château Regnier after that night; the rooms and halls were opened to the daylight—there was romping and laughing of children from one end of it to the other. The Count de Regnault was sent for on the very next day after that happy Christmas, and was embraced by the baron as a son— and evermore thereafter, with great splendor and merriment, was that feast held at the château; so that the Christmas festivals of Château Regnier became famous throughout France.

As for the young priest—that night, after he had seen Clemence once more in her father's arms, he left the château and never returned to it. He went away to Toulouse, and wrote from thence to the baron, telling him that his love for him and his was unalterable, but his mission at the château was accomplished; the voice of duty called him elsewhere; and he begged the baron's consent to depart. The baron gave his acquiescence reluctantly. Père Rudal soon after entered the order of the Trinitarians, for the redemption of captives, which had been recently established, and perished on a voyage to Tunis.

DOÑA RAMONA.

FROM THE SPANISH.

In an empire whose name history has failed to record, there lived in a miserable stable a poor laborer and his wife. Juan and Ramona were their names, though Juan was better known by the nickname " Under present circumstances," which they gave him because in season or out of season that phrase was continually dropping from his lips. Juan and Ramona were so wretchedly poor that they would have had no roof to cover them unless a laborer of the province of Micomican had taken pity upon them, and given them a hut to live in, which in other days had served as a stable, and was now his property.

" We are badly enough off in a stable," said Juan : " but we ought to conform ourselves with our lot, since under present circumstances God, though he was God, lived in a stable when he made himself man."

" You are right," replied Ramona. So both worked away, if not happy, at least resigned—Juan in going out day after day to gain his daily reward of a couple of small pieces of money, and Ramona in taking care of the house, if house be a proper term to apply to a stable.

The emperor was very fond of living in the country, and had many palaces of different kinds in the province of Micomican. One day Juan was working in a kitchen garden near the road, when far away he saw the carriage of the emperor coming at a rate almost equal to that of a soul that the devil was trying to carry off.

" I'll bet you," said Juan, " that the horses have escaped from his majesty, and some misfortune is going to happen ! It would be a great pity, for under present circumstances an emperor is worth an empire."

Juan was not mistaken. The emperor's horses had escaped, and the emperor was yelling :

" God take pity on me ! I'm going to break my neck over one of those precipices ! Isn't there a son of a gun to save me ? To whoever throws himself at the head of these confounded horses, I'll give whatever he asks, though it be the very shirt on my back."

But no one dared throw himself at the horses' heads ; for they tore along at such a furious rate that to rush at them was to rush into eternity.

Juan, enraged at the cowardice of the other workmen, and moved by his love for the emperor as well as his natural propensity to do good without looking at the person to whom he did it, threw himself at the horses' heads, and succeeded in stopping the coach, to the admiration of the emperor himself, who at that moment would not have given a brass farthing for his life.

" Ask whatever you like," said the emperor to him, " for everything appears to me small as a recompense to the man who has rendered me so signal a service."

" Sire !" said Juan to him, " I, under present circumstances, am a poor day laborer, and the day that I don't gain a couple of *pesetas* my wife and I have to fast. So, if your majesty will only assure me my day's labor whether it rains or whether it is fine weather, my wife and I will sing our lives away in happiness, for we are people content with very little."

"That's pretty clear. Well, go along, it's granted. The day that you have nothing to do anywhere else, go to one of my palaces, whichever you like, and occupy yourself there in whatever way you please."

"Thank you, sire!"

"What! No; no reason for thanks, man. That is a mere nothing."

The emperor went on his road happy enough, and Juan went on his, thinking of the great joy he was about to give his wife when he returned home at night, and told her that he had his day's work secured for the rest of his life whether it rained or was fine weather.

In fact, his wife was greatly rejoiced when he carried her the good news. They supped, and went to bed in peace and in the grace of God, and Juan slept like one of the blessed; but Ramona passed the whole night turning about in the bed like one who has some trouble or desire that will not let him sleep.

"Do you know what I have been thinking the whole night long, Juan?" said Ramona, the following morning.

"What?"

"That yesterday you were a fool to ask so little from the emperor."

"Indeed! What more had I to ask?"

"That he would give us a little house to live in, something more suitable and decent than this wretched stable."

"You are right, woman; but now there is no help for it."

"Perhaps there may be."

"How?"

"Look here; go and see the emperor, and ask him."

"Yes; now is the time to go on such an errand!"

"Go you shall, and quickly, too!"

"But, woman, don't get angry. My goodness! what a temper you have! Well, well; I will go, and God grant his majesty does not send me off with a flea in my ear, although, under present circumstances, he is a very open-hearted, outspoken gentleman."

Well, Juan set out for the palace of the emperor; and the emperor granted him an audience immediately on his arrival.

"Hallo, Juan!" said his majesty. "What brings you this way, man?"

"Sire!" replied Juan, twirling and twirling the hat which he held in his hand, "my wife, under present circumstances, is as good as gold; but, you see, the stable that we live in is gone to rack and ruin, and we wish to get it out of our sight. So she said to me this morning: 'If your majesty, who is so kind, would only give us a little house, something better than the one we have, who dare sneeze at us then?'"

"Does your wife want nothing more than that? Well, it's granted. This very moment I will give orders that they place the little white house at her disposal. Go into the dining-room, and take a mouthful and a drop of something; and, instead of going afterwards to the stable, go to the little white house, and there you will find your wife already installed."

Juan returned thanks to the emperor for his latest kindness, and, passing on to the dining-room, filled himself with ham and wine.

Our friend commenced his journey home, and, when he arrived at the white house, his wife rushed out to receive him with tears of joy.

And indeed it was very natural

for poor Ramona to find herself so merry, for the little white house was a perfect jewel. It occupied the summit of a gentle acclivity, whence the whole beauty of the plain was spread out before it. A large Muscatel vine covered the whole of the porch, and beneath it there were seats and little plots of pinks and roses. The apartments of the house were a little drawing-room, very white, and clean, and pretty, with its chairs, its cupboard, and its looking-glass; an alcove with its bed, so soft and clean and beautiful that the emperor himself might have slept in it; a little kitchen with all its requirements, among which were included the utensils, which shone like gold; and a little bewitching dining-room, with four chairs, a table, and a sideboard. To the dining-room there was a fairy entrance, adorned without by an arc of flowers, and through this entrance you passed into a garden, where there were fruits, and flowers, and vegetables, and a small army of chickens clucked; and every egg they laid was as big as Juan's fist.

When night came on, Juan and Ramona took their supper like a couple of princes in their little dining-room, and soon after laid them down in their beautiful bed. They both slept well, particularly Juan, who stirred neither hand nor foot the whole night through.

Ramona began to find fault the very next day, and Juan noticed that every night her sleep was more disturbed.

"Woman, what the devil is the matter with you, that all night long you are twisting like a reel?" asked Juan, one morning. "Why, there are no fleas here as there were in the stable."

"Fleas hinder my sleep very little."

"Well, then, what hinders it, woman?"

"What hinders it? Your stupidity in asking the emperor so little hinders it."

"In the name of the Father, and of the Son! . . . And you still think it little that I have asked, and he granted us?"

"Yes, indeed I do. This little house is so small that one can scarcely turn in it; and if to-morrow or some other day we have children, what shall we do with them in a hut like this?"

"Say what you like about it, there is no help for it now."

"Perhaps there may be."

"And how, I should like to know?"

"Going back and seeing his majesty, and telling him to give us a larger house, of course."

"Go to Jericho, woman. You don't catch me going on an errand of that kind!"

"Well, go you shall, then; or we'll see who is master here."

"But, wife, don't you see that my very face would drop from me with shame?"

"Now, that's enough of talk on the matter. All you have to do is, run along to the palace as fast as you can, if you care to have a quiet time of it."

"Well, well; since you wish it, I'll go."

Juan, who did not possess an ounce of will of his own—a thing which is the greatest misfortune that can befall a husband who is not blessed with such a wife as God ordained for him—set out once more on his road towards the palace of the emperor.

"Indeed," said he to himself, with more fear than shame, "it is very possible he will send me down-stairs head foremost, because it is only natural that this abuse of his good-nature will prove too much, even for him.

And it will serve me right for my unfortunate weakness of character."

Juan's fears were not realized. So soon as he sought an audience with his majesty it was granted, and the emperor asked him, with a smiling face:

"How goes it at the little white house?"

"Not badly, sire!"

"And your wife, how does she find herself there?"

"Not badly, sire, but your majesty knows what the women are. Give 'em an inch, they'll take an ell. My wife, under present circumstances, hasn't a flaw in her; but she says that, if to-morrow or the day after we have youngsters, we shall all be crowded there like bees in a bottle."

"You are right. So she wants, of course, a house a little larger?"

"You've just hit it, sire!"

"Well, turn into the dining-room till they give you a snack of something; and, instead of returning to the white house, go to the Azure Palace, where you will find your wife installed with the attendance befitting those who live in a palace."

Juan returned the emperor thanks for his great goodness, and, after stuffing himself till he looked like a ball in the dining-room, off he set, as happy as could be, to the Azure Palace, which was one of those that the emperor had in that district.

The Azure Palace was neither very large nor furnished with great wealth; but it was very beautiful and adorned with becoming elegance. A servant in livery received Juan at the door and conducted him to the apartment of the lady. The lady was Ramona, whom her maid had just finished dressing in one of the beautiful robes which she found in her new dwelling. Juan could do nothing but open his mouth and

stare in amazement at seeing his wife in such majestic attire.

Juan and Ramona feared they would go mad when they found themselves lords of a palace, well fitted, elegant, and waited on by four servants: namely, a coachman, a footman, a maid, and a cook.

"Take off that clown's dress," said Ramona to Juan. "Aren't you ashamed to show yourself in such a trim before our own servants?"

"This is a new start," said Juan, astonished at the sally of his wife. "So I, who, under present circumstances, have passed all my life in digging the earth, and things even worse than that, must feel ashamed of the clothes I have worn all my life long!"

"But, you stupid head," replied Ramona, "if you have costume corresponding to your rank, why didn't you put it on?"

"My rank! . . . Come, this woman's head is turned."

"Juan, go to your apartment and change your things, and don't try my patience so much, for you know already that my temper will not stand too great a trial."

"Well, there's no need to put yourself out, woman. Here I'm going now, said Juan, turning to the room from which he saw Ramona come out.

"Blockhead!" said she, catching hold of him and showing him another room, "this apartment is mine, and that is yours."

"Hallo! this is another surprise. So my wife's room is not mine also?"

"No; that is only among common folk; but in people of our rank, no."

Juan gave up the dispute, and, entering the room which she had pointed out as his, found therein a wardrobe with a quantity of fine changes befitting a gentleman, and came out again transformed into a milord.

There passed fifteen days since Juan and Romana came to live in the Azure Palace, and Ramona grew day by day more captious, and slept less and less every night.

"What the deuce ails you? One would think the ants were at you," said Juan to her, one morning.

"What ails me is that I have the biggest fool for a husband that ever ate bread."

"Hey for the sweet tempers! So you are not yet content with the sweet little fig that your husband gathered for you?"

"No, sir, I am not. One must be a dolt like you to content herself with what we have, when we might have much more only for the asking."

", But, woman alive, have you lost your senses? Can the emperor grant us more than he has granted us, or do we need more to make us happy?"

"Yes, he can give us more, and we need it."

"Explain yourself, and the devil take the explanation, for you're going to drive me mad with your ambition."

"Explain myself! I'll explain myself, and very clearly, too; for, thank God, there are no hairs on my tongue to prevent me speaking to anybody, even to the emperor himself. To make you happy, all that is wanting is what common folk want— a good table where you may stuff yourself with turkey all the day long; but for us who have higher aims, we want something more than chunks of meat and wine that would make an ox dance a hornpipe. You can swell yourself out and look big when you walk out here, and hear them calling you Don Juan; but as for

me, I could eat myself with rage when they call me Doña Ramona."

"Well, and isn't it better for them to call us that than Juan and Ramona, as they used to call us before? What more do you want, woman?"

"I want them to call me lady marchioness."

"Have you lost your ears, Ramona? Now I tell you, and tell you again, that that wicked ambition of yours has deprived you of your senses."

"Look here, Juan, you and I are not going into disputes and obstinacy. You know me well enough already, or if you don't you ought to, to be certain that it doesn't take long for my nose to itch. I want to be no less than the Marchioness of Radishe and the Countess of Cabbidge, who at every turn fill their mouths with their grand titles, and, when they meet one, don't seem to have time to say with their drawling affectation, 'Adios, Doña Ramona.' Now, since the emperor has told you, when you saved his life, that you might ask him even for the shirt that he had on his back, go and see him, and ask him to make us Marquises."

"Go and ask him if he has a head on his shoulders, why don't you say? But there's enough about it. Even in fun I don't like to hear such nonsense."

"Juan, don't provoke me; take care that I don't send you with a flea in your ear."

"But, woman alive, however much of your husband's breeches you may wear, could you even imagine that I was going to agree to this new start of yours?"

"I bet you, you will agree."

"I tell you I am not going again to see the emperor."

"Go you shall, though you have to go on your head."

"But, wife, don't be a fool—"

"Come, come; less talk, and run along."

"Well, I'm going, then, since you are so anxious about it. The saints protect me, if I don't deserve to be shot for this chicken-hearted weakness of character!"

Juan took the road to the court, and solicited a new audience with the emperor. Though he took it for certain that his majesty would send him to Old Nick if he did not throw him to him over the balcony, he found that his majesty was very ready to grant him an audience.

"Sire, your majesty will pardon so many impertinences—" he stammered out, full of shame, when he drew near the emperor.

"Why, man, don't be ashamed and a fool," interrupted his majesty kindly. "Well, how goes it in the Azure Palace?"

"Beautifully, sire."

"And how is that little rib of yours, eh?"

"Who—she? Oh! very well, under present circumstances."

"And content with her lot? Is it not so?"

"Well, as for that, sire! Well, your majesty knows what the women are. Their mouths are like a certain place I wouldn't mention before your majesty, always open, and there's no getting at the bottom of it."

"Well, and what does the good Doña Ramona ask now?"

"What, sire? But there—one is ashamed to say it."

"Go on, man; out with it, and don't be bashful. To the man that saved my life I'd give anything, even the crown I wear."

"Well, then, sire! She wants to be a marchioness."

"A marchioness! Is that all? Then from this instant she is the Marchioness of Marville."

"Thank you, sire."

"Keep the thanks for your wife and look into the dining-room to see if there is anything to lay hands on. And when you go back you will find your wife already installed in the palace belonging to her title, for the Azure Palace is not good enough for marquises."

Juan passed into the dining-room, and, after running the danger of bursting, he made his way for the palace of Marville. The palace of Marville was not such a very great wonder as its name might lead one to believe; but, for all that, one might very well pass his life in it!

A crowd of footmen and porters received Juan at the gates of the palace, addressing him as my lord marquis; and Juan, for all his modesty, could not but feel a little inflated with such a reception and such a title.

But there was nothing to hold the pride of his wife (though one might be as big as the bell of Toledo, under which one day there sat down seven tailors and a shoemaker) at hearing herself called by her maids lady marchioness here, and lady marchioness there.

"Well, so you are at last content, wife?" said Juan to her.

"Yes, of course, I am. And indeed it was very provoking to hear one's self called Doña Ramona, short like, as though one were only the wife of the apothecary or the surgeon. You see the truth of what I have said; if one has only to open her mouth in order to be a marchioness, why shouldn't she? Now you see that his majesty did not eat you for asking such a reasonable thing."

"Well, do you know, now, that it cost me something to ask it of him?"

"Ah! get out of that; men are good for nothing."

"But it gave me more courage

when his majesty said to me : ' Don't be bashful, man ; for to the man that saved my life I'd give even the crown I wear.' "

" Whew ! so he said that to you ? "

" As sure as I'm here."

" Then why didn't you ask him more ? "

" There we are again ! What more had I to ask ? "

" You are right ; for, as somebody said, ' there are more days than long sausages,' and

' A horse and a friend
No work can spend.' "

On the following day the Marquis and Machioness of Marville took a turn in their grandest coach, and it was a sight to see how they rolled along, at every hour in the day, all around those parts, the very wheels seeming to say envy ! envy ! to the Marchioness of Radishe and the Countess of Cabbidge. Some little trouble took place on account of the actions and complaints of the country folk, who prevented them from passing in their coach over this and that road, or by this and that property. But the marchioness quite forgot all these annoyances when, for example, at meeting the wife of the apothecary or surgeon, she said to them from her coach wherein she reclined in all her glory, " Adios, Doña Fulana," and the other answered her, trotting along on foot, " Good-by, my lady marchioness."

After some time the marquis thought he noticed that his wife was not perfectly happy, because he found her every day more capricious, and she never slept quietly.

One morning, when the day was already advanced, the marquis slept away like a dormouse, and the marchioness, who had passed a more restless and sleepless night than ever, lay awake at his side impatiently waiting for him to awake.

" S. Swithin ! what a sleeper !" exclaimed the marchioness ; and, no longer able to restrain her impatience, she gave her husband a tremendous pinch, and said, " Wake up, brute."

" Oh ! ten thousand d——!" yelled the marquis.

" Are you not ashamed to sleep so much ?"

" Ashamed ! of something so natural ?   More ashamed should the one be who does not sleep, for sleeplessness bespeaks an unquiet conscience.   What the devil is the matter with you that you have not ceased the whole night from turning and twisting about ?"

" Yes, indeed, if one only had a soul as broad-shouldered as you."

" I don't understand you, woman."

" Well, then, you shall understand me, blockhead though you are. Now, tell me, Juan, an emperor is greater than a king ?"

" Why shouldn't he be ?"

" That is to say, that emperors can make kings ?"

" I think so.   For instance, suppose his majesty the emperor wished to say to us, ' Ha, my good friends the Marquis and Marchioness of Marville, I convert the province of Micomican, which belongs to me, into a kingdom, and I make you the monarchs of my new kingdom, I believe nobody could hinder it."

" Very well, then ; I wish his majesty to say and do this at your petition."

The very house seemed to fall atop of Juan at hearing this from his wife ; but this latest caprice of Ramona was so absurd that he had courage to hope in its all being a joke.

" Don't you think his majesty would give the person a nice slap in the face who was so impudent and barefaced as to go to him with such a petition as this ?" he said.

"If you go, he will not; since he has said that he cannot deny even his crown to the man who saved his life. So go along, ducky, hurry and see his majesty."

"But you mean this ?"

"Why shouldn't I mean it ? I have a nice temper for jokes! I want to be queen, in order to let those little folks know their proper places, who pass their lives in digging the earth and eating potatoes, and have the impudence to dare face gentlefolk who condescend to pass wherever they please."

"Well, well, now it's clear that you have lost your wits altogether !"

"What you are going to lose, since you have no wits, is your teeth, with a slap in the face, if you don't make haste and hurry off to the court."

"I'd lose my head before I'd commit such an absurdity. There. I've given way enough already."

"Indeed ! Then from this day forward know that you have no longer a wife. This is my room, and you shall never set foot in it again, nor I in yours."

"But, woman !"

"No, no; remember we are strangers to each other."

"Come, don't be obstinate, my own Ramonita."

"Don't I tell you, sir, that all is over between us ?"

"Now, look here, pigeon."

"Stop your prate !"

"The dev—! Well, come, you shall be satisfied; I will go and see his majesty, and tell him that you want to be queen, though I know he will shoot me on the spot."

Ramona bestowed a caress on her husband in reward for his consent, and our good Juan made his way to the court cursing his own foolish weakness of character.

Contrary to his expectations, the emperor hastened to grant him an audience, and received him with the accustomed smile.

"Well, marquis, what is it ?" he asked.

"What ought it to be, sire ? A fresh impertinence."

"Come, out with it man, and don't be bashful. Something concerning the marchioness, eh ?"

"You've hit it again, sire. These foolish women are never content."

"Well, what does yours want ?"

"Nothing, sire. She says, would it please your majesty to make her queen ?"

"Queen ! nothing more than that ? Well, she is queen already, then. Now, go into the dining-room, and see if there is anything there you can destroy ; and, instead of returning to the palace of Marville, go to the palace of the Crown, where you will find your wife installed as becomes the Queen of Micomican."

Juan outdid himself in thanks and courtesies, and, after treating himself in the dining-rooms right royally, made his way home. On his arrival at the palace of the Crown, a salvo of artillery announced his coming. The troops were drawn up around the palace, where he entered to the sound of the Royal March, and amid the *vivas* of the people, who became mad in the presence of the husband of their new sovereign.

Her Majesty, the Queen Doña Ramona the First, was holding a levée at the moment when her august spouse arrived at the palace, and he, seating himself by her side, gave also his royal hand to kiss; but it was so dirty that as many as kissed it hurried out of the chamber spitting. To be king, it is necessary to keep the hands very clean.

The King and Queen of Micomican amused themselves mightily during the first weeks of their reign : so that all was feasting and rejoicing in celebration of their happy coming to the throne. But so soon as the festival passed, the Queen Doña Ramona began to grow sad and weary.

The king summoned the chief physician of the court, and held a deep consultation with him.

" Man alive," said he to him, " I have summoned you in order to see what the devil you have to say to me touching the sorrow and evil state in which I have noticed my august spouse to be for some time past. She is always turning and twisting about in her bed, so that she neither sleeps herself nor lets me sleep, and the worst part of it is, that every day she is sadder, and everything irritates and exasperates her."

" Well, sire, in the first place, we must please her in everything and by everything."

" I agree with you there, man; but there are things beyond human power. If it rains, she is put out because it rains ; if it blows, she is put out because it blows ; if we are in the winter, she is put out because the spring has not come, and her mind is so turned that she cries out: ' I command it not to rain,' ' I command it not to blow,' ' I command the spring to come at once.' Now, you see that it is only by being God one can secure obedience of orders like these. Well, then, to what the deuce do you attribute these whims of my august spouse ?"

" Sire, it is very possible that they may presage a happy event."

" Ah, ah! I take you. Well, to be sure, and I never thought of such a thing. And wouldn't it be a joy to me and to my august spouse to find ourselves with a direct successor ? For, if not, there is no use in deluding ourselves : the day that we close our eyes, in comes civil war, and the kingdom is gone to Old Nick."

So the Queen Doña Ramona remained watching to see what would happen. But months and months passed, and the queen grew every day sadder and more capricious.

One day the king decided on interrogating very seriously the queen herself, to see if he might draw from her the secret of her sadness and capriciousness.

" Well, let us know, now, what the deuce is the matter with you," he said, " that you neither sleep nor let me sleep, and remain for ever like the thorn of S. Lucy."

" I am very unhappy," answered the queen, beginning to weep like a Magdalen.

" You unhappy ?—you who lived in a stable as empty and bare as that which Our Lord lived in when he became man, and under present circumstances you find yourself the somebody of somebodies, a queen clean and complete ? What the deuce do you want ?"

" It is true, I am a queen. But I die of sadness when from the throne I look back and see nothing of what other queens see."

" Well, and what do other queens see ?"

" For instance, the Queen of Spain sees a series of great and glorious kings, named Recaredo, Pelayo, San Fernando, Alonso the Wise, Isabel the Catholic, Ferdinand the Catholic, Charles V., Philip II., Charles III.—and those kings had blood of hers, and seated themselves on the throne, and loved and made great the people that she loves and makes great."

" You are right, wife. But you wish to do what is impossible, and that God alone can do."

" Well, then, those impossibilities are the very things that tease and exasperate me. What is the use of being a queen, if even in the most just desires one sees herself constrained, and unable to realize them? It is a fine afternoon, for instance, and I begin to get ready to go out for a walk in the palace gardens, but a wretched little cloud appears in the sky, as though to say to one, ' Don't get ready !' And when one wishes to go out, that insolent cloud begins to pour down water, and one is obliged to remain at home, disgusted and fretting. What I want is to have power enough to prevent a miserable little cloud from laughing at me."

" But, woman, don't I tell you that this power God alone can have ? "

" Then I want to be God."

Juan made the sign of the cross on himself, filled with shame and horror at hearing his wife give utterance to such a thing, whose head was undoubtedly turned by the demon of ambition. But he did not wish to exasperate the poor crazed being with lessons which, had she been in her right senses, she would have deserved.

" But don't you know, child," he said to her with sweetness, " that the fulfilment of that desire is as impossible as it is foolish ? The emperor has granted us whatever we have asked, but what you want now he cannot grant."

" Still, I want you to go and see him, and say so to him ; for perhaps between him and the Pope they will be able to manage it."

" But if there is and never can be more than one God, how can you be made God ?"

" I have always heard say that God can do everything. If the emperor consults with the Pope, and the Pope has recourse to God, then you'll see if God, who can do everything, will disappoint them both."

" But if God cannot ?"

" Hold your tongue, Jew, and

don't say such awful things. God can do everything."

Juan thought it would be more prudent to abstain from contradicting his wife any further. So he retired and summoned the chief physician of the court, in order to lay before him the new and extraordinary phase which the moral malady of the queen displayed. The physician said that in his long professional career he had met with cases of mental aberration even more extraordinary than that of the queen ; and insisted that, far from contradicting the august invalid, they should comply with her every wish as far as it was humanly possible.

The king returned soon after to the chamber of his august spouse, who the moment she saw him became a perfect wasp.

" How, sire ?" she exclaimed. " So you are the first to disobey my orders ?"

" How disobey ?"

" Yes, sire ! Did I not tell you that I want you to go and see the emperor, and implore him to place himself in communication with the Pope in order to see whether between them they could so manage that I might be God ?"

" Yes, you told me so, but—"

" There are no buts for me. How is it that you are not already on the road to comply with my orders ? Now, none of your nice little jokes with me, if you please—you, who are no more than the husband of the queen—and, if you ruffle my feathers, I'll send you off to be hanged as soon as look at you."

" Come, child, don't be angry, you shall be obeyed instantly."

" Remember, none of your pranks, now ! And listen : go and tell that health-killer whom you seem to have made one of your council, that if you don't go to see the emperor, and

perform in every point the commission which I charge you with, he
shall serve you as partner in your
dance in the air."

The king withdrew; and when he
reported to the chief physician what
his wife had just said to him, the
physician insisted more than ever on
the necessity of pleasing the august
invalid in everything.

So the king set out on his journey
to the imperial court. The extravagant and impious nature of his mission disturbed him greatly; but the
consideration gave him comfort that
he was no longer a Juan nobody, as
on other occasions when he had
made the same journey, but a monarch about to consult with another
monarch. The only thing that
weighed at all on his mind was the
question of etiquette.

"I don't know," said he, "for the
life of me what shoes to tread in
when I address the emperor. I
have heard it said that all we sover-
eigns call each other cousins, though
not a bit of cousinship exists between us: but how do I know, if I
call the emperor cousin, that he may
not give me a blow that would send
all the teeth down my throat?" Occupied with such thoughts, he arrived at
the imperial court, and the emperor
hastened to receive him when he had
scarcely set foot in the palace.

"How is her majesty, Queen
Doña Ramona?" asked the emperor
kindly.

"Bad enough, under present circumstances."

"Man, that is the worst news yet!
And what ails her?"

"What the devil do I know?
The evil one alone understands these
women. If your majesty could only
guess the commission she has given
me—"

"Hallo, hallo! Well, let us hear
it."

"She says—but pshaw! One is
ashamed to say it. She says to see
if your majesty could consult with the
Pope, and between you manage to
make her God."

"Eh! That is a greater request.
Make her God, eh!'

"Your majesty sees already that it
is a piece of madness; for a woman
can't complain of the small advance
in her career who to-day is a queen,
and not a year ago lived in a stable.
A stable is a disgrace to nobody, sure
enough; for, after all, Our Lord,
though he was God, lived in one
when he made himself man."

"So the good Doña Ramona
wishes to be God, eh!"

"You've hit it, your majesty."

"Well, we will please her as far as
we are able. Let your majesty step
into the dining-room and drive the
wolf from the door, and on returning you will find your wife, if not
changed into God, changed into
something which is like to him."

The royal consort turned into the
dining-room, but, do what he would,
he could scarcely swallow a mouthful. Everything seemed to disagree
with him, and the cause of it lay in
his feeling within him a restlessness
which seemed to forebode some misfortune. He made his way home-
wards, and on arriving at the palace
of the crown he saw, with as great
sorrow as dismay, that the palace
was closed and deserted.

"What has happened here?" he
inquired of a passer-by.

"The emperor has put an end to
the kingdom of Micomican, re-estab-
lishing the ancient province, and re-
incorporating it with the empire."

Juan had neither courage nor
strength to ask more. He wandered
about for hours and hours like one
demented without knowing whither,
when suddenly he found himself at
the door of the stable where he had

lived with his wife, and on pushing open the door, which revolved on its hinges, he found his wife installed there once more. The only thing Godlike which the woman who had entertained the criminal ambition of becoming like to him, consisted in the similarity of her dwelling to the stable which God occupied when he became man.

.

.

AN EVENING IN CHAMBLY.

SOME years ago, upon occasion of a visit to Rev. F. Mignault, at Chambly, we were most agreeably surprised to meet an old and valued friend whom we had not seen or even heard from for many years. We had known him as a Protestant physician in Upper Canada, and our surprise was none the less to see him now in the habit of a Catholic priest.

After the first salutations, tea was served, when we all withdrew to the cosey parlor of our reverend host—which none can ever forget who have once participated in its genial warmth, and inhaled the kindly atmosphere of its old-time hospitality—and settled ourselves for a long winter evening of social delight.

Our chat was opened by eager inquiries of the friend, whom we had known as Dr. Morris, touching the change in his religion and profession. After some hesitation, and smiling at the urgency of our request for his narrative, he complied, saying:

"Should the tale tire you, let this challenge stand
For my excuse."

My medical course was completed in a Scotch university, at an earlier age than was usual with students of the profession.

Immediately after receiving my diploma, I joined a colony of my countrymen who were leaving for the wild regions of Upper Canada. After our arrival, not relishing the rough life in "the bush," I decided to settle in the little village of Brockville, instead of remaining with the colony.

During the progress of the last war between Great Britain and the United States, I had a professional call to go up the St. Lawrence, a two days' journey.

It was a glorious morning in June when, having accomplished the object of my visit, I set out on my return trip. I was then a stranger to that region, and, attracted by the peculiar beauty of the scenery on the river, I determined to leave the dusty highway, and enjoy a stroll along its banks for a few miles. Accordingly, dismissing my man with the carriage, and directing him to await my arrival at a little inn some miles below, I turned my steps towards the majestic stream, whose flowing waters and wide expanse formed a leading feature of the charming andscape before me, and an appropriate finish or boundary upon which the eye rested with ever-increasing satisfaction and delight.

I had loitered on, absorbed in contemplation of the shifting scene, pausing occasionally to watch the changes wrought by the wing of the passing zephyr as it touched the polished mirror here and there, leaving a ripple more like a magic shadow upon its surface than any ruffling of its peaceful bosom, and peering into its abysses, with the eye of an eager enthusiast, to see—

"Within the depths of its capacious breast
Inverted trees, and rocks, and azure skies,"

lulled, the while, by the blissful consciousness of present beauty, to forget that—

"Garry's hills were far remote,
The streams far distant of my native glens"—

over the thoughts of which my homesick spirit was but too prone to brood.

I had reached a close thicket of low bushes that skirted the water's edge, when my steps were suddenly arrested by a rustling sound a little in advance of me. Peeping cautiously through the leafy screen of my secure hiding-place, I saw what seemed to my excited fancy more like an apparition from another world than aught that belonged to this. Upon the gentle slope of a hill which descended to the water, and close upon the bank, stood a gigantic tree that threw its shadows far into the stream, and at the foot of it sat a youthful maiden with a book in her hand, the rustling leaves of which had first attracted my attention. She seemed at times to pore intently over its pages, and at others to be lost in reverie, while her eyes roamed anxiously up and down the river.

As she reclined on the bank, her slight form enveloped in the cloud-like folds of a white morning-dress, it was easy to imagine her the *Undine* of those wild solitudes, conning the mystic page that was unfolding to her the mysterious lore, hidden from mortal ken, through which the power of her enchantments should be gained and exercised. While I gazed with admiring wonder upon the serene intelligence and varying light which played about her fair features, and rested like a glory upon her uplifted brow, I was surprised by the soft tones of a voice proceeding from the tangled underwood that clothed the upward sweep of the hill : " Sits the pale-face alone on this bright summer morning ?"

" O Magawiska! how you startled me, breaking so suddenly upon my dreams! I was indeed sitting alone under the shade of this old tree, pondering over a page in history ; counting the white sails far up and down among the Thousand Islands ; watching the boiling whirl-

pools in the waters of our dear old St. Lawrence; and thinking of more things than I should care to enumerate, when your voice broke the spell, and disenchanted me. How is it, Magawiska, that my sisters of the wilderness always approach so softly, taking us, as it were, unawares ?"

" In that, we do but follow the example given by all things which the Great Spirit has created to inhabit the forest. But come away with me, my White Dove, to the wigwam. That page in history is turned, and strong hands are even now writing the next one in letters of blood ! Many a white sail has glanced through the mazes of the Thousand Islands that will never thread that fairy dance again, and the waters, so pure below, are already tinged further toward their source with the heart's blood of many a brave soldier ! Let my fair one come away ; for old Honey Bee, the medicine-woman, has just returned from Chippewa, and may bring some news of the gallant young captain who commands the *Water-witch*. Floated not the thoughts of my pale sister to him from the folds of the white sails she was so busy counting ?"

" Nonsense, Magawiska! But your words alarm me. Surely the Honey Bee has no bad tidings for me from him you name! What can she know of him ?"

" I know not ; only I heard her whispering to my mother in the Indian tongue, and was sure she uttered the name of the Lightfoot more than once."

" Well, I will go with you, and hear whatever news she has for me."

" Will my sister venture through the Vale of the Spirit-flowers, by crossing which the distance to the wigwam is so greatly shortened ?"

" Yes, if you are sure you know

the way perfectly; for I have never traversed its dreary depths myself."

"Never fear! the Dove shall be as safe in the home of the wild bird as in the nest of its mother." Saying which, the young daughter of the woods glided away over the hill, fol-.owed by her fair companion.

As they vanished, I quietly emerged from my hiding-place and followed them at a distance, creeping cautiously along to avoid awakening any sounds in the echoing forests, into which we soon entered, that would reach the quick ear of the young native, and at the same time making a passing note of her appearance. She was quite young and beautiful for one of her race. Her form was very slight and graceful in every motion, while her light, elastic step seemed scarcely to press the tender herbage and moss under her feet in her noiseless course. As she passed along, she ever and anon cast a sly glance over her shoulder, smiling mischievously to see the difficulty with which her companion kept pace with her rapid movements through the tangled recesses of the forest. After descending the opposite side of the hill, they entered the dingle at its base to which the young squaw had alluded. I was startled when I found myself enshrouded in its dim shadows. So faint was the light therein on this cloudless June morning as to make it difficult to realize that the hour was not midnight! I could discern something white upon the ground that I conjectured was mould which had gathered in those damp shades. Upon examining more closely, I found it to be a vegetable growth, embracing in form every variety of wild flowers that abounded in the neighboring woods, but entirely colorless, owing to the total absence of light. I gathered a quantity of these singu-

lar "spirit-flowers," which presented the appearance of transparent crystallizations, hoping to inspect them by the full light of day; but the moment they were exposed to the sun, to my great surprise they melted like snow-flakes, leaving only fine fibres, like wet strings, in my hands.*

When they reached the wigwam, I secreted myself in a thicket near by, where I could hear the conversation between the old squaw and the beautiful stranger; for having then less knowledge of the Indian character than I afterwards acquired, I could not feel quite safe to leave her so entirely in their power. "Magawiska tells me," she said, with the blushing hesitation of maidenly reserve, "that you have just returned from a distant voyage, and may know something of events which are taking place far up the wilderness of waters."

"And if the Honey Bee knows, and should fill your ear with tales of bitterness, would not the pale-face say she was more ready to sting the child she loves than to nourish her with sweetness? No, my White Dove! return to the nest of thy mother, and seek not to hear of ills for which there is no cure!"

"I must know, and I will not go until you have told me!" she vehemently cried. "For the love of heaven! my mother, if you know aught of the Lightfoot, tell me; for I can bear any ills I know better than the dread of those I know not."

"Even so; if the Bee must wound the heart she would rather die than grieve, even so; the will of the Great Spirit must be done, and may he heal what he has broken! There has been a mighty battle; the foes of thy father are the victors. The *Water-witch* went down in the midst

* A fact.

of the fight. The Lightfoot was known to be on deck and wounded when it sank. Thy father is maddened at the triumph of his foes, but rejoices over the fall of him whom he hated for his bravery in their cause, for his religion, and for the love the young brave had won from the only daughter of the old man's heart and home."

How my bosom throbbed in painful sympathy with the moans and stifled sobs that burst from the young heart, crushed under the weight of this series of dire calamities, knowing that no human aid or pity could avail for its relief! After some time, she whispered faintly: "Is there, then, no hope for the poor broken heart, so suddenly bereft of its betrothed? Oh! tell me, my good mother of the wilderness, is there no possibility that he may have escaped? If I could but see him, and hear his gentle voice utter one assurance of constancy and affection, even if it were his last, I think I could be reconciled. But this terrible, unlooked-for parting! Say, mother, may he not have escaped? May I not see him once again in life?"

"The hand of the Great Spirit is powerful to heal as to bruise! Since it was not raised to protect and snatch thy beloved from death when no other could have saved him, look to it alone, my child, for the comfort thou wilt seek elsewhere in vain! Were there not hundreds of my brethren who would gladly have given their heart's blood for the life that was dearer than their own, and had been offered in many conflicts to shield them and theirs from danger? I tell thee, pale daughter of a cruel foe, that wailing and lamentation went up from the camp of the red men when the eyes of its fiercest warriors were melted to women's

tears at the sight I have told thee of!"

Nothing more was said, and soon after the young stranger departed accompanied by Magawiska.

A few days later, I was summoned in the night to attend upon a wounded soldier on the American shore of the St. Lawrence. I entered a bark canoe with a tall Indian, whose powerful arm soon impelled the light vessel across the broad, swift stream. After landing, he conducted me into a dense and pathless forest, through which I had extreme difficulty in making my way with sufficient speed to keep within ear-shot of my guide. To see him was out of the question; the interlaced and overhanging foliage, though the moon was shining, excluded every ray of light, so that my course was buried in bewildering darkness. A long and fatiguing tramp through the woods brought us at length to a cluster of wigwams, and I was conducted to the most spacious one—the lodge of the "Leader of Prayer"—where I found a remarkably fine-looking young officer lying, faint from loss of blood and the fatigue of removal. A Catholic missionary, whom I had frequently met by the bedside of the sick, and in the course of his journeys from one encampment to another of his Indian missions, was sitting by him, bathing his hands and face in cold water, and whispering words of encouragement and consolation during every interval of momentary consciousness.

From him I learned that the Indians from the scene of action up the lake had brought the wounded man thus far on the way to his friends, at his earnest request. So anxious was he to reach home that he would not consent to stop for rest after they left their boat, although the increased motion renewed the bleeding of the wound, which had been partially checked, until he was so far exhausted as to become wholly unconscious, when they halted here, having brought him through the woods on a litter. The priest had given him some restoratives, but had been unable to check the flow of blood, which was fast draining the vital current. He had administered the last sacraments to the young man, who belonged to a family of Catholics who had recently removed from Utica to a new settlement on the borders of Black Lake.

I made a hasty examination, and soon discovered the position of the bullet. I succeeded in extracting it, after which the bleeding was speedily and in a great measure staunched.

From the moment I looked upon him, however, I regarded his recovery as more than doubtful. Had the case received earlier attention, and the fatigue of removal been avoided, there was a possibility that youthful energy might have carried him through the severe ordeal; though the wound would have been critical under the most favorable circumstances.

When he became conscious for a moment during the operation, and looked in my face, he comprehended the office I was performing, and read in my countenance the fears and doubts which possessed my mind.

" Do not leave me, doctor, until all is over," he faintly said. " This reverend father will acquaint my friends with my fate, for he knows them."

I assured him I would remain with him, and he relapsed into the stupor which I feared would be final.

We watched by him with silent solicitude. While the priest was deeply absorbed over the pages of his breviary, my thoughts wandered from the painful present back to the dear old land from which I was a lonely, homesick exile; to bright scenes of the past, fond memories of which neither time nor absence could obliterate, and drew a vivid contrast between them and the circumstances of my new life, especially at this hour. What would the dear friends with whom I had parted for ever think if they could see me in the midst of this wild and dismal scene, surrounded by the rudest features of savage life? With what dismay would they not listen to the howling of wolves and the shrieking of catamounts in the woods around us? How sadly would the continually repeated plaint of the " whippoorwill " fall upon their ear; while, to heighten the gloomy effect of the weird concert, the echoing forests resounded with the shrill notes of the screech-owl, answered, as if in derision, by their multitudinous laughing brothers, whose frantic " Ha! ha! ha! " seemed like the exulting mockery of a thousand demons over the anxious vigil in that Indian wigwam. I was gloomily pursuing this train of thought, when a slight movement near the entrance of the lodge arrested my attention, and aroused me from my reverie. Turning my eye in that direction, I perceived by the dim light the form of old Honey Bee entering softly, accompanied by a female, in whom, as she approached the wounded man and the light fell upon her face, I recognized, to my astonishment, the *Undine* of my former adventure. But, oh! the change a few short days had wrought in that fair face! The very lineaments had been so transformed from their radiant expression of careless joy to the settled pallor and marble-like impress of poignant anguish that I could scarcely bring myself to believe it was the same.

Calmly she approached and knelt

by the sufferer, taking his hand and bowing her fair forehead upon it. Thus she remained for some time in speechless agony, when my ears caught the whispered prayer : " O my God! if there is pity in heaven for a poor broken heart, let him look upon me once more! Let me hear his gentle voice once again!" Then, placing her mouth to his ear, she said clearly, in a low, pleading tone : "Will you not speak to me once again, my own betrothed ?"

Slowly, as if by a painful effort, the drooping eyelids lifted the long lashes from his cheek, and his eyes rested with unutterable tenderness upon the pale face which was bending over him. "Oh! speak to me! Say if you know me!" she pleaded, with convulsive earnestness.

Repeatedly did the colorless lips vainly essay to speak, and at length the words were wrenched from them, as it were, in broken sentences, by the agonized endeavor :

"My own, my best beloved! May God bless and comfort you! I leave you with him! He is good to the living and the dying. Trust in him, my own love, and he will never fail you. I am going to him, but I will pray for you ever, ever!" Then, with another strong effort, while a sweet smile stole over the features upon which death had set his seal, "Tell your father I forgive all!" A gurgling sound—a faint gasp—and the light went out from the large dark eyes, the hand which had held hers relapsed its grasp, and, before the holy priest had closed the prayers for the departing spirit, all was over!

It was the old, old story, repeated again and again, alike in every village and hamlet, on the bosom of old ocean, in the city and in the wilderness, through all the ages since the angel of death first spread his wings over a fallen world, and car-

ried their dark shadow into happy homes, banishing the sunlight, leaving only the cloud. The same story, "ever ancient and ever new," which will be repeated again and again for every inhabitant of earth until "time shall be no longer," yet will always fall with new surprise upon the ears of heart-stricken survivors, as if they had never before heard of its dread mysteries! Thank God that it closes for those souls whose loved ones "rest in hope" with consolations that become, in time, ministering angels over life's dark pathway, smoothing the ruggedness, lighting up the gloom, even unto the entrance of the valley whose shadows are those of death, and supporting them with tender aid through the dread passage.

Long did we remain in a silence broken only by bitter sobs pressed from the bleeding heart of that youthful mourner. One by one the Indians, each with his rosary in his hand, had entered noiselessly and reverently knelt, until the lodge was filled with a pious and prayerful assemblage.

In the course of my profession, I had witnessed many death-bed scenes, but had never become so familiar with the countenance of the pallid messenger as to be a mere looker-on. A sense of the "awfulness of life" deepened upon me with each repetition of the vision of death. But I had never before been present at one that so entirely melted my whole being as this—so striking in all the attributes of wild and touching pathos!

God forgive me! I had hitherto lived without a thought of him or his requirements, and wholly indifferent to all religion. My life, though unstained by vice, had been regulated by no religious motives, and, so far as any interest in religion was in question, beyond a certain measure of decent outward respect, I might as well have claimed to be a pagan as a Christian. I resolved by that death-bed, while I held the cold hand of that lifeless hero in mine, and mingled my tears with those of the broken-hearted mourner, that it should be so no longer! Then and there I resolved to begin a new life, and offered myself to God and to his service in whatever paths it should please his hand to point out to me.

As the morning dawned, old Honey Bee, with gentle persuasions and affectionate urgency, drew the afflicted maiden away, and I saw her no more. I assisted the good priest to prepare the remains of the young officer for the removal, which he was to conduct, and then sought his advice and guidance in my own spiritual affairs, freely opening to him the history of my whole life. After receiving such directions as I required, and promising to see him again soon at Brockville, I returned by the way I went, and never revisited that vicinity.

Some weeks later, I was called to the residence of a well-known British officer, a leader of the Orangemen in Upper Canada, to attend a consultation with several older physicians upon the case of his daughter, who was lying in a very alarming state with a fever. Upon entering the apartment of the patient, I was again surprised to discover in this victim of disease the lovely mourner of that sad scene in the wilderness. She lay in a partial stupor, and, when slightly roused, would utter incoherent and mysterious expressions connected with the events of that night, and painful appeals, which were understood by none but myself, who alone had the key to their meaning.

If I had formerly been amazed to see the change a few days had accomplished, how much more was I now shocked at the ravages wrought by sorrow and disease! Could it be possible that the shrivelled and hollow mask before me represented the fair face that had been so lately blooming in beauty—shining with the joy of a glad and innocent heart?

The anguish of her haughty father was pitiful to see! Determined not to yield to the pressure of a grief which was crushing his proud spirit, his effort to maintain a cool and dignified demeanor unsustained by any aid, human or divine, was a spectacle to make angels weep. Alas! for the heart of poor humanity! In whatever petrifactions of paltry pride it may be encrusted, there are times when its warm emotions will burst the shell, and assert their own with volcanic power! When the attending physician announced the result of the consultation, in the unanimous opinion that no further medical aid could be of any avail, he stalked up and down the room for some time with rapid strides; then, pausing before me, and fixing his bloodshot eyes on my face, exclaimed violently, "It is *better so!* I tell you, it is *better* even so, than that I should have seen her married to that Yankee Jacobin and Papist! At least, I have been spared that disgrace! But my daughter! Oh! she was my only one; peerless in mind, in person, and in goodness; and must she die? Ha! it is mockery to say so! It cannot be that such perfection was created only to be food for worms! As God is good, it may not, *shall not*, be!"

While he was uttering these frantic exclamations, a thought struck me like an inspiration. The image of old Honey Bee arose suddenly before my mind. I remembered that she had gained the reputation among the settlers of performing marvellous cures in cases of this kind by the use of such simples as her knowledge of all the productions of the fields and forests and their medicinal properties had enabled her to obtain and apply.

Therefore, when the haughty officer paused, I ventured to suggest to his ear and her mother's only, that the Indian woman might possibly be able to make such applications as might at least alleviate the violence of the painful and alarming symptoms. He was at first highly indignant at the proposal of even bringing one of that hated race into his house, much less would he permit one to minister to his daughter. But when I respectfully urged that she be brought merely as a nurse, in which vocation many of her people were known to excel, and which I had known her to exercise with great skill in the course of my practice, failing not to mention her love and admiration for the sufferer, the entreaties of the sorrow-stricken, anxious mother were joined with mine, and prevailed to obtain his consent. I was requested to remain until she should arrive. Nothing was said of the matter to the other physicians, who soon took their leave.

When the old friend of the hapless maiden arrived, she consented to take charge of the case only upon condition that she should be left entirely alone with the patient, and be permitted to pursue her own course without interruption or interference. It was difficult to bring the imperious officer to these terms; but my confidence in the fidelity of the old squaw, and increasing assurance that the only hope of relief for the sufferer lay in the remedies she might use, combined with the prayers of her mother, won his reluctant consent, if I could be permitted to see his daughter daily, and report

her condition. This I promised to do, and found no difficulty in obtaining the permission of the new practitioner to that effect.

Whether the presence of a sympathizing friend assisted the treatment pursued I do not know. There are often mysterious sympathies and influences whose potency baffles the wisdom of philosophers and the researches of science. Certain it is that, to my own astonishment, no less than to that of the gratified parents, there was a manifest improvement in the condition of their daughter from the hour her new nurse undertook the charge.

In a few weeks, the attendance of old Honey Bee was no longer necessary. The joy and gratitude of the father knew no bounds. He would gladly have forced a large reward upon her for services which had proved so successful, but she rejected it, saying: "The gifts that the Great Spirit has guided the Honey Bee to gather are not the price of silver and gold. Freely he gives them; as freely do his red children dispense them. They would scorn to barter the lore he imparts for gold. Enough that the daughter of the white chief lives. Let him see that he quench not the light of her young life again in his home!"

"What does she mean?" he muttered, as she departed. "Does she know? But no, she cannot; it must be some surmise gathered from expressions of my daughter in her delirium."

In accordance with my promise, I had called daily during the attendance of the Indian woman, who found opportunity, from time to time, to explain to me the circumstances attending the rescue of the Lightfoot.

The Indians, by whom he was

greatly beloved, supposed, when they saw his vessel go down, that he was lost, as they knew him to have been badly wounded. A solitary Indian from another detachment was a witness of the catastrophe while he was guiding his canoe in a direction opposite to that of the encampment, and on the other side of the scene of action. He dashed at once with his frail bark into the midst of the affray, to render assistance, if possible, to any who might have escaped from the ill-fated vessel. While he was watching, to his great joy he saw the young officer rise to the surface, and was able to seize and draw him into the canoe. As he was passing to the shore, he was noticed by the father of the officer's betrothed, and the nature of his prize discovered. A volley of musketry was immediately directed upon the canoe, and the Indian received a mortal wound. He was so near the shore that he was rescued by his party, but died soon after landing.

I told her that I had heard the remainder of the story from the missionary at the wigwam.

She then informed me that, after she came to take charge of the maiden, as soon as her patient became sufficiently conscious to realize her critical condition, she had implored so piteously that the priest might be sent for that it was impossible to refuse. When he came —privately, of course, for it was too well known that her father would never consent to such a visit—she entreated permission to profess the Catholic faith without delay. After some hesitation, the priest consented when he found her well instructed in its great and important truths, heard her confession, her solemn profession of faith, and administered conditional baptism ; following the rite by the consoling and transcend-

ent gift which is at once the life and nourishment of the Catholic soul and the sun of the Catholic firmament.

The squaw dreaded the violence of her father when he should discover what had transpired, and enjoined it upon me to shield the victim, if possible, from the storm of his wrath. Alas! she little dreamed how powerless I should prove in such a conflict!

Before the strength of the invalid was established, that discovery was made. I had known much of the unreasoning bigotry and black animosity which was cherished by the Orange faction against Catholics ; but I was still wholly unprepared for his savage outbreak. He heaped curses upon his daughter's head, and poured forth the most bitter and blasphemous lamentations that she had been permitted to live only to bring such hopeless disgrace upon his gray hairs.

Despite the mother's tears and prayers, he ordered her from the house, and forbade her ever to return or to call him father again. Once more did old Honey Bee come to the rescue of her *protégée*. Her affectionate fears had made her vigilant, and, when the maiden was driven from her father's house, she was received and conducted to a wigwam which had been carefully prepared for her reception. Here she was served with the most tender assiduity until able to be removed to Montreal, whither her kind nurse attended her, and she entered at once upon her novitiate in a convent there.

The day after her departure, I also took my leave of that part of the country, and, proceeding to a distant city, entered the ecclesiastical state. In due time, I was ordained to the new office of ministering to spiritual instead of physical ills, my vocation to which was clearly made known to me by that death-bed in the wilderness.

And now that I have related to you how the Protestant doctor became a Catholic priest, I must ask, in my turn, how it happened that you and your family became Catholics.

"The story is soon told," we replied. "Very probably our attention might never have been called to the subject but for a great affliction which was laid upon us in the sufferings of our only and tenderly cherished daughter. She was blest with rosy health until her tenth year, and a merrier little sprite the sun never shone upon.

"Suddenly disease in its most painful and hopeless form fastened itself upon her, and, while sinking under its oppressive weight, she felt more and more deeply day by day, with a thoughtfulness rapidly matured by suffering, the necessity for such aid and support as Protestantism failed to furnish. It was, humanly speaking, by a mere accident that she discovered where it might be found.

"During an interval between the paroxysms of the disease, and a little more than a year after the first attack, a missionary priest visited our place, and her Catholic nurse obtained our permission to take her to the house of a neighbor where Mass was to be celebrated.

"She was deeply impressed with what she saw, and the fervent address of that devoted and saintly priest melted her young heart. She obtained from him a catechism and some books of devotion. From that time her conviction grew and strengthened that here was the healing balm her wounded spirit so much needed. After long persuasion and many entreaties, we gave our reluctant consent that she might avail herself of its benefits by making profession of the Catholic faith. To the sustaining power of its holy influences we owe it that her life, from which every earthly hope had been stricken, was made thenceforth so happy and cheerful as to shed perpetual sunshine over her home and its neighborhood.

"By degrees she drew us, at first unwillingly, and at length irresistibly, to the consideration of Catholic verities. Through the grace of God operating upon these considerations, our whole family, old and young, were soon united within the peaceful enclosure of the 'household of faith.'

"When the work of our dear little missionary was thus happily accomplished, she was removed from the home for which she had been the means of procuring such priceless blessings to that other and better home, the joys of which may not even be imagined here. With grateful hearts we have proved and realized that for those whom God sorely afflicts his bountiful hand also provides great and abundant consolations."

THE CANADIAN PIONEERS.

FROM THE FRENCH OF M. L'ABBE CASGRAIN.

I.—DETROIT.

ARE you familiar with that fertile, laughing country, so rich in historical souvenirs, whose virgin soil was first trodden by our French ancestors? Are you familiar with these green and undulating prairies, watered by limpid streams, and shaded by maples, plane-trees, figs, and acacias, in the midst of which rises, brilliant in youth and prospective greatness, the flourishing city of Detroit? If you wish to enjoy fully the enchanting picture that this charming country presents—whose climate need not be envious of the Italian sun—ascend the Detroit River some fresh spring morning, when Aurora has shaken her dewy wings over these vast plains, and when the bright May sun has thrown its luminous rays through the transparent mists of morning. Nowhere is there a clearer sky or more ravishing nature. Nowhere are the wavy lines of the blue horizon more distinctly traced. Here are wild and uncultivated sites, romantic landscapes, little wooded islands, like baskets of verdure, all re-echoing the mocking laughter of multitudes of birds. Pretty promontories whose round arms encircle gulfs full of shadows and sunlight; whose waves, caressed by these warm breaths, deposit along the shore a fringe of silver foam. Hills and valleys, covered with luxuriant verdure, mirror themselves in the neighboring wave. On either side the shore stretches along, covered with pebbles or fine gray sand; sometimes embroidered with a lace-like turf, or bristling with tall reeds, crowned with little tufts, among which the timid kingfishers perch, and take flight at the least noise. Here the fresh murmuring rivulets flow under the flowery arches of interlacing boughs; there tiny paths, edged with strawberries and forget-me-nots, wind over the brow of the hill; and, more distant, the fresh spring zephyr trembles on the green meadows, and perfumes the air with a delicious fragrance. The thousand confused noises of the water and the rustling foliage, the warbling of birds, the buzz of human voices, the lowing of herds, and the distant and silvery echo of the bells of the steamers that ply along the river, ascend from time to time through the air, and diffuse an indefinable charm in the soul and through the senses. At short distances apart, pretty little villages stretch along the shore, or group themselves on the banks of a stream, or again on the slope of a hill, or crowning its summit like a diadem. Finally you arrive at Detroit, with its steeples and roofs glittering in the sunlight. Hundreds of boats, engaged in commercial interests, are constantly arriving at or leaving its quays, furrowing the river in every direction. Were I a poet, I would compare this charming city to the superb swan of this country, which, on awakening in the midst of the rushes on the river's bank, shakes its white wings in taking flight, and showers around a rain of dew and down; or, better still, to the stately magnolia growing on the banks of the stream, when, shaken by the aromatic breath of the morning breeze, it covers the wave in which it is mirrored with the fertile dust of its corolla.

II.—THE PIONEER.

Founded in the· year 1700, by M. de la Mothe-Cadillac, Detroit remained for a long time under the Canadian government. It was taken by the English in 1760, and remained in their possession until the war of 1812. Then the United States became the happy possessor of this charming country, which F. Charlevoix has so justly called " the garden spot." " Detroit," says the Canadian historian, " has preserved, in spite of its many vicissitudes, the characteristics of its origin, and French is still the language of a large portion of its population. Like all the cities founded and settled by this great people— the monuments of whose genius are landmarks in America — Detroit is destined to become a great business centre, on account of its favorable situation between Lake Huron and Lake Erie." * Toward the year 1770 or 1780, Detroit was far from presenting the flourishing aspect which it offers to the stranger to-day. It was only a small fort surrounded by weak ramparts, and a stockade in which lived a few hundred Canadian colonists—a veritable tent in the wilderness. The fort was the advanced sentinel of the colony, and by consequence constantly exposed to the attacks of the Indians. Around the fortifications the colonists had cleared a few acres of land, which they could only cultivate at the risk of their lives, holding a pickaxe in one hand, and a gun in the other; while beyond, before, behind, to the

* *Histoire du Canada.* Par M. F. X. Garneau, ii. 23.

right, to the left, everywhere a wilderness, everywhere interminable forests, whose gloomy shades concealed multitudes of beings a thousand times more cruel, a thousand times more formidable and to be feared, than the wild beasts and reptiles which shared alike the tenebrious shelter. It is easy from this to imagine what indomitable courage these hardy pioneers possessed who dared to come and plant the standard of civilization in the midst of these distant solitudes, in the face of such multitudinous perils. One of the grandest pictures that the history of the New World presents, after the sublime figure of the missionary, is that of the Canadian pioneer. He is the father of the strongest race that has been implanted on the American continent—the Canadian race; and the noblest blood that has ever flowed in human veins, flows through his— the French blood. Everywhere on the continent the Canadian pioneer is to be found, and everywhere can be traced by his blood. Travel through North America, from Hudson's Bay to the Gulf of Mexico, from Halifax to San Francisco. and on the snows of the North Pole and the golden sands of California, along the Atlantic strand, and on the moss-covered slopes of the Rocky Mountains, you will find the print of his footsteps. An insatiable activity consumes him. Onward! is his watchword, and he only rests when he has reached the goal of his ambition. But it is not alone the love of adventure nor the violent thirst for gold that stimulates him to action : a nobler ambition urges him on, a more legitimate instinct animates and guides him. He has a mission to accomplish—a mysterious apostleship. Turn for a moment to the pages of our history, and especially to the accounts of the Jesuits, and you will see the Canadian pioneer throughout animated by the most admirable zeal for the conversion of the savages, opening a way for the missionaries by the most heroic efforts, and frequently himself making the most wonderful conversions. We find united in him the three grandest types of manhood: priest, laborer, soldier. Priest!—by his ardent piety, his lively faith, his zeal for the salvation of vacillating souls and obdurate hearts, drawing to the faith entire settlements. Was there ever a more admirable priesthood? Laborer!—before his powerful axe the great forests fall with a crash around him, and his plough tracks, through the fallen trunks, the furrow where the green germ of the future harvest will soon begin to tremble. Soldier! —by years of mortal combat, he has conquered the soil that his hand cultivates. Ah! were I only an artist, to trace on canvas this noble figure in his triple character of priest, laborer, and soldier. In the background of the picture, immense forests, in all their savage grandeur; nearer, the waving grain, growing between the charred trunks. In the foreground, a portion of the great river, with its emerald waves sparkling in the sun. On one side, an angle of the old fort, with its ramparts and stockade, whence rises a modest little belfry surmounted by a cross. On the other side, a band of Indians flying toward the edge of the wood. The centre-piece would be my brave pioneer, his eyes flashing, his hair blown by the breeze, and his forehead bleeding from a ball which had just grazed it, near him his plough, and holding his gun, whose muzzle still smokes from a recent conflict. At the right, he would be pouring the water of baptism on the head of his vanquished and dying enemy, whom he had just converted to the faith. Oh! how could I attempt to paint this vigorous figure in the various attitudes of a soldier-laborer, with his iron muscles, and the calm, serene strength of the man of the fields; the invincible courage of the soldier, and the sublime enthusiasm of the priest! Verily, this picture would not be unworthy of the pencil of a Rubens or a Michael Angelo. Faith, toil, courage; priest, laborer, soldier—this is the Canadian pioneer. It is Cincinnatus, the soldier-laborer, become a Christian. It is the Spartan warrior, who has passed through the Catacombs. The Canadian reader who peruses these lines can raise his head with noble pride, for the blood that flows through his veins is the blood of heroes. He can look attentively at the palm of his hand, and see there still the unction of earth, of powder, and of the priesthood. The pioneer has nobly filled his mission: yours remains to be accomplished. A people to whom God has given such ancestors is necessarily destined for something great, if it faithfully corresponds with the designs of divine Providence. But let us leave these teachings, which properly belong to venerable heads, and return to our story.

III.—EVENING

At the remote period which we describe, the fur trade of Detroit was immense; and the Indians, aided and encouraged by the facilities for reaching there, came in great numbers to sell the products of their hunting expeditions. There were representatives from the various tribes—Iroquois, Potawatamies, Illinois, Miamis, and a host of others. M. Jacques Du Perron Baby was at that time Indian superintendent at Detroit. This was an extremely important and responsible position at that period.

M. Baby had realized a handsome fortune there in a few years. Almost all the land on which the Detroit of to-day stands was then owned by him and a Mr. Macomb, the father of General Macomb, who commanded a portion of the American troops during the war of 1812. At the close of this war, the entire property of M. Baby was confiscated in consequence of his political opinions, which were declared in favor of Canada *versus* the United States. His fine mansion stood in the centre of the fort, surrounded by a beautiful garden. Having luxurious tastes, he embellished it with all the requirements of refined and cultivated life. The garden was on raised ground, surrounded by a sodded terrace; the house stood in the centre, half concealed by a dense foliage of maple, pear, and acacia trees, which waved their branches coaxingly over its roof. A number of birds, sometimes hidden in the branches, sometimes flying through the air, crossing, pursuing each other, describing a thousand bewildering circles, abandoned themselves to joyous song, while the little *ramoneur*,* complaining on the chimney-top, mingled his shrill, harsh cry with their melodious voices. It was evening. The last rays of the setting sun colored with rose and saffron tints the tops of the forests. The heat had been intense throughout the day. The evening breeze, coquetting among the roses, dahlias, and flowering eglantine, refreshed exhausted nature deliciously, and perfumed the air with the most intoxicating fragrance. Tea was about being served in the garden, and the table was most invitingly covered with tempting viands and lovely flowers. The superintendent and his family were seated around; a young

officer who had been several months in Detroit had been invited to join the family party. Two colored servants waited most assiduously at the repast. "What a charming evening!" said the officer—he was a handsome young man, with light hair, noble and expressive features, and rather a high forehead. There was a proud, intelligent expression in his bright eyes, and yet at times something vague and dreamy. "Truly," he continued, "I have never seen anything in Italy more delightful than this; such a climate, and such ravishing scenery, such fine effects of light and shade! Look there along the horizon, and at those fleecy clouds which float through the azure sky; they resemble a superb scarf fringed with purple and gold."

"It is indeed a magnificent evening," replied the superintendent. "We really enjoy a very fine climate in this section of country. I have never seen anywhere a clearer sky or more transparent atmosphere, and nature so grand; but, against all of this, we are deprived of nearly all of the luxuries and comforts of the old country, to say nothing of the constant dangers to which we are exposed from the Indians; for we are on the utmost limits of civilization. You, who have just left the civilized shores of Europe, can scarcely form any idea of the cruelty of these barbarians. Life is indeed very severe in this new country."

"Yes," said his wife, whose fine physiognomy indicated her great force of character; "it is only a few years ago that I was obliged to do sentinel duty, and stand at the entrance of the fort with a gun in my hand, while the men were occupied in cultivating the fields around it."*

The conversation was here interrupt-

* Chimney-swallow.

* Fact.

ed by one of the servants, who came to say that a stranger was waiting to see the superintendent and his wife. They all arose from the tea-table.

"You look very sad this evening, mademoiselle," said the officer, addressing a young girl of sixteen or eighteen years of age, and who, from a strong resemblance, could be easily recognized as the daughter of M. Baby. "What can have happened to cause such a shadow to fall on your fair brow; while all are smiling around you, your heart seems full of sorrow? It is almost impossible that any one could contemplate this lovely scene, and not experience a feeling of interior peace. Nothing so completely bewilders me like an evening of this kind. This graceful harmony of light and shade is for me full of a mysterious intoxication."

"Alas!" said the young girl, "a few days ago I too could have enjoyed this scene; but to-day, as it were, every object is covered with a funereal pall. This beautiful sky, these green fields, the flowers and fruit, these vermilion roses, which charm your sight, all make me shudder. I see blood everywhere."

"My God!" cried the officer, "what misfortune can have happened to you?"

"Oh! only a few hours ago, I witnessed such a distressing scene that it is impossible to imagine it. I cannot obliterate it from my mind, or distract my thoughts in the least from the shocking spectacle. But I ought not to distress you by this sorrowful recital. I had rather let you enjoy tranquilly these hours that afford you so much pleasure."

"Continue, continue," exclaimed he. "Relate to me this tragic story. Happiness is often so selfish, but we should always have our sympathies ready for the sorrows of others."

The young girl then continued:

"Day before yesterday evening, a party of Indians half intoxicated came into the fort to see my father; they brought with them a young girl, whom they had captured several days before. Oh! if you could only have seen the despair on her countenance! Poor child, her clothes were in rags, her hair hung in tangled masses, and her face was all scratched and bleeding. She did not utter a complaint, nor did she weep; but stood with fixed eyes, mute and immovable as a statue. We might have believed her dead but for a slight trembling of the lips that betrayed the life that was not visible. It was a fearful sight. I have never seen anything like it. Great misfortunes are like severe wounds; they dry up our tears as terrible and sudden wounds arrest the blood in our veins. Compassionating her distressed situation, my sister and myself made her come in and stay in our room through the night; but we did not deceive ourselves with the slightest hope that anything could be done for her rescue, for we knew too well the character of these savages. Nevertheless, we tried to sustain her with a little hope that something might possibly be done. Perhaps our father could succeed in inducing the Indians to let her go. At last she gradually recovered from her state of stupor, and told us her sad, sad story."

IV.—AGONY.

"I have lived for some time," said she, "near Fort Wayne with my married sister. One morning, while her husband was at work in the field, several Indians suddenly entered our house. 'Where is your husband?' they inquired roughly of my sister. 'He is at Fort Wayne,' she replied, frightened by their sinister aspect; and they went out again. Full of anxiety, we followed them with our eyes for some time. 'O my God! sister,' exclaimed I, trembling, 'I am so frightened, so terrified. Let us fly; these savages appear to me to be meditating some dreadful act. I am convinced that they will return.' Without paying any attention to my words, she continued to watch them as they went off in the direction of Fort Wayne. The road which they took lay only a short distance from the place where her husband was quietly at work, not having the slightest idea of the danger that threatened him. Fortunately, a clump of trees hid him from their sight. We began to breathe more freely, for they had now gone beyond the field; but suddenly one of them happened to turn around. 'They have discovered him! they have discovered him!' shrieked my sister, almost fainting with terror. And really they had all stopped, and were looking in the direction where Joseph was stooping down, gathering up the branches of a tree which he had just cut down. He had no suspicion of danger. The Indians, concealed by the trees, were now only a short distance off. Suddenly we heard the report of a gun, and Joseph fell to the ground. Believing him dead, they advanced boldly; but the ball had only grazed his head, and he was stunned for the moment. He quickly recovered himself, and, making a breastwork of the branches of the felled tree, seized his gun, and in an instant two of them were stretched stiff corpses on the ground. The others, alarmed, made a precipitate retreat toward the edge of the woods, and then a quick firing commenced on both sides. Joseph was a fine marksman; at each shot, he disabled an enemy. Three had already fallen. We

awaited, in an agony of apprehension, the result of the mortal combat, which would not have been doubtful had it been only an ordinary enemy that the savages had to contend with. But Joseph was a formidable adversary. He fired rapidly, reloading his gun with the most perfect coolness, while the balls were whistling all around him. Placing the muzzle of his gun between the branches, he made the sign of the cross on his breast at the moment of taking aim; then, pulling the trigger, we counted another Indian less. Every time I saw a new victim fall, I could not repress a tremor of delight. Joseph's unerring ball had just struck a fourth enemy. We began to hope, when we discovered one of the savages creeping along on the ground behind him. No serpent could have advanced with more cunning or address. Without shaking a pebble or disturbing a leaf, he approached slowly; at one time concealing himself behind a little knoll, then under a thicket of brambles, only exposing himself when he saw Joseph busy taking aim. Finally he arrived within two steps of him without being seen. Then, stopping, he waited until Joseph had reloaded his gun. Without suspecting the danger behind him, he raised his gun to his shoulder to take aim; then we saw him lower it quickly, and look around. He had heard a slight noise in the bushes near him. He raised his head and listened an instant, then leaned toward the right, and then toward the left, without perceiving anything; for the savage was lying flat on the ground, behind a pile of branches. Feeling entirely reassured, he again raised his gun to take aim. At the same moment, the Indian, with an infernal smile, raised himself from the earth, and, just as Joseph was preparing to immolate another enemy, he brandished his knife. A last shot was heard, a last Indian fell; but Joseph had also fallen, struck to the heart by the cowardly fiend. The wretch then proceeded to scalp him, after which he plundered him of his clothes, in which he arrayed himself.

V.—LAMENTATION.

"Paralyzed with horror and fright, we thought no longer of saving ourselves. My sister, in her despair, pressed her baby to her heart, and threw herself at the foot of a crucifix, which she seized in her hands, and mutely covered it with tears and kisses, while I, too, utterly overcome, threw myself on my knees beside her, and mingled my tears and prayers with hers. Poor mother! she did not tremble for herself, but for her child— that dear little angel, whom she loved so tenderly, whom she so adored. It was indeed a beautiful babe, scarcely eighteen months old, and had already begun to lisp 'Mamma.' 'O my God!' cried my sister between her sobs, 'if I must die, I willingly give up my life; but save, oh! save my child!' Then, embracing it, and bathing it in her tears, she clasped it to her heart, and sank to the floor insensible. Although more dead than alive myself, I tried to sustain her, and had her in my arms, when Joseph's murderer entered, followed by his cruel companions. Without uttering a word, he advanced toward us, and violently snatched the child from its mother. She had not heard them enter the room, but, when they tore the child away from her, she shuddered and suddenly recovered her consciousness. The savages, exasperated at having lost seven of their comrades, now only thought of blood and vengeance. The assassin of Joseph, holding the child at arm's length, looked at it with the diabolical expression of a serpent charming his victim before striking him. It was an angel in the grasp of a demon. The monster smiled—Satan alone could have laughed as he did. The baby, as if to supplicate his pity, smiled also, with that angelic expression of innocence that would have moved the most hardened and obdurate of hearts. But he, seizing it by the leg, whirled it round for an instant, and then—oh! horror!—dashed its head against the heavy edge of the huge stove. Its brains spattered over its mother's face. Like a tiger she sprang at the murderer of her child. Maternal love gave her superhuman strength, and, seizing him by the throat, she buried her fingers in his flesh. He tottered; his face turned black, and he fell heavily to the floor, suffocated by the strength of her desperate grasp. She would have undoubtedly strangled him, had not another savage at that instant struck her a blow on the head with his hatchet. My poor sister! her death was indeed a cruel one, but her agony only lasted a moment—her troubles are ended, and she is now in heaven. But I— what will become of me? You see the condition that I am in. O my God, my God! have pity on me."

And the young girl, wringing her hands in despair, threw herself sobbing into my arms, pressed me to her heart, and implored me not to abandon her into the hands of these brutal savages. But, oh! what is more heart-breaking than to witness misfortune without the power of alleviating it! We spent the night in weeping and trying to encourage her, but I could not help feeling at the time that it was cruel to inspire her with a confidence that I had not; for I knew these savages too well. I knew that the monsters never abandoned their victims. The next day, my father tried in every way to conciliate them, and then interceded in behalf of the young captive. He offered any amount of ransom for her, but in vain; nothing would tempt them. The effects of the liquor had not entirely worn off, and they were sullen and obstinate. My father used in turn prayers and threats to move them; but neither presents, prayers, nor threats could rescue her from their merciless hands. The wretched girl threw herself at their feet, and, embracing their knees, besought them to listen to her supplications; but the monsters only replied to her entreaties by bursts of laughter; and, in spite of her prayers, and sobs, and supplications, they carried her off with them.*

"Alas!" said Mlle. Baby, looking sorrowfully at the young officer, "are you surprised now at my sadness, and that I could not smile and be gay after having witnessed such a scene?"

"The demons!" exclaimed the officer, stamping his foot in horror and indignation. "This infamous, bloodthirsty race should be exterminated—exterminated to the last man. Why did I not know this sooner? Yesterday, a Potawatamie came to my quarters to sell some furs. He asked three times as much as they were worth, and I declined buying them. He hung around for some time, annoying me very much, until I finally ordered him to leave. He refused to do so; then, losing all patience with the fellow, I rose from my seat, and, leading him to the door, I kicked him out. He went away muttering, and threatening me with his knife. I had a stick in my hand, and I now regret that I did not knock him down."

"How imprudent!" said the young girl. "You ought not to have provok-

* A fact. She was never heard of afterwards.

ed that Indian; don't you know that a savage never forgets an injury? He may wander around the fort for a year, spying all of your movements, watching your footsteps, tracking you everywhere, hiding in the woods and among the rushes in the river, until an opportunity offers, and he will approach with all the *finesse* and cunning of a serpent, spring upon you like a tiger, and strike you a death-blow, when you least expect it. I see that you go every day out of the fort to fish on the banks of the river. I advise you not to go any more; it is not safe, and something terrible might happen to you."

"Pshaw!" said the young officer, "you are too timid. I saw the fellow leave this morning with a number of warriors belonging to his tribe; they were going to Quebec to sell the furs, which they could not dispose of here."

VI.—THE DREAM.

The clock in the *salon* had just struck one. Mme. Baby and her daughter were seated sewing in the deep recess of an open window, with a little work-table in front of them. M. Baby had gone away that morning, to look after some land that he had just bought on the other side of the river. The streets were deserted; nearly all the inhabitants of the fort were at work in the fields in the vicinity. The heat was intense. Not a breath agitated the trees in the garden, whose motionless branches drooped languidly toward the earth, as if imploring a refreshing breath or a drop of dew. A negro servant was spreading some linen out to dry on the bushes, and put to flight, in her perambulations, some chickens that were panting with the heat under the sheltering foliage of the trees and shrubs. The silence was only broken by the buzzing of insects,

and the noisy whirr of the grasshop-
per as it danced through the sunlight.
The open window, filled with bou-
quets, looked into the garden, and
the pale, melancholy face of Mlle.
Baby could be seen between them,
bending over an open flower which
imaged her loveliness in its fragrant
corolla. "Mamma," said she at
last, raising her head, "do you think
papa will be away a long time?"

"I think he will be back in four or
five days at the latest," replied her
mother. "But why do you ask such
a question?"

"Oh! because I am so anxious
to have him back again. I want
him to take us immediately to
Quebec, instead of waiting until
next month. The trip will divert my
thoughts; for, since those Indians
were here the other day with that
poor girl they had captured, I have
not had a moment's peace of mind.
She is always before my eyes. I see
her everywhere; she follows me
everywhere. I even saw her in my
dream last night. I thought I was
sitting in the midst of a gloomy and
immense forest, near a wild, rushing
river that dashed over a precipice
into a bottomless chasm a few steps
from me. On the opposite bank,
which was covered with flowers, and
charming to behold, stood the young
captive, pale and tranquil, in a halo
of soft, transparent light. She seemed to be in another world. She
held in her hands an open book,
and, bending towards me, she slowly
turned over the leaves. She turned
at least sixteen; then she stopped
and looked at me with an expression
of the greatest sorrow and distress,
and made a sign to some one, who
then seemed to be standing near
me, to cross the torrent. At the
signal, all his limbs trembled; his
knees knocked together, and his eyes
dilated, his mouth gasped with terror,

and a cold perspiration stood upon his
forehead. He tried to draw back,
but an invincible power drew him
toward the abyss. He turned toward
me, and besought my help most
piteously. I experienced the greatest
commiseration for him, and tried
in vain to extend my hands to help
him; invisible cords bound all my
limbs, and prevented any movement
whatsoever. Vainly he tried to cling
to the cliffs along the shore; a relentless force impelled him towards
the abyss. He had already reached
the middle of the stream, whose
deep and foaming waters reared
around him, as if impatient to swallow him up. He tottered at every
step, and came near losing his equili-
brium; but, rallying his strength, he
struggled on. At last a great wave
broke over him, and he lost his
balance. His feet slipped; he looked
toward me with a glance of the
most inexpressible anguish, and fell.
In an instant, he was borne to the
brink of the precipice; he threw out
his hands, and grasped at a piece of
rock that jutted out of the water,
burying his fingers in the green and
slimy moss which covered it. For
an instant, he hung on with the
strength of despair; his body, stopped
suddenly in its precipitate course, appeared for an instant above the waves.
The foam and spray enveloped it like a
cloud, and the wind from the fall blew
through his dank and dripping hair.
His dilated eyes were fastened on
the rock, which little by little re-
ceded from his convulsive grasp.
Finally, with a terrible shriek, he disappeared in the yawning gulf below. Transfixed with agony and
horror, I looked across at the young
captive; but she, without uttering a
word, wiped away a tear, and silently pointed to the last page in the
book, which seemed to me to be
covered with blood. I screamed

aloud with fright, and awoke with a start   My God ! will it be a page in my life ?"

VII.—BLOOD.

Scarcely had Mlle. Baby finished speaking, when the sound of hasty footsteps was heard at the door, and a man, covered with blood, and with a terrified look, rushed in. It was the young officer. His right arm was broken, and hanging at his side.

"Hide me quickly," cried he. " I am pursued by the Indians."

" Up in the attic, quick," said Mme. Baby to him, " and do not stir for your life."

In another moment, the savages nad entered the room ; but, before they could say a word, Mme. Baby pointed to the next street, and they went out again quickly, believing that the officer had escaped in that direction. The admirable composure of Mme. Baby had completely deceived them. Not a muscle of her face betrayed her excessive agitation, and, happily, they did not have time to notice the mortal pallor of the young girl, who, still leaning among the flowers on the window-sill, had almost fainted away. It was one of those moments of inexpressible anguish when a chill like death strikes the heart. Mme. Baby hoped that the savages, fearing the superintendent, would not dare to force themselves into the house ; and yet, who could stop them if they did, or who could foresee what these barbarians, once having tasted blood, might do ? She hoped that their fruitless efforts might induce them to abandon their search, or, if they persisted, that she would have sufficient time to obtain help, in case they again entered the house. Making a sign to a servant who was at work in the garden, she ordered him

to run as fast as he could, and notify some men belonging to the fort of the danger which threatened them. Some anxious minutes elapsed, but the savages did not return. "Do you think they have really gone ?" asked the young girl, in a low tone. A faint glimmer of hope appeared in her countenance.

" Even if they should return," answered Mme. Baby, "they would not dare . . ."

She did not finish, but leaning toward the window, she tried to catch the sound of human voices which were heard in the distance. Was it the help that she expected, or was it the voices of the Indians coming back ? She could not distinguish. The sound drew nearer and nearer, and became more distinct as it approached. "They are our men," exclaimed Mlle. Baby. " Don't you hear the barking of our dog ?" And she drew a long breath of relief, as if an immense weight had been taken from her heart.

Mme. Baby did not reply ; a faint smile played over her lips. She, too, had heard the dogs barking ; but another noise that she knew only too well had also reached her ears. Very soon the voices became so distinct that it was impossible to be deceived any longer. " Here they are, here they are !" shrieked the young girl, sinking into a seat near the window, as the different-colored feathers with which the savages decorated their heads appeared between the trees.

" Don't tremble so," said Mme. Baby in a quiet voice to her daughter, " or you will betray us. Look out of the window, and don't let them perceive your emotion."

Courage and coolness at a critical moment are always admirable, but when a woman possesses these qualities, they are sublime. Calm and impassive, without even rising from her seat, Mme. Baby tranquilly continued her work. The most practised eye could not have detected the smallest trace of emotion, the least feverish excitement or agitation, on her commanding and noble countenance. A heroine's heart beat in her woman's breast, and it was thus that she awaited the arrival of the savages. "Tell us where you have concealed the white warrior," cried the first one who entered the room. It was the Potawatamie whom the young officer had so imprudently offended. He was dripping with perspiration, and out of breath with his long and fatiguing quest. You could see the rage and exasperation of his disappointment in his ferocious glances, his scowling brow, and the excitement that made every feature quiver.

"Comrade," replied Mme. Baby, in a tranquil tone of voice, "you know the superintendent well; and, if you have the misfortune to misbehave in his house, you will get into trouble."

The Indian hesitated a moment, then said, in a feigned mildness of voice, "My white sister knows that the Potawatamie loves peace, and that he never makes the first attack. The white warrior is on the war-path, or the Potawatamie would not have pursued."

"I have not hidden the white warrior," answered Mme. Baby. "It is useless to search here; you had better look elsewhere, or he will escape you."

The Indian did not reply, but, looking at Mme. Baby with a smile, he pointed to a little stain on the floor that no one but an Indian would have discovered. But the sharp eye of the savage had detected there a trace of his enemy. It was a drop of blood, which Mme. Baby had taken the precaution to wipe away

most carefully. "My sister has told the truth," said the Indian, in an ironical tone. "The white warrior has not passed this way; that drop of blood, I suppose, she put there to persuade the Indian that she had concealed the white warrior." Then, assuming a more serious tone, he continued: "My sister, know well that the Potawatamie will do the white warrior no harm; only show us where he is hidden, and we will go away; we only want to take him pris . . ." He stopped, and, bending his head forward, looked through an open window at the other end of the apartment; then, giving a hideous yell, he rushed across the room, and leaped out of the window that opened into the garden. His ferocious companions followed him, howling like a troop of demons. Without seeing what had happened, Mme. Baby understood all. The young officer, hearing the Indians return, and believing himself lost, had the imprudence to jump out of one of the windows into the garden. He ran toward a covered fountain in the centre of the *parterre* to hide, when the Indian perceived him. How can I describe the scene which followed? The pen drops from my hand. In two bounds, they had reached him, and one of the savages, striking him a terrible blow with his fist, sent him reeling to the ground. He fell on his broken arm, and the excruciating pain caused him to utter a deep groan. They then seized hold of him, and bound his hands and feet. Poor young man! what resistance could he make to his cruel enemies, with a broken arm, and totally disabled and weakened by the loss of blood. He called for help, but the echoes in the garden only answered his cries, and redoubled the horror of the scene. Mlle. Baby, bereft of her senses, threw herself at her mother's feet, and, hiding her face on her knees, she covered her ears with her hands, to shut out, if possible, from sight and hearing the frightful tragedy. While the rest of the savages were tying their victim down, the Potawatamie drew out his knife, and deliberately commenced to sharpen it on a stone. His face betrayed no excitement whatever; not even the horrible pleasure of gratifying his vengeance, which caused his heart to palpitate with an infernal joy, could change his stoical countenance. " My brother the white warrior," said he, continuing to whet his knife with the utmost coolness, "knows very well that he can insult the Potawatamie with impunity, because the Potawatamie is a coward, and would rather run than fight. . . . Does my brother now wish to make peace with his friend, the Potawatamie? He can speak if he wishes, and name his terms, for he is free." Then, suddenly assuming a ferocious air, he straightened himself up, and, fixing his inflamed eyes on the young officer, said: " My brother the white warrior can now chant his death-song, because he must die." And brandishing his knife, he plunged it into his throat, while another of these monsters caught the blood in a little copper kettle. The rest of the savages then kicked and stamped upon the body with the most infernal yells and contortions. The death-rattle of the poor victim, mingling with these howls, reached the ears of the young girl, and she shook in a convulsion of horror. At last it all ceased. The victim had been immolated. Pushing aside the corpse with his foot, the Potawatamie, followed by his companions, came again toward the house. " Ha! ha! so you would not tell us where your friend, the white warrior, was?" cried the Indian, as he entered the room.

" Very well, since you love him so much, you shall drink his blood." Mme. Baby, pale as a marble statue, drew herself up firmly. " You can kill me," said she, " but you can never make me drink it!" The young girl had fainted, and was lying at her mother's feet. They seized hold of Mme. Baby, and tried to force open her mouth; but failing in their efforts, they threw the contents of the vessel in her face, and left the house. *

VIII.—THE SERPENT.

Several months had elapsed since the events had taken place which we have just narrated. It was night. In the centre of the garden, a simple black cross had been erected on the spot where the unfortunate young man had been massacred. No inscription revealed to the passer-by either the name of the victim or the fatal circumstances of his death. Alas! it was written for ever in characters of blood on the hearts of the family. Every evening, the superintendent, with his wife, children, and servants, assembled at the foot of this cross, to pray for the repose of the soul of his unfortunate friend. On this especial evening, all the family had as usual visited the grave, and returned to the house, except the young girl, who, dressed in deep mourning, still remained kneeling at the foot of the sombre monument. She was very pale, and there was an expression of the most ineffable sadness on her face. The evening dew had almost entirely uncurled her long ringlets, which now hung in disorder around her cheeks. You might have mistaken her for a statue of grief. From the clear, high heaven above, the moon poured floods of melancholy light. Its dreamy rays fell on the sod at the

* Horrible as this scene is, it is nevertheless perfectly true, even in minutest detail,

foot of the cross and on the face of the young girl like a thought from beyond the tomb—like a silent and grateful sigh from the innocent victim whose memory had left so tender and anguishing an impression in her soul. Her lips moved in ardent prayer—prayer, that celestial solace of the grief-stricken heart, the smile of the angels through the tears of earth. For a long time she thus silently held communion with her God, breathing out her prayers with sighs and tears, as she knelt at the foot of this cross, on the sod still damp with the victim's blood. At last she rose, and was about to leave, when, raising her eyes for a moment, she thought she saw a shadow moving across an opening in the wall of a shed near by. A cloud, at that moment passing over the moon, prevented her from distinguishing what the object was. She waited a moment until the cloud had passed over, when what was her astonishment to see a human face in the aperture! It must be a robber, she thought, and yet she knew positively that the gate was well secured. "He will find himself nicely caught when the servants come to lock up," said she to herself. By degrees, however, the head was pushed more and more through the air-hole, and gradually emerged from the obscurity. At the same moment, the moonlight fell clear and full on the face. The young girl actually shivered. She recognized it but too well; it was impossible to be mistaken. It was he; she recognized perfectly his copper skin, his hard, ferocious features, and his yellowish eyes, rolling in their sockets. It was indeed the Potawatamie, the murderer of the young officer.[*]

Her first thought was flight, but an invincible curiosity fastened her

to the spot. The Indian continued to work through the aperture; one arm was already out, and he held something in his hand which she could not discern. He tried for a long time to get through the air-hole, which was too small for his body. Finally, while making a last effort, he suddenly turned his head, and fixed his eyes with a very uneasy expression on a little bush near him. He seemed undecided what to do; then, letting go the object, he rested his hand on the ground, and, pushing it against the earth with all his strength, tried to force himself back again through the hole. But his broad shoulders, compressed on both sides by the wall, held him like a vice, and he could neither move one way nor another. Then his uneasiness increased, and he looked again anxiously toward the bushes. A slight rustling of the leaves was then perceptible, and a small head emerged slowly from the shadow of the branches, and extended itself toward the savage. It was a rattlesnake.[*] Immovable and with fixed eyes, the Indian watched the least movement of the reptile, which advanced softly and cautiously, as if aware of the strength and power of his redoubtable adversary. When within a few feet of the savage, it stopped, raised itself up, and, throwing out its forked tongue, sprang toward his face; but, before he could touch him, the Indian, as quick

---

[*] Persons familiar with the Indian character well know their thieving propensities.

[*] These reptiles were still so numerous in this part of the country not many years ago that it was extremely dangerous to leave the windows open in the evening. My mother related that, while she was living at Sandwich with her father, one of the domestics was imprudent enough to leave a window open. During the evening, they had occasion to move a sideboard which stood against the wall, and a large snake was discovered behind it fast asleep. Another day, when playing truant, a snake sprang upon her, and tried to bite her waist; but happily her clothes were so thick that its fangs could not penetrate them. While she ran in great terror, her companions called to her to untie her skirt. And that advice saved her life.—AUTHOR.

as thought, gave him a violent blow with the hand that was free, and the reptile fell a short distance from him. Then he began again to make every effort to disengage himself; but in vain. The snake, now furious, advanced a second time to recommence the attack, but with more caution than before. Approaching still nearer to his enemy, he threw himself forward with much greater violence, but without success; for the hand of the savage sent him rebounding further off than before. The Potawatamie then gathered all his strength for a final effort of liberation, but of no avail: he remained fast in the opening of the air-hole. Quick as lightning, the reptile, now foaming at the mouth, with blazing eyes, and jaws swollen with rage, his forked tongue extended, sprang with renewed strength toward his prey. His scaly skin glistened and sparkled in the silvery light of the moon, and the slight noise made by his rattles resembled the rustling of parchment, and alone broke the silence of the night. This mortal combat in the stillness of night, between a serpent and a savage more subtle than the serpent, had an indescribable fascination; it was more like a contest between two evil spirits, in the shadow of night, over some unfortunate victim. The serpent now approached so near the Indian that he could almost have seized him with his hand; he raised himself a last time, and, throwing back his head, sprang forward. The

savage, guarding himself carefully with his one hand, had followed with his eyes the least movement of the writhing body. It was plain to see that the final fight had begun, and could only terminate in the total vanquishment of one or the other of the combatants. At the instant that the snake sprang like an arrow upon his enemy, the Indian raised his hand; but this time the attack of the reptile had been so rapid and instantaneous that, before he could strike him a blow, his fangs had entered his cheek. A hoarse cry died away in the throat of the savage, who, seizing the serpent with his hand before he could escape, raised him to his mouth, and in his rage tore him to pieces with his teeth. A vain reprisal—the blow had been struck. A short time after, the most horrible cries and fearful convulsions announced that the mortal venom had entered his veins. The victim writhed with despair in the midst of his excruciating agony. It was thought at first that he had finally succeeded in getting out; but subsequently they found the body, enormously swollen, still held in the aperture of the air-hole. His blood-shot eyes were starting from their sockets, his face as black as ink, while his gaping mouth revealed two rows of white teeth, to which still clung the fragments of the reptile's skin, and flakes of bloody foam. Providence had indeed terribly avenged the assassination of the young officer.

MISS ETHERIDGE.

WHILE I was spending a summer in a pleasant town in Connecticut, I became very much interested in an invalid lady, who used to be drawn past my window in one of those small vehicles which seem both chair and carriage. The lady did not look ill by any means. She sat erect, and gazed about her with a lively air, betokening good health and spirits. She was always richly dressed, and wore her silks, velvets, and laces with the air of one well used to such raiment. Many of those meeting her bowed with deference, which she returned with courteous grace and a high-bred manner. Sometimes she would stop her little carriage while a friend chatted with her, and seemed always to make herself very agreeable, as I judged from the pleased faces of her listeners. Frequently I would see ladies and gentlemen walking by the side of her carriage as her maid slowly pushed it along. I met her very often in my walks, and sometimes I strolled a little way behind, observing this stately dame, so afflicted and yet so favored apparently by fortune and misfortune.

She was a very handsome woman of about fifty years of age. Her silver-gray hair was abundant and beautiful, crowning her with a dignity beyond the power of any artificial adornment to bestow. The carriage of her head was proud and erect. Her features were clear cut and handsome, and the delicate tint of her complexion seemed almost to belong to youth. She appeared to me like a fine picture of a court dame in some bygone time, because, with all the air of style investing her, she was not dressed in the fashion of the day. In this was shown a fine, nice taste; whatever was her infirmity, it seemed to place her so removed from the frivolity of her sex that an affectation of fashion in her attire would have been unbecoming.

Being so much interested in this lady, I made inquiries, and soon learned much of her former history. She was a Miss Etheridge, afflicted with incurable rheumatism, of that kind which renders the victim almost helpless. She could not stand on her feet or change her position without the help of others. She could only imperfectly use her hands, and yet her health was good and her intellect vigorous. She had been, only a few years before, an active, energetic woman, remarkably self-reliant and helpful to others. She had been a beauty and belle in her girlhood, and always a woman commanding the homage and respect of all who knew her.

But now, what a sad ending of a favored life! " Bound with chains," she said to me, for, waving ceremony in view of her great affliction, I called upon her and cultivated an acquaintance which I never regretted. Debarred as she was from all occupation, she was very fond of society. Her hands, once very beautiful, as former portraits showed, were now so distorted and weakened as to be unable to hold any but the lightest books or pamphlets for reading, and that not very long at a time. So, in her luxurious apartments, surrounded by every alleviation that wealth could bestow, this lady passed many lonely hours and days—hours of intense weariness of both body and mind. Sitting in her massive, high-backed chair, she looked like a fine picture and showed no sign of her infirmity ; yet how her poor limbs ached from the mere lack of change of posture, only those similarly affected can tell. An intimacy sprang up between us so easily that I was often present at times when her attendants moved and dressed her ; and then it was that I became aware of the extent of torture to which she was subjected by the mere moving of a limb. Much of her time she passed lying in her bed, from an intense dread of the severe ordeal of being moved. I have passed hours sitting by her bedside, reading to her and in conversation with her, and by this means came to know much of her state of mind and religious feeling.

I admired the fortitude and pati-ence with which she bore her burden, yet it did seem to me quite as much Spartan endurance as Christian meekness or acceptance of the will of God. Hers was a heroic nature, with some pious yearnings uncultivated. She chafed like a caged lioness, but was too proud to whine or repine in any cowardly fashion. She was an Episcopalian of the firm, old-fashioned type that eschews both Ritualism and Evangelicalism. To be as the bishops and clergymen of her family, who had supplied the church of her affections for generations with clerical stock, seemed to her just the right medium, and in clinging to this standard she simply starved her soul. She knew me to be a Catholic, a " Roman Catholic "—for she also claimed to be a Catholic, an "Anglican Catholic," as I also had once done. I, being a recent convert, felt enthusiastic even while timid on this subject. I had passed through the ordeal of estrangement from friends, been exposed to misunderstanding of my motives and all the whips and stings to which those who take this step are subjected, too recently not to be very sensitive about laying myself open to the charge of endeavoring to proselyte another. I loved Miss Etheridge and her society too well to risk her displeasure, or by speaking overmuch of my own faith to give any handle for her relatives to turn against us. She, on her part, was too truly polite to ever make any unpleasant allusions to the subject. And yet how much I longed for her to know what a sure trust and support she *could* have if she only *would!* When I heard her involuntary moans, my prayers went up for the intercession of the Mother of Sorrows, again, and yet again. And I knew all the time that *that* intercession she rejected with scorn. Nothing I could have said to her would have been so unwelcome as a prayer to the Blessed Virgin in her behalf. Yet I did ask that tender intercession, and I believe the All-Pitying Woman above was touched with compassion for the proud, suffering woman who would not ask her aid.

On one occasion, when our conversation had drifted along to the subject of the next life, she remarked that to *her* the bliss to be desired was to be "unchained—'delivered from the body of this death.'"

"My dear friend," said I, "if you die before I do, my regrets will be tempered by the thought that your 'earthly clogs' are cast off."

"Ah! if there is a purgatory," she often said, "I am enduring mine here. What has been my sin more than another's, that this should be thrust upon me!" And at these times the tone of her voice and the expression of her face showed the impatient, unchastened fire of the haughty, rebellious spirit.

But had she none of the consolations of religion? Protestants are not pagans. No, indeed. This lady had her books of devotion in profusion. Her elegant Book of Common Prayer and her Bible lay always at hand. Other books also were on her table— "Counsel for the Sick-Room," and kindred works, of which she contemptuously remarked that they were written by persons in good health, who found it very easy to bear patiently the pains and crosses of other people, but who might possibly not be such fine Christian philosophers if they had to endure all this themselves.

In her palmy days of health and strength she had been a communicant in the Episcopal Church, and now, when, according to the teaching of that church, she needed still more the nourishment for her soul's health, she declined availing herself of the privilege. This always seemed to me very strange, knowing full well as I did what her church taught her, and what in all consistency she should do. But on this topic my lips were closed. Her pastor was a timid young man, who visited her at intervals, but who was afraid to urge anything upon her which she seemed not to wish. I found from her own and others' conversation concerning him that he regarded his highest duty to his flock to be that of preaching to them, and their highest duty to come to church and listen to him. To give him as little trouble as possible, and leave him as much time to himself as they could, was to make themselves agreeable parishioners. He delighted in having certain enthusiastic and well-disposed ladies conduct Sunday-schools, societies, charities, visiting of the sick, and all other troublesome matters; thereby relieving him of all need to bother himself and take his thoughts from the fine sermons which he delighted to elaborate in his study. His wife and children claimed much of his attention, and through them society had its demands on him. In short, he liked to be very comfortable, and much money "donated" by good and kind people went to put him and his family in the enjoyment of ease and refinement, which money might, I often thought, have helped to build schools and charities. I, however, cared for the success of this reverend gentleman's ministrations only as they affected my friend Miss Etheridge. I think he regarded me with distrust and disfavor. He always spoke of me as a *pervert* and *Romanist*, but as he was a thorough gentleman, and as Miss Etheridge was a lady who always had her own way accorded her, no unpleasant collision ever occurred between us. I was one who never listened to his preaching, and therefore was uninteresting to him, except as I might influence one of his fold.

Seeing no signs of this dire result of ry intimacy, he accepted it passively as one of the circumstances which he must submit to, if not approve.

One day I was returning from Miss Etheridge's house, when I met two Sisters of Charity, just about entering a poor, low dwelling not far from the rich one I had just left. Having a slight acquaintance with the sisters, I stopped to exchange a few words with them, and to ask what was their mission of mercy in this abode.

"Oh! we are going in to see poor Mrs. McGowan," said one of them. "Her time passes very tediously at the best, and she likes to have us come and read to her. Will you go in and see her?"

"What is the matter with her, sister?" I asked, as I turned in at the gate, responding to the invitation.

"Chronic rheumatism," said Sister Francina—"the saddest case! so helpless and so lonely as she is! She has had it five years, growing worse all the time."

And now we were at the door of this victim of the terrible tyrant whose power I had witnessed in the house of her rich neighbor. I need not say how interested I was at once.

Poor, ignorant, Irish, and childless was Mrs. McGowan—but a Catholic. Very mean were all her surroundings, but very decent and cleanly. She was a woman but little older than Miss Etheridge, and in some respects not unlike her. Education and high breeding and polish were lacking, but some look in her face and complexion, and especially in the poor twisted hands, constantly reminded me of my friend. Here the silver-gray hair was almost covered by the hideous wide-frilled cap which elderly Irish women consider so decorous. Her plain dark cotton gown presented a contrast to the rich massive folds of Miss Etheridge's heavy silk robe. No high,

carved, cushioned chair supported her, but she sat on the side of her bed, with her hands patiently folded in her lap. Miss Etheridge always had her maid within call.

Bright-eyed, rosy Maggie Maloney I see her now, tenderly brushing a fly from her mistress' forehead, or fanning her, or handing her books, a handkerchief, glass of water, or whatever else was required. But here, from morning till night sat poor Mrs. McGowan, depending for all such little offices on the kindness of her humble neighbors and their children. Her husband was a poor mechanic, who left her every morning after assisting her to dress, and lifting her from her bed to the seat by the bedside. After this, a kind woman, her nearest neighbor, performed all the services necessary for her.

And so her weary hours passed. Equally helpless with Miss Etheridge, how very different were her surroundings! No fine pictures upon which to rest her weary eyes hung upon these walls. Here only a low ceiling and bare walls, with one small window from which she gazed, seeing what she might of the passers-by. No maid to obey her slightest demand; no exquisite music-boxes, to the low, sweet tinkling notes of which she might listen; no birds, pictures, books, flowers, fine furniture, hangings, and carpets contributed what they might to soften *her* hard lot. Poor Mrs. McGowan had none of these. Bare, cold, hard, and pitiless seemed her position, and yet she appeared to me the happier woman of the two. A serene contentment and cheerful acceptance of God's will seemed to sustain her. Miss Etheridge was surrounded by relatives who vied with each other in their attentions to her, and were devoured by jealousy of each other as her favor inclined capriciously, sometimes to one, sometimes to another. Indeed, I often thought this lady could not really tell between them all what was done for love of her and what for interested motives, she having a fortune to bestow as she pleased. Mrs. McGowan also had her relatives, but they were hard-working people, nieces and cousins who lived at service, and who came to see her at intervals of time and stayed as long as they could be spared. Stout men would lend their strong arms occasionally to carry her to some other part of her little dwelling. This was all the change of scene she had been able to obtain for years.

The similarity and dissimilarity in the lot of these two women chained my attention. My interest in the one increased my interest in the other, and I was thus led to compare their different ways of bearing their sufferings.

I could not help seeing that Mrs. McGowan was the happier of the two, despite her poverty. Why was this? I could not think it entirely proceeded from a more cheerful temperament, because Miss Etheridge was far from being a morose or despondent woman. But Mrs. McGowan performed to the best of her ability all her religious duties. Regularly her parish priest came to her to hear her confession and administer to her the Blessed Sacrament. To all of us comes a time in our lives when we feel the need of something more than our own or any human support, and such aid from above this humble sufferer accepted in simple, childlike faith and trust, while her proud sister-in-need disdained to receive it. No wonder that one was stronger to bear her heavy affliction than the other. Of what avail was Miss Etheridge's superior education and cultivation to loosen or lighten her "chains"? They clasped her quite as closely and

pitilessly as those of her ignorant neighbor. And while Christ himself was the soul's health of the one, only a cold, bare formula of religious observance was offered to the other.

I longed to bring Miss Etheridge to the sense of this, so plain to myself. But hesitating always in my sensitiveness as to how my motives might be construed, I mused long upon the best way of introducing the subject. I at last concluded to get her to pass Mrs. McGowan's door in my company. This was very naturally and easily accomplished, and I, walking by her side, told her of Mrs. McGowan, and pointed out her little dwelling. Mrs. Etheridge was interested at once, and, stopping her carriage by the gate, I went in, and told Mrs. McGowan to look out of the window at her guest. She already knew of Miss Etheridge and her affliction, and, with the keen, quick sympathy of her race, responded at once to the demand upon her. I felt the tears come up to my eyes so involuntarily and uncontrollably, that I stepped back so that Miss Etheridge might not perceive my agitation. It was touching to see these two, so far removed in social position, so near in a common suffering, talking of their feelings to each other. Miss Etheridge never forgot her dignity for an instant, and Mrs. McGowan, who had been a servant in her youth, did not presume, but acknowledged by her manner her appreciation of the superiority of her visitor, and yet with delicate tact tendered her pity and sympathy. Through the open window her voice came kindly, and her face looked cheerfully to Miss Etheridge, who was able to perceive also how homely and mean were all the surroundings of her fellow-sufferer.

"You are better cared for than I am, ma'am, and likely you will last longer; but sure, my pains would be as great in a palace as they are here. It is the Lord's will, and I must be content."

"May the good Lord help you, and me too," said Miss Etheridge. Her proud face softened with a tender pity, and her voice had a tremulous vibration in it, as of some hidden chord in her heart stirred now, perhaps, for the first time. She seemed very thoughtful and silent on our way back, and I thought she was more patient with her attendants as she was lifted out of her carriage and placed in her usual chair.

After this she sent or carried to Mrs. McGowan many presents of little delicacies and comforts, and the gratitude which the poor woman freely expressed seemed to please Miss Etheridge more than anything else. It became a hobby with her to contrive some new comfort and pleasure for Mrs. McGowan.

"Ah! ma'am," said the poor soul, "an' what can the likes of me do for you? I have nothing to give you but my prayers," which I doubt not she did give in no scant measure. I often thought that she enlisted powerful intercessions in behalf of Miss Etheridge which that lady would not have secured for herself.

One day, as we stopped by the little window, the sweet face of Sister Francina looked out at us. I glanced quickly at Miss Etheridge, but that high-bred lady showed no prejudice, whatever she might feel. She was looking kindly and courteously, bowing her head to the sister, even before I could speak the words of introduction. The sister, led on by Miss Etheridge's cordial manner, and her sincere interest in one of whom she had heard so much, held quite a sprightly conversation with us. She spoke of the frequency of her visits to Mrs. McGowan, and

praised the poor woman's uniform patience and cheerfulness and piety.

A few days after this, I was astonished by Miss Etheridge asking me if it would be against rule for Sister Francina to visit her. I replied, "As you are an invalid, I think not." Then Miss Etheridge asked me if I thought I could not induce her to come. "I will try," I replied.

"I wish it," she said—"I wish it very much. I think I may have the few comforts I can enjoy, and I *will.*"

This was uttered in a tone of such decision and defiance that I almost felt that I myself was supposed to oppose her in the matter. But the tone was really against the bitter opposition she knew she was courting, both for herself and me, from her anxious and affectionate relatives. The having of her own way and asserting herself on any subject, only added a spice to her enjoyment of what she attained, but it placed me in an awkward position toward her family. I knew that it would seem to them that I had urged this visit of Sister Francina, or at least brought it about by more direct means than was really the case. True, I was the instrument, but Miss Etheridge used me more voluntarily than they would believe. I did not like to be regarded in the light in which I was sure I would be viewed—as an undermining and scheming emissary of Rome. But, on the other hand, I did not like to be cowardly in refusing to procure for Miss Etheridge so very innocent a pleasure. If she were merely whimsical in her wish to have the sister visit her, still, why not let her be indulged? It was the sister's mission to visit the afflicted, and here was an appeal to her charity, and to mine too. So I plucked up my courage, which was backed up by my affection for Miss Etheridge, and soon brought Sister Francina to her. It was as we anticipated. The family were up in arms about this visit. One would have supposed that I had brought a wolf, or "roaring lion, seeking whom he might devour," to Miss Etheridge, instead of meek, gentle, innocent Sister Francina, strong only in her holy faith. But if no one else was brave, Miss Etheridge certainly was. She expressed herself so pleased at the sister's visit, that she asked it as a personal favor and charity to herself that the sister would come often. With great delicacy, the sister was urged to accept a generous gift for the mission in which she was engaged. And Sister Francina did come; not very often—Miss Etheridge and her family could not think she presumed upon the encouragement she received—but still often enough to endear herself to Miss Etheridge more and more. The family were rampant, but powerless. Still Miss Etheridge chose to have me walk by her carriage. Still she would go and talk to Mrs. McGowan, and, doing so, she met at last Father B——. He was going in at the gate just as we, from an opposite direction, came around the corner of the house. I knew him at once, and told Miss Etheridge, asking if we should go on, which I supposed she would prefer. I was surprised at her expressing her intention to stop. She had in her lap a basket of fruit which she wished to leave for Mrs. McGowan, and, "if the priest would not object to her, she certainly would not shun him."

Father B—— was a convert himself from the Anglican ranks. He bore about him all the genial *bonhomie*, the polished bearing, and gentle dignity which is characteristic of that class of Protestant clergy. Miss Etheridge had never been personally acquainted with him, but, having heard him preach in the bygone days when she went to church and his eloquence charmed Protestant audiences, she retained still a curiosity, if nothing more, concerning him. This at least was no stern-browed ascetic with the odor of a sanctity she could not appreciate about him, but a kindly, social gentleman, with many little points of sympathy whereon to begin an acquaintance. Father B——, seeing no repulse, readily responded to Miss Etheridge's overtures of good-will. She certainly found her mind disabused of many previous notions of this priest at least. On the whole, I felt glad of the meeting. It thawed some remaining reserve on our part in discussing the differences between us in faith. I told her frankly how I had been led, step by step, into the fold wherein I now rejoiced to be. How my first dissatisfaction in the Episcopal Church had arisen from witnessing the utter inability of the pastor to withstand lay interference in matters which belonged exclusively to the clergy. How two wardens in open enmity still partook of the sacrament, in defiance of the rubric which bears upon the case, and which the rector never dared to enforce. How I had heard such various teaching and explaining of the creed, services, articles of religion, and everything appertaining to the whole system, that it seemed to me like the confusion of tongues "worse confounded." That the desire to embrace in the Anglican fold such opposing elements as Calvinism on the one hand, and pure, "primitive," and mediæval Christianity on the other—to be Ritualistic and Evangelical at the same time, worked such mischief and rebellion that I had longed for some authority, some utterance which had the ring of the true metal, and some fold wherein I might be *at rest*.

Miss Etheridge listened very patiently, very thoughtfully. I hardly expected so little opposition to all I said. She granted the force of my objections, but wondered at my being able to acquiesce in all which I had now accepted. I replied that perhaps what I had accepted would not seem to her so very unreasonable if she came to examine and understand it as I did; that nothing dispelled prejudice like an acquaintance with and analysis of the objectionable subjects; that the effect was frequently like that produced by examining some supposed spectre which has frightened us in the dark, and which we find to be only an innocent optical illusion.

After this, I refrained from obtruding any more of my religious views upon Miss Etheridge, until one day when she asked me to read *Morte d'Arthur* to her, and I came upon the passage:

"Pray for my soul. More things are wrought by prayer
Than this world dreams of. Wherefore let thy voice
Rise like a fountain for me night and day.
For what are men better than sheep or goats
That nourish a blind life within the brain,
If, knowing God, they lift not hands of prayer
Both for themselves and those who call them friend?
For so the whole round earth is every way
Bound by gold chains about the feet of God."

I remarked that Tennyson had, with a poet's insight, spoken like a true Catholic. Miss Etheridge denied that it was Tennyson's own belief advanced, but only that of King Arthur, the words being put into his mouth by the poet as fitting for him, the same as any writer would make any Catholic speak, or as he might put very evil words into the mouth of a blasphemer.

"True," I said; "but while an author must make his characters speak according to their supposed faith, he is not obliged to give such forcible words to them in opposition to his own private belief. He is

hardly likely to do so. He may screen himself behind his characters, or he may betray himself through them. We may guess at his own leanings more or less accurately, and he may contradict himself. Here certainly the poet seems in favor of prayers for the dead."

"But is it prayer for the *dead* Arthur, after all?" said she. "Was he not only going away 'to the island-valley of Avilion?'"

"Tennyson has named the poem *Morte d'Arthur*, and it is so accepted and understood," I replied.

She acquiesced in this, but still opposed with true Protestant unbelief and persistency the idea that any good could come from prayers for the dead.

I told her that, even while I had been a Protestant, this had always seemed to me a tender and affectionate practice of Catholics to try to reach and help those on the other side of the grave, and that, even if it were unavailing, it was at least harmless, and I could never understand why it should be denounced as wicked. That it benefited the souls of those who prayed, at least, if not those for whom they prayed.

"My dear Miss Etheridge," said I, "is the thought that I might pray for the repose of your soul after your death offensive to you now in life?"

She was silent only a moment. That she could be the object of such prayer was probably then presented to her mind for the first time, and startled her somewhat. Then she said:

"Why, no; certainly not. I cannot but regard it as a kind and loving thing to do, even if a useless one."

"But you would not do as much for me," I rejoined.

"Ah," she said evasively, "you will not be neglected; be sure of that."

Only about a week after this we heard that Mrs. McGowan was ill. The blinds were closed at her window, and Father B—— and the sisters went oftener than usual to see her. I too went back and forth, and brought Miss Etheridge tidings of how Mrs. McGowan bore her sufferings; of all that was done for her spiritual and bodily comfort, of all that was hoped and all that was feared, and at last of her death. This affected Miss Etheridge more than one could have supposed possible. It was touching to witness her sadness. That this proud lady, so widely separated in everything but the same infirmity from this poor Irishwoman, should truly grieve for her awakened in me a greater admiration for Miss Etheridge's noble heart than I had before entertained. She seemed restless and anxious to be doing something still for the poor woman. She asked me if I did not think it could be managed that she could see Mrs. McGowan once more before her burial.

I told her it could without difficulty, and so it was done. Respectfully the crowd parted for her little carriage as it made its way through the humble assemblage which is sure to be around the house of death among the Irish. Willing arms carried her to the side of the coffin, whereon her own gifts—a cross and crown of beautiful flowers —had been placed.

In silent dignity she gazed at the face and hands of the dead—curiously at the lighted candles and emblems of the faith of the departed, and at the habit which covered the body, now straightened in the rigidity of death.

She was very composed, and soon signified her desire to be conveyed to her carriage, and in silence she returned to her home. I thought Miss Etheridge showed, in this act of going

to pay the last mark of respect to her humble friend, true heroism and charity. She was a mark of curious observation to a crowd of people with whom she had no sympathy, and her helplessness and peculiar infirmity made her more sensitive to the notice and notoriety which she knew her going would bring upon her; and yet she had the courage to brave such results. Only a true lady, lifted above all vulgar fears and considerations, would have done this. No *mean* soul would have desired so to do.

"The chains have fallen off her now," she said to me. "I wonder if she remembers and thinks of me. You think of her as being in a different state from that which I have been taught to believe as that of the departed; but we will not argue about it now. I only want to do for her yet—something which I do believe she would, poor soul, have done for me, had I gone first. It pleases me to do what she would in life have liked to think would be done for her, whether availing or unavailing."

And with this apologetic remark, Miss Etheridge actually placed in my hand a large sum of money to convey to Father B—— for Masses to be said for the repose of the soul of Mrs. McGowan. I was truly astonished. Was this the fruit of our reading of *Morte d'Arthur?* If so, I blessed the day we did it. But I was afraid of being hopeful overmuch, Miss Etheridge might never advance beyond this liberal yielding of a stubborn prejudice. It was the last thing she could do for her poor friend, and her generous soul took pleasure in doing it. I was afraid that this was all; and for a time it seemed to be all.

The summer passed into autumn, and I was recalled to my city home. I parted with Miss Etheridge with great regret, and the more so because

she could not write to me, save by
the hand of another. I promised to
write to her, and she said that I should
get tidings of her from time to time
in some way. "According to my
message shall my scribe be," she said,
and so we parted.

I did write from time to time, and I
had a brief note now and then, written
by Miss Etheridge's business agent,
telling me of her continued good
health, but increasing infirmity. But
during Easter-tide I received a longer
missive, written in the delicate pen-
manship of Sister Francina. "According to my message shall my
scribe be," she had said to me, and
now I knew her meaning, for the message was that she was a Catholic.

As I folded up the letter, the words
came to my mind:

"These through great affliction came."

AMBROSIA.

A LEGEND OF AUGSBURG.

We were talking of our travels, my friend Archer and I, and of the lessons travelling brings to those who go a little out of Murray's beaten track. And especially, so we were pleased to think, these lessons might be learnt in little out-of-the-way nooks, hidden centres of ignored life, none the less busy for that, and none the less full of exciting life-dramas. I was telling him of Pavia—for my wanderings had led me chiefly through Italy—of the desolate, enchanted look of the wall-enclosed court-yards round the gloomy and picturesque palaces; of the lonely walk on the former ramparts, now 'planted with fine horse-chestnuts; of the many tapestries of romance I had woven in my mind about the silent-looking houses and the dark-eyed maidens I occasionally met in the streets. It was while Pavia was in Austrian hands that I passed through it, and perhaps the military occupation tended to make the sleepy city still more sombre and dull. Yet what additional elements of romance that circumstance contributed! For it was not impossible that some fair, mild German, with his dreamy sentimentality, yet fresh from college, might have been drawn to feel a holy, wondering love for the bright southern beauty whose childhood had been fostered in indignant hatred of his land and race; and between these two how many complications of pathetic interest might we not imagine, how many shades of feeling and degrees of circumstances might we not conjure up! "But," said Archer, interrupting my fine flow of language about the joys and sorrows of the town of the *Certosa,* "you know Italy, strictly speaking, is rather the land of passion than of romance. Could you think of an Italian 'Gretchen'? The one character most like her, the Cenci, is so different despite the likeness! Religion seems more spiritual in Germany; in Italy they do as the Greeks of old, put their own human feelings into heavenly representatives and then pay homage to them, thinking unconsciously that they are honoring supernatural attributes. There is too much earthliness about their ideal—in fact, I do not believe they have an ideal at all."

"Come, come," I answered, "you are too hard on the southern temperament. You do not know Italy well enough to speak with authority on the subject. After all, as long as their way of feeling religion does them good, the Italians are quite as well off, spiritually, as your Teutonic ideals. I am not sure but what I prefer warmth and impulse to passive tenderness, however reliable the latter may be throughout a lifetime. But this question of the relative merits of various races will always be an open one, and no one wishes to leave it so more than the church herself, for she wisely sees how much the glory of God gains through this blending of various natures in his service."

"No doubt," answered my enthusiastic Teutomane, "as far as that side of the question is concerned. You have been saying something equivalent to telling me that the orchestra is preferable to a single violin or cornet, while *I* was speaking of the intrinsic merit of each of those individual instruments."

"Well," I said, "now tell me something about the tone of these instruments. You know I have been very little in Germany, and I should be

glad to hear something worth hearing, something that one would not find in the guide-book, nor in the volume of self-important nonsense occasionally thrust upon the public by a gushing sister or a city alderman."

"You are very caustic," said my friend with a laugh. "If I must travel so far out of the beaten track to please you, why not plunge at once into a volume of mediæval legends?"

"Is it in print? Because in that case I could see for myself, and therefore would not care to hear it," I answered teasingly.

"It is *not* in print, Sir Doubter, and, what is more, it is not even in manuscript."

I began to feel interested. "A popular tradition, then?" I asked.

"Exactly. It is not worth much, only I happened to see the places mentioned, the quaint house that is standing yet, though very much disguised of course, and the dark street leading to the cathedral. It happened in Augsburg, and the cathedral, as you know, is Protestantized, though still very well kept. I was only in the town for two days, so you may imagine I know little of it beyond what my narrator told me."

"And pray who was your narrator?"

The father of a girl in an old book-stall, where I had stopped attracted by some rare copy of a Catholic work, of which she did not seem to know the value. Equally surprised at seeing the book there and at finding her ignorant of its worth, I asked her how she got it. She lifted up her head, which had been bent on some mysterious turning-point of her knitting, and said smilingly:

"*Mein Herr* is a Catholic, then?"

I answered that I was, and repeated my former question.

" It must have been one of my great-uncle's books," she said, " he was going to be a priest, but he died before being ordained. We were al-ways Catholics."

" And how came you to keep this stall, child ?" I asked, becoming in-terested.

" It is my father's," she answered quickly ; " and he has been ill for two months, so I keep it for him. His uncle left him all his books."

" And is your father so poor, then ?"

" Very poor, *mein Herr*," said the girl, with a longing glance at the book I still held in my hand, as if she were thinking of the price a con-noisseur might be tempted to give for it. " His father and grandfather were booksellers," she continued, " but not like him ; they had large libra-ries and plenty of men working un-der them. That was long before I was born, *mein Herr*.'

" And I suppose your father got into difficulties. But anything would have paid better than this, my poor child."

" My father would not go to work for any other bookseller, not if he were the king," laughed the girl, more merrily than I thought the case war-ranted ; " and he is a regular student. My mother used to earn money in many ways, teaching, writing, sew-ing ; and I did the housework. She died two years ago, and we have nothing but the book-stall now to keep my sick father and my little crippled brother."

I thought to myself, Why, here is a regular romance ; perhaps the in-evitable lover of German stories is going to peep out next, from the frank revelations of my new friend. At any rate, let us follow it up. So I said aloud : " If your father is will-ing to part with this book, I should like to buy it. But I should be very glad

to see him and chat with him abou it. Do you think he could see me ?"

" Oh! yes, of course," answered the girl with a hearty smile ; and for the first time I noticed her features and expression. She was not beauti-ful—I hope you did not expect the romance to be perfect ?—but there was a pure, calm steadiness in her look, and an air of unconscious dig-nity about her that made her strik-ing to the eye. She seemed made for fidelity and helpfulness, and as to external charms, if you admire hair, she simply had superabundant mass-es of it. German-like, it was put up in broad plaits, tightly coiled round the head, without a shadow of co-quettishness, and just as if she thought it no ornament at all. Now I have noticed your Italian girls know how to make a good deal more of their advantages. I have seen poor girls in Venice with as elaborate a coiffure—ringlets, puffs, plaits, and wavings—as any Parisian hair-dresser could ex-hibit on his waxen models."

" Libels again !" I answered. " I have seen the very contrary at Na-ples, and there are women there like Grecian statues. Venice is half Eastern, you know. But to go on with your impromptu romance."

Well, when evening came, I went to the address the young girl had given me, and as you may imagine, it was not a palace that I entered. The neighborhood was as common-place as any in an old German city can be, that is, picturesqueness itself compared with our modern " back slums." Still, through the pictu-resqueness, there stared the most un-mistakable poverty. I went up a good many flights of steep, narrow stairs, with curious balusters that would have driven a dealer in old carv-ing wild with delight, and knocked at a door that I recognized by the rude cross and bit of palm over the archway. There was just such another cross and sprig of green inside the door, and a little holy-water vessel in stamped brass hung at the side nearest the door-handle. There was nothing very peculiar about the room, except that it had an air of freshness and cleanliness, which, considering its sick inmates and its cramped locality, was the more pleasant because it was a surprise. A great German bed, with a feather-bed of traditional height, filled one side of the room, and there was a stove in the middle. The remains of the supper were on a side-table, and a lamp drawn close to the father's arm-chair stood on a centre-table laden with domestic "mending." The little crippled brother sat in a low easy-chair by the stove, which chair was the only luxury in the room. My friend, the young girl, came quickly forward and said:

"My father is so glad you have come, *mein Herr.*"

I sat down beside him, and soon got into conversation with the old scholar. He was still very weak, but seemed to feel better when excited. I found him a thorough bookworm, full of knowledge that, in another man's hands, would have made his fortune. I discovered, or rather forced him to tell me, that in that press (pointing to a common painted chest of drawers) were manuscripts ready to be published, if a publisher could be found to undertake the risk, but the author had no ambition, though he was full to the brim of literary enthusiasm. His researches had lain chiefly among works of mediæval ecclesiastical lore, legends and poems, etc. The emblems borne by the various saints were a favorite subject of his. His uncle's theological collection and the libraries in which he had spent his youth, had furnished him with

means to prosecute his studies even after his father's reverses in fortune—the public libraries had done the rest. His wife's help had been very important, and piles of her notes and references lay among his own manuscripts. He spoke with pride of his little crippled son, whom he said he had made as good a scholar as if the poor boy had been to the universities; and as to his daughter, his looks said more than his words, as he gazed at her across the table, she sitting so calmly there amid her heap of "mending," her dark-blue dress reminding me of the coloring of a mediæval virgin martyr in the stained-glass window of some old cathedral. She was more queenly than slender in figure, and neither her face nor her hands were small, though they were perfectly shaped; there was more majesty than grace in her whole air, yet she was thoroughly girl-like. I unconsciously invested her in my mind with royal robes, heavily jewelled, like the Byzantine saints, or with the ample cloak of the brave and learned Portia. Presently she went into a smaller room, opening into the one where we were sitting, and during her absence I ventured to hint to the father that for her sake he should try to make those literary treasures of his more remunerative. He smiled; I asked him if she were already provided for, or if he did not feel it his duty to put by some kind of fortune for her.

"My child is watched over from heaven," he said; "she will never come to harm."

"What is her name?" I asked. I had already ascertained his family name to be Reinhold.

"Ambrosia," he answered.

"Rather an uncommon name," I remarked, well pleased, somehow, that it should be so.

"Yes," said the father, "and I dare say it will interest you to hear the reason why she has that name. She was born on the anniversary of the day that a young girl called Ambrosia came to life here in the sixteenth century. This was how it happened. The troubles of the Reformation were just beginning, and this young girl, who was the burgomaster's daughter, was famous through the town for her holiness and modesty. She was betrothed to a young merchant who had been her playmate in childhood. Did you notice that great building on the corner of the street to the right of the cathedral? That was her father's house; it is a hotel now. Her bridegroom lived two or three streets further off, on a corner too; and under the corner window, which was beautifully carved and painted, stood a wooden image of the Mother of God, with a lamp before it which was never allowed to go out. It began to be whispered about that Engelbrecht, the young lady's betrothed, and a very handsome, dashing young fellow, was rather inclined to the new doctrines which Luther was then preaching all over Germany. Every one wondered how Ambrosia would take this, but no one knew anything positive until it became the talk of the city that one night Engelbrecht and a few companions, heated with wine and singing profane songs, had broken and extinguished the votive lamp before the image under his window, and thrown the image itself into the gutter. The next day it was known that Ambrosia was very ill, and had sent for her lover. He came, and, as he really was very fond of her, the sudden alteration in her looks frightened and subdued him for the moment. She took off the betrothal ring he had put upon her finger, and very gravely and sweetly told him that she could

never be his bride on earth, but that she fervently hoped that she had indeed won his soul's final salvation, through the joyful and willing sacrifice of her own life. She said she should die on the day that was fixed for their wedding, but that from the dead she would speak to him yet, and in public. Then a year would go by, and she told him that it was not given to her to know if he would repent or not during that time, but that on the anniversary of her death she would come to life again and walk from her tomb to the cathedral and back; and she summoned him to meet her there. It was her hope that, after that second call, he would surely be won back to God. So when her wedding day came, although she seemed happy and looked only very grave and pale, she called her father and mother and her lover to her, and there, sitting by the window that looked on the cathedral, she passed away without agony, and just as the hour struck which should have seen her a new-made wife. She was not buried for several days, for the scoffers said she was deceiving the people and simulating death. Doctors and priests watched the body for a week, and Mass was said in the room where she lay, surrounded with flowers and tall tapers. Exorcisms were even read over her, but the placid expression of her alabaster face seemed to grow only more heavenly day by day. At last signs of decomposition appeared, as if to make the marvel more certain, and those who had watched the body drew up a legal declaration of her undoubted death. She was brought to the churchyard, the family vault was opened, and the coffin, which was still uncovered, was just going to be finally closed, when she raised herself suddenly to a sitting posture, and, seemingly transfigured into greater beauty than had ever been hers in life, she gazed slowly round the crowd and beckoned to her lover. He stood transfixed, and the people fell back from him and left him face to face with his bride. She only said in a clear, pitying voice that was heard by all, 'Remember, Engelbrecht, thy tryst with me one year from this day. God be with thee until then.'

"She fell slowly backwards into her narrow couch, and when the people had taken courage again, they came hurriedly and closed the coffin in great awe. A year went by, and Engelbrecht, uneasy and remorseful, plunged into worse excesses than ever, went heart and soul, at least outwardly, into the Lutheran movement, and became the head of a band of young men whose dissoluteness was spoken of with disgust by the licentious reformers themselves. The day came, and with it crowds flocked to the grave of Ambrosia. Those who had gone at sunrise found a white-robed figure kneeling there, its face hidden in its hands, and two long plaits of golden hair streaking its drapery. Those who had watched all night and gone there the evening previous after dusk, could tell nothing save that the grave had been the same as ever, but they thought they must have slept for a few minutes before midnight, since they had heard the quarter strike from the cathedral, and had looked at their timepieces directly after, and found it was half an hour *after* midnight. The radiant, silent figure was there then, and an odor as of incense filled the night air. As soon as the cathedral doors were open (it was in June), Ambrosia rose and turned towards the church. Some sceptics who saw the strange procession, rushed at once to the grave, and, hastily disinterring the coffin, found it empty. Crowds joined the procession to the cathedral, which the young girl reached during the first Mass, for the priests still had possession of it then. Every one wondered if her lover would meet her, but no sign of him appeared. Ambrosia looked incomparably more beautiful than in life; her eyes were cast down, and she wore a golden betrothal ring on her finger. She moved like a spirit, yet there was no doubting the reality and substance of her presence. There were many in the crowd who were scoffers and libertines, men whom no virtuous maiden's eye would as much as glance upon, yet even they were silenced, and the marvellous beauty of Ambrosia seemed to have no other effect upon them than one of awe and unconscious restraint. The people followed her in and lined the aisles through which they knew she would walk on leaving the cathedral. She knelt for a moment before the high carved tabernacle, with a lovely miniature spire, quite in a separate corner from the altar—you have seen those tabernacles of ours in old Catholic churches in other parts of Germany, *mein Herr?*—and then she turned slowly back. There was no hurry, no anxiety nor expectancy, in her manner; still Engelbrecht had not been seen. She had come to the middle of the left aisle, still with her eyes persistently cast down, and though the people had all asked her many questions as to their future spiritual fate and that of others dear to them, yet she had never answered a word. Now, she stopped deliberately, yet never raising her eyes. A sob was heard in the crowd, and the serried masses heaved to and fro as a young man forced his way violently through. It was Engelbrecht, but he was unrecognizable. A cloak covered him from head to foot — evidently a studied disguise—yet what was more unlike him was his agitated, humble manner, the look of passionate self-accusation in his drawn features, and his impetuous disregard for appearances. As Ambrosia stopped, he rushed forward with his arms extended, but some unseen power stayed his progress, and though she was not a foot distant from him, he could not touch her. For the first time she lifted her head, and a look of love, pure as an angel's over a repentant sinner, lighted up her ethereal face and mingled with an expression of deepest gratitude. She pointed to the betrothal ring on her finger, and then glanced upward without uttering one word. This second warning from the world of souls was of too solemn a nature to admit of even the holy yet too human expression that her words had given to the first, but it was unmistakably borne in upon the mind of her lover that as long as he kept true to the faith, he might hope to claim her as his spiritual bride in the kingdom of God. And, as she continued her journey toward her grave, he did not even follow her, but went straight to the Dominican convent and asked for the habit of the order. Those who accompanied Ambrosia to the churchyard could tell nothing as to the manner of her disappearance; all they knew was that they saw her one moment, and the next they saw nothing. Engelbrecht gave all his riches to the church to found a seminary somewhere beyond the bounds of the heretical countries of Germany, for the instruction of missionaries; the foundation eventually became a house of his order. He wished his own dwelling to be used for monastic or hospital purposes, should religion again revive in Augsburg; but his wish was not fulfilled. The house was forfeited to the state, and

became successively a warehouse, a barrack, a prison, and a factory. Now, it is a great printing-office, and plenty of lies are coined into money within its walls, through the partisan newspapers that issue from it. You can see the corner window still, with its beautiful carving hardly injured by time, and the empty niche beneath it where the image of the Mother of God once stood. Have you noticed it, *mein Herr?*"

"No," I said, hardly liking to answer, for fear of losing some further detail. "But what of Engelbrecht?"

The old German looked surprised.

"Why, I have told you he became a monk."

"But did he distinguish himself against the reformers?"

"Ah!" said Reinhold, reverentially, "God knows, and his bride, but he left no record for the world to read. No doubt he worked out the will of God."

I was silent, for I was ashamed of myself in the presence of this man, to whom the hidden life of the soul seemed so all-sufficient a history.

Ambrosia, his daughter, had come back long before this story was finished, and was sitting sewing diligently, and listening to it with all her father's pride and personal enthusiasm in the matter.

"So," continued Reinhold, "the day of this wonder was remembered, and among those who remained Catholics, it became a custom to christen girls born on that day by the name of the holy maiden Ambrosia. My child, thank God, was one of them."

After listening to this peculiar and interesting legend, I led the conversation to the book I wished to purchase, and which Ambrosia had brought home with her on purpose. Reinhold knew the value of it perfectly well, and firmly resisted my well-meant attempts to fix a price upon it beyond what even its merits warranted. I was hardly able to indulge in such extravagance, yet *bibliomania* had always been my be-setting sin, and I had curtailed our little household in many ways to feed my library. Besides, here was a charity as well-deserved as it seemed well-placed; how else, with my lim-ited means, could I help my poor friends? But my fellow-bookworm was proof against all such artifices, and I was reduced to ask him, point-blank, was there anything which he would allow me to do for him? Without the least show of fussy pride, but with a quiet, manly grati-tude that was immeasurably more dignified, he answered at once, his voice shaking as he looked at his lit-tle son:

"A very little would make my child's life happy and useful, and, *lieber Herr*, that little I have it not."

"How stupid of me!" I exclaim-ed. "I might have thought of that myself. Is he to be a scholar, or an artist, or what?" I said, stroking his hair, while his great eyes were fixed hungrily on mine.

"Books are his passion," said his father, "and he knows all our poets by heart. He should have a literary education, I think."

"But," said I, "he could not go alone to the university, and if you do not mind leaving Augsburg, would it not be best for you all to go together? I have some English friends at Bonn, Catholics and rich people; they will do much for your child that I cannot do, though my heart would rejoice to do it, so sup-pose we start to-morrow?"

Reinhold looked up incredulously. Ambrosia laughed, and the poor lit-tle cripple clapped his hands in ecs-tasy. I watched the girl to see whether a shade of regret denoted ties of a tenderer or more passionate

nature than her strong, calm family affections; but there was no sign of anything save quiet joy and a grati-tude that in its fulness made me feel quite ashamed. I kept thinking of what could be done for her; whether my English friends at Bonn could or would be kind to her in any practi-cal way, and whether in that case she and her father would ever sub-mit to being provided for by the kindness of strangers. She seemed too self-reliant for that; and although she evidently longed for the same education her brother was to have, and had, indeed, already amassed in the intervals of her active work such miscellaneous knowledge as mere reading could give her, yet I felt sure that she would insist on earning her bread and helping to support her father. I decided on introducing the old man to the notice of some great publisher, with whom an ar-rangement about his manuscripts might perhaps be made; but of this we did not speak just now. I left the room full of our new projects, and spent the early part of the next day in carefully visiting the scenes of Ambrosia's life, death, and mar-vellous resurrection. In the after-noon I went back to Reinhold's old-fashioned abode, and found every-thing nearly ready. The books were packed in a curious old chest, which was certainly a quaint contrast to the trunks and valises of modern tour-ists; this and some of the old furni-ture, endeared to Reinhold and his daughter by the associations of a lifetime, were to be forwarded to their new destination through the care of the good "Pfarrer" (parish-priest), and a few little necessaries (a very slender amount in the eyes of our "girls of the period," I fan-cy!) together with the precious man-uscripts, were to go with us in a large leather hand-bag, which I volunteered to carry. I asked to be allowed to take charge of the little brother too, as we were too near the railway to need a carriage, but Ambrosia laughingiy caught him up, and, with gentle deftness, insisted on carrying him, telling me to give my disengaged arm to her invalid father. As soon as we were seated in the train, Ambrosia began to tell me that she had never been in one before. I asked if she were sorry to ˮ the old town.

ʼ ʾh! no," she said, " I know I shaʌɪ go back there one day, when I know more than I do now."

I wondered if there were any hidden meaning in the words. Reinhold and I talked "shop" all the ˮay, till our fellow-passengers must ɪave been bored with our enthusiastic bibliomania. Ambrosia sat chatting gayly to her little brother, whose glee and wonder were sometimes gravely expressed in questions that made our neighbors laugh. When we got to Bonn, and were comfortably settled at a quiet, old-fashioned hotel, absolutely perfect in its appointments, but as unobtrusive of its merits as its gaudy, noisy rivals were shrilly eager about theirs, I set out to find my friends. They were out of town. Without their influence I was powerless, so I had to wait a few days for their return. They took up the matter as warmly as I could have wished, and were particularly anxious to do something for Ambrosia; the difficulty was to find something she would accept. In the meantime, the crippled child was recommended to the college authorities with plenty of guarantees, seen to by the priest, who was my friend's adviser and fellow-worker in all his good schemes, and Reinhold was quietly put in the way of good opportunities for the publication of some of his accumulated writings.

The little boy promised well, and I was more anxious about Ambrosia, who wanted to support herself by needlework.

" You see," she said to me, a week after our arrival, " some of the work will be knitting, and I can read as I knit; then I will go to school at night and on Sundays, and pick up what I can, and twice a week I will make time for the singing-class. There is a very good one, and so cheap, attached to our church here, and the master is a really great artist, though he is old and very poor now. He and my father will be friends, I know, so you see I shall be as well off as it is possible."

Nothing could move her from her resolve, and as I had to leave Bonn shortly after, I was obliged to take things as they were. I received monthly bulletins of my little *protégé's* conduct and progress, and sometimes heard from Ambrosia and Reinhold, through their rare but warm letters, though oftener from my friends established at Bonn. After awhile, I heard that the girl had consented to take music lessons twice a week, in the evening, with Miss L., my friend's niece, and sometimes to share her French and Latin lessons. English she already knew. The needlework was not abandoned, however, and Ambrosia, I was told, seemed to gain new energy with each new pursuit she undertook. Reinhold's works were in a fair way of being successfully published, and his circumstances were actually beginning to mend. I never heard of such a lucky venture as that hurriedly made at the Augsburg book-stall! Everything and everybody favored it, and my quiet old sister at home used to make me tell the story over and over again, as we turned over the pages of the book that had been the first *deus ex machinâ* of the romance. She was certainly disappointed in the want of a lover for Ambrosia, and, to console herself, would sometimes so arrange the little we knew as to make it the frame of a possible love-story that we did not, and never might, know.

A year passed by in this way, when business called me up from my cottage in the Isle of Wight to London. It was May, and the exhibitions were just open. I went to Burlington House, and saw very little that was worth seeing; then to Pall Mall, to some of the minor galleries. The French collection of paintings was pretty upon the whole, but suddenly I came upon a picture that was really striking. An old German town and a cathedral painted to the very life formed a most varied background, upon which a conventional "crowd," that is, a few picturesque groups of burghers and peasants in the costume (accurate to the slightest detail) of the early part of the sixteenth century, was represented, gazing at the central figure, a maiden dressed in white, with two thick cords of golden hair streaking the snowy robe. I looked at once for Mephistopheles and his victim Faust, taking this for a novel and very artistic representation of Goethe's masterpiece; and turning to the catalogue I looked for the name of the painter—"Franz Eichenthal." But the painting itself was marked "Ambrosia, a Legend of Augsburg," and in a few brief words beneath the story was told as Reinhold had told it to me. Strangely interested, I looked at the white figure; I saw the likeness which had before escaped me; it was Ambrosia's face, her abundant hair, her grand form; the repose, the dignity that I so well remembered were there, but over the whole was thrown an air of etherealized peace and beauty which was a fitting tribute to the entirely spiritual essence of the

story. I looked to see if Engelbrecht were anywhere represented, and thought I could discover him in a corner, half hidden by the shadow from a buttress of the cathedral. There was a wonderfully energetic expression about this face, which made me single it out from the rest as being probably meant for the unhappy lover. There was strength and nobility in the features, and an almost feminine grace in the figure, while the look of horror and remorse struggling with unbelief was in painful contrast with this courtly exterior. Underneath, on the buttress, was carved, in antique characters, the name of the painter, "Franciscus Eichenthal, pinxit." It certainly happened to be the most obvious place for this traditional signature of the artist, yet I could not help fancying, almost hoping, that there was more in it than a mere chance, and that "Engelbrecht" was, in fact, the portrait of the painter himself. Ambrosia's face drew me to it again; the likeness was life itself, yet such as an American authoress describes as "not the man that we are, but the angel that we may be." She says that "as to every leaf and flower there is an ideal to which the growth of the plant is constantly urging, so there is an ideal to every human being, a perfect form in which it might appear, were every defect removed and every characteristic excellence stimulated to the highest point." She likens this to the image of St. Augustine, as his mother, with her spiritual prophetic sight, saw him all through his reckless youth, and then says: "Could a mysterious foresight unveil to us this resurrection form of the friends with whom we daily walk, compassed about with mortal infirmity, we should follow them with faith and reverence, through all the disguise of human faults and weaknesses, waiting for the manifestation of the sons of God."*

The German artist seemed to have had some such revelation vouchsafed to him concerning Ambrosia. The picture was unspeakably beautiful, and I felt instinctively that in the future it would become literally true. And yet the girl had never before struck me as having so exalted a nature; perhaps it was that she was so utterly unlike the usual ideal of a perfect woman.

I made inquiries as to whether the picture was an " order," or simply a speculation, and learned that it had been the latter, but was now destined for the hall of the " Young Men's Catholic Society " at Augsburg. An English nobleman had been so struck with it abroad that he had induced the artist to have it exhibited in London, and had himself ordered engravings and photographs from it. I felt very much inclined to go in for another extravagance, and have it copied on a reduced scale for my library, but I thought it most prudent to consult my sister first. I went home full of my discovery, and at once wrote to Reinhold for an explanation.

I received a very happy letter from Ambrosia herself in return, telling me of her engagement to the painter Eichenthal, who was an Augsburg man, and had lived for many years quite close to their old home, without either family having the remotest knowledge of each other. At the singing-class these two had met, their fellow-citizenship had first drawn them together, and the old master, whose favorite pupil the artist was, had brought him to see Reinhold. The result was natural, and my sister was innocently enthu-

* Mrs. Beecher Stowe, *Minister's Wooing.*

siastic over the ending in so pleasant a reality of the romance she had begun in imagination many months before.

There was a quiet wedding at Bonn, and my friend's niece, Ambrosia's companion in her studies, was bridesmaid. My sister and I went over to be present, and the dear old father, now quite strong again, gave his daughter a copy of his first published work for a wedding gift. Next to the dedication leaf, which was addressed to your humble servant, and overflowing with affectionate expressions, there was a cheque for half the proceeds of the work (and the sum was not to be sneered at, I can assure you).

Ambrosia and her husband then went to Rome, where Eichenthal identified himself with the school of Overbeck, and became very popular among the foreign visitors and patrons of art. The Englishman who had taken such a fancy to his picture of the Augsburg legend chanced to come across him again in Rome, and, having succeeded to his father's property, lavishly encouraged his artist friend. A *replica*, full size, of the original " Ambrosia " was painted for his chapel in England, and a large picture, representing a group of the patron saints of his family clustering round the throne of the Virgin and Child, was also ordered. The painter's wife was the model for a St. Catharine of Sienna, and the Englishman himself, a thorough Saxon in build and features, made a magnificent St. Edward the Confessor.

Several years later, the young couple settled in Augsburg, where Eichenthal established a flourishing school of Christian art, and used to give lectures on the subject in the very hall where his first successful work was hung. Ambrosia's brother got on so wonderfully that at twenty he was made professor of belles-lettres at Bonn, and was famous for writing the most beautiful religious poetry that had been known for many years. Ambrosia's children gather round their young crippled uncle in the spacious, old-fashioned house where Reinhold lives with his daughter, and make him repeat wonderful mediæval legends clothed in verse of his own. This is how he spends his vacation. Reinhold is always at his manuscripts, and the same books that used to be his pitiful stock in trade are now the cherished ornaments of his large library. The Christmas-tree gathering in that house is a poem in itself. The children of Ambrosia's friend, the English girl of Bonn, are often there playing with the artist's beautiful boys, for there is no Ambrosia the younger among Eichenthal's children. The best society of Augsburg Protestant and Catholic alike, delight to honor the successful artist; the musical soirées given in his house are as perfect in their way as each of his own paintings, and never is anything purely worldly allowed to appear under his roof.

"When I first saw my wife," he says, "I was a Lutheran or rather a so-called philosopher, but since I won her, I vowed to make her my arbiter and my conscience; you see the result. 'Seek first the kingdom of God, and his justice, and all these things shall be added unto you.'"

"And this is the end?" I said regretfully, as Archer paused.

"Not quite," he answered with a peculiar smile; "the end will not really come till Ambrosia has grown to be the counterpart of her spiritual portrait. But she is growing towards that standard every day. Would that you and I were, old friend!"

"There is time yet," I said; "let us try.'

KATHLEEN WARING.

THE loveliest of autumn days shed its warmth and brightness over magnificent Rome, while the bells from many towers announced the hour of twelve, and a still more emphatic reminder of mid-day boomed from Castle Sant' Angelo, the firing of whose cannon frequently startles strangers, though even they soon become unconscious of its loud report. Citizens meeting complained of 'the horrible sirocco day; visitors congratulated one another upon such beautiful weather for the fulfilment of their plans; and a very perceptible thing was that not even in the Eternal City can every individual be satisfied. In no way could an unbeliever be better convinced of this solemn truth than by a peep into the principal parlor of the Hôtel d'Angleterre, where a travelling party had just arrived. An elderly gentleman stamped up and down the apartment, furiously gesticulating, and undoubtedly making use of rather forcible language, consigning hotels in general, and the Hôtel d'Angleterre in particular, to pretty uncomfortable quarters. At every approach to a small tête-à-tête placed near the window he fiercely glared upon a lady, evidently his wife, whose sweet, smiling face served to exasperate her husband beyond endurance. A large fan, plied industriously, stirred not only the black feathers of her own bonnet, but the scarlet ones jauntily stuck in a dark gray hat that persistently drooped, for no reason in the world but to conceal a very amused countenance which might have added fuel to the fire of the gentle-man's anger. Though for a time he is denied the gratification of a peep at so winning a face, we will take it ourselves, and see what is under that gray hat with the scarlet plumes: A pair of dark eyes sparkling with fun, which all those curling black lashes cannot hide, while a few saucy rings of hair, lying here and there on the forehead, cause a surmise as to whether they are the result of nature and warm weather or curl-papers nightly twisted up. It would be difficult to form an estimate of a mouth whose under-lip is being held in bondage by two rows of exceedingly white teeth, but we will imagine it a rose-bud, and hasten to make the acquaintance of yonder thunder-cloud, who pouts so abominably, and is still so like her of the mischievous aspect. Agathe Waring leaned on the back of her chair, and, when her father stamped his feet, she did likewise; when his frown deepened and voice waxed louder, her pout became more decided, and very beautiful hands doubled into fists that shook defiantly at invisible landlords. Mrs. Waring, observing this, remarked: " I think, Agathe, you have chosen a dangerous employment for hands so valued as yours. Do you not fear your vehemence will be the cause of a sprained wrist or finger? Then where will be our delightful evening music. A young lady who, at the faintest suspicion of danger ahead, generally clasps her hands behind her, is to be wondered at when seen bravely challenging our most dreaded enemies."

" It may be very amusing to you

and Kathleen, mamma; but I confess to not perceiving the joke," replied Agathe, glancing complacently at her formidable weapons. "How you can see papa so worried, and be perfectly unconcerned, is more than I understand."

"But, my dear, would it mend matters in the least were your sister to weep tears of vexation, and I to vociferate against the unfortunate people of this hotel, who were never less in fault than now? If your father had taken my advice, and telegraphed for rooms, this occasion for trouble would have been avoided; but, as he considered such a precaution unnecessary, we need not regard ourselves as dreadfully-injured travellers."

"Am I not sufficiently annoyed, madam, by this turn of affairs," shouted the elderly gentleman, "that *you* should consider it essential to remind me what your advice was in Florence? I have never yet met the woman who did not delight in being able to say, 'I told you so.'"

"Now, papa," said Kathleen with a merry glance from her bright eyes, "I look upon that speech as a calumny and an injustice to Agathe. When all our luggage was left in Paris, simply because you would not heed her injunction to be very careful in looking after it, she did not gratify herself by any such malicious words as 'I told you so.' Indeed, her sympathy was far greater than ours, as we only felt indignant at having nothing to wear."

This boldly-uttered sentence proved quite soothing to Mr. Waring, who ceased his restless walk to twine an arm about his daughter's waist, whose head leaned fondly against the dusty sleeve, and desired no sweeter resting-place.

"Yes, whatever my faults, whatever my grievances, this little daughter is ready and willing to share them," said he, gently patting Agathe's cheek. "It has always been a wonder to me that a brute like myself should possess three treasures such as my wife and daughters. But the more valuable the treasure, the more difficult its keeping. If that atrocious landlord will only give us an apartment for this afternoon, I'll go in quest of permanent quarters, and leave you to rest until my return."

An immediate ringing of the bell brought the attendant, who was requested to inquire into the possibility of procuring at least a single room for the remainder of the day, during which time other accommodations might be sought. An answer, to the effect that there was a small chamber, engaged by a party who would arrive that night, which until then was at the service of the American gentleman, caused a gathering together of bags, boxes, and baskets, an ascent of several stairs, and a happy entrance into the nicely-furnished and exceedingly pleasant apartment. The waiter, before his departing bow, made many apologies for the crowded condition of the house having rendered it impossible to receive monsieur, and hoped their inability to please would be forgiven. Mr. Waring's wrath, until then on the wane, appeared gradually gaining ascendency, and a convenient lunch-basket would certainly have made the acquaintance of the waiter's head had not the latter prudently withdrawn. "The impudence of that dog in presuming to beg my pardon! What do I care how crowded the house may be or how impossible it is to accommodate us? I don't suppose this hotel is the only habitable place in Rome; if so, I'll just take up my abode in the Colosseum, and be done with it."

Neither Mrs. Waring nor Agathe could resist smiling at this outburst, while Kathleen laughed outright.

"I shall consider it my first duty, on entering the Colosseum, to set you up as a statue of Perversity, surrounded by imps of contradiction. During the last half-hour you have been in a towering passion because the Hôtel d'Angleterre could not contain you. Now the poor waiter humbly laments the numerous visitors and non-elastic material of the house, and you are ready to annihilate him for supposing us anxious to remain in it."

"Are you not ashamed of yourself, Kathleen Waring?" cried Agathe. "Were I papa, you should not speak to me in that rude manner. You surely do not approve of it, mamma?"

"My dear Agathe," said her mother, "I cannot disapprove when I so fully appreciate the spirit in which your sister thus addresses her father. Do not imagine you are alone in your affection for him, and that the sole mode of expressing that affection is by unvarying respectfulness in language and constant caressing. We all know you to be more dignified than Kathleen, and to possess much greater stability of character; then how can you expect her to be otherwise than more thoughtless and much saucier than yourself?"

This last sentence, accompanied by a meaning smile, brought a crimson flush to Agathe's cheek and an angry retort to her lips, the utterance of which was stayed by a kiss from her sister, who whispered:

"Never mind, Aggie; just be as firm and stable and dignified as you choose. I'll be your admiration-point for ever, and I am sure mamma is as proud of her model of strength and her impersonation of sauciness as she can be; then why need we quarrel?"

"Well, it *would* be a waste of ammunition, mavourneen," replied Agathe; "so, instead of letting loose my tongue, I'll exercise my arms. Be good enough to get me the clothes-brush from your bag, that I may dust papa's coat."

By plentiful application of soap and vigorous use of towels Mr. Waring now appeared resplendent, and announced his intention of at once going in search of rooms. "In my absence," said he, pausing at the door, "I desire the three treasures to repose, and hope to find them bright and sparkling this evening."

The ladies did retire, and slept soundly several hours, while Mr. Waring made every effort to obtain a suite of rooms, first at the different hotels, which were all full, next at two or three *casas* recommended by his banker. At last in a small house, opening on the Piazza di Spagna, he succeeded in engaging five bright, cheerful apartments, though at quite a high price, since the number of visitors at Rome increased rents far beyond their usual rate. Leaving orders with his *padrone* to secure a man-servant as soon as possible, he next made arrangements with the proprietor of the nearest restaurant to supply him with the necessary breakfast and dinner, which must be daily occurrences to sustain the vitality of even the most enthusiastic tourist. With a sigh of relief that his preparations were complete, Mr. Waring returned to the hotel, and found his wife and daughters radiant in their fresh toilets and expectant eagerness. There is nothing so destructive of beauty as fatigue added to the dust and soot of railway travelling; and an individual emerging from this double ordeal deserves the congratulation of friends. Mr. Waring bestowed a gaze of admiration upon each lady in turn, kissed his wife, pulled one of Agathe's curls, and whirled Kathleen round and round to the tune of a cracked. hand-organ stationed beneath the window, which just then ground out a very fine waltz. Breathless and panting, Kathleen soon sank on the sofa, while her mother came to the rescue with a fan, and Agathe opened the window to throw the musician some coppers.

"There is little need to inform us of your success," said Mrs. Waring, "as this emphatic greeting tells its own tale. I am really glad you were able to return before dark, as we feared you might be detained later."

"Well, you cannot fail to like the rooms," said Mr. Waring; "for they are five in number, quite handsomely furnished, and two overlook the Piazza di Spagna. I think, as it is a mere step from here, we had better walk, and have our luggage sent by these people. If you are half as tired riding as I am, you will infinitely prefer proceeding to our destination on foot."

"We should like nothing better!" cried the three ladies, and immediately began to collect their scattered property. This being duly disposed of, the black bonnet and gray hats donned, our party set out. The Ave Maria was ringing, and the sweet sound of many bells penetrated the hearts of even these Protestants, who understood so imperfectly its beautiful significance. Dusk was fast changing into darkness, while black clouds chased each other over the sky, and the rising wind betokened the sure approach of a storm. Our travellers hastened their footsteps, and only reached their parlor when a terrific flash of lightning poured through the windows, and the rain fell in torrents. Mr. and Mrs. Waring at once went on a tour of investigation, in which neither of the girls could be induced to join. Agathe approached the window and gazed upon the outdoor fury, with only clasped hands and awe-stricken countenance to betoken her feeling. Kathleen buried a miserably pale face in the cushions of her armchair, and sobbed most piteously; for the poor child dreaded nothing so much as thunder and lightning. After a short lapse of time, Agathe turned impatiently from her post of observation, and exclaimed:

"Without exception, Katy, you are the greatest goose I ever met, to be sitting there crying when you might have the benefit of yonder magnificent panorama. It is *too* absurd that the least sign of a storm must send you into hysterics. Do you not suppose there is quite as much danger for me as for you? Yet let me sob as you are doing, and how foolish you would think me! Do control yourself this once, or your eyes will be red and ugly to-morrow, and you not presentable."

Agathe had intended simple expostulation; but anger got the better of her, and her last words were very commanding—so much so as to rouse Kathleen, who cried:

"I am sure I don't care for eyes, or appearance, or anything else, and I wish you would let me alone. Because you have a reputation for courage and firmness, you imagine you are justified in persecuting me; but I tell you you are not. I cannot see any great courage and firmness in facing that lightning. If there should ever be a call upon me for such qualities, I will beg the good Lord to give them to me, but not for the purpose of staring at a storm." With this the dark head again took refuge in the cushions, and Agathe returned to her former position. The scene was indeed magnificent, and fully compensated for any uneasy feeling she might have experienced in thus exposing herself. The entire sky within range of vision seemed one dense, black cloud, hanging but a few feet above the house-tops, every moment sending forth flashes of light, at times sharp, forked, fearful, again soft, widespread, and of sufficient duration to illumine the entire piazza beneath. The pouring rain could not conceal surrounding objects, but rather served to enhance their beauty, since they appeared through a mist that served to screen the hard, substantial reality. High up, beyond the fine steps which are a prominent feature in this piazza, rose the church and convent of the Trinità di Monte, looking, in its elevation and noble strength, a fit emblem of a religion so true and sublime. Inclining from its height to the level beneath, the aforesaid steps were lonely and deserted, deprived of their lounging idlers, but nevertheless beautifully reflecting from their wet surface the brightness above. One might have imagined the piazza, with its brilliant shops, *caffes*, hotels, and booths, to be the noisy, bustling world, having in its midst those steps so numerous, so difficult of ascent, but in the end leading to rest, peace, heaven! How pitiful, then, to see no foot ascending! And if this little picture be one of sorrow, how much worse the great, real world, where so few mount the stairs within reach of all! Some walk round, others glance up and promise a beginning to-morrow;

but how many heed the warning? Now, *now* is the time; to-morrow may never come!

It is not probable, however, that such thoughts found favor with Agathe, whose Protestant mind was in no way addicted to pious musing, since her church furnishes such meagre food for heart and brain. Her eyes, roving restlessly about, suddenly became fixed upon the tall, muffled figure of a man hurrying through the rain with bent head and quickening speed. Devoid of fear, of suspicion, she watched until he neared the piazza's centre, when, after one long, blinding streak of lightning, a fearful crash followed, and she distinguished the object of her curiosity lying prostrate on the ground. A sharp cry from her lips brought Mrs. Waring, to whom, with trembling limbs and horror-stricken face, she pointed out the prostrate form. Kathleen, who had crept up behind her mother, no sooner beheld it than she ran from the room, and, meeting her father in the hall, breathlessly exclaimed: "O papa! do go quickly. . . . There is a poor man lying in the street who has been struck, . . . and nobody seems to know it. Please go to him. . . . Bring him here. Get some one to help you; for he may not be quite dead."

Before she had ceased speaking her father was down-stairs ordering a servant to follow him; and from their position Mrs. Waring and Agathe saw the two rush into the driving rain, gently raise the body, and carefully bear it towards the entrance. Kathleen had hastily arranged pillows and blankets on the sofa; so there was no delay in fixing something on which to lay the poor fellow, and very soon the entire family were making a desperate effort to restore animation, as Mr.

Waring declared there was life in the body. His assertion was verified when, after a while, the young man drew a long breath, and opened such bewildered, astonished eyes as made every one smile.

"Ah! my fine fellow," cried Mr. Waring, "I'll wager you you are on the road to life again, and we are spared the trouble of attending your funeral—a thing, I candidly assure you, I had expected to do not very long ago."

"O papa!" whispered Kathleen, glancing timidly at the pale face, blue eyes, and curling brown hair, "don't talk to the poor fellow about funerals when he has been so near the grave; it cannot be pleasant."

"Never mind, Miss Puss, I will set him straight," replied her father. "Now, my friend, I have always heard, and there is an indistinct idea of my having read it, that people struck by lightning never feel it. As you are a living witness to the truth or falsehood of this statement, I would like to have your views on the subject."

This, delivered with the air of a man thirsting for knowledge, brought a smile to the patient's mouth, and caused a general laugh.

"I am truly grieved," replied the lightning-struck, "that my knowledge is of questionable authority, because I cannot tell whether I felt a blow on the head or not, though there is a half-defined recollection of some one pounding me there, and producing about five hundred simultaneous sensations; whether really so or the fruit of my active imagination I am unable to avow."

"Well, for our own satisfaction, we will believe you *did* have five hundred feelings jumbled together, and take it as a warning to avoid like strokes."

"Such profanity shall not be allowed!" said Mrs. Waring; "and I really think, Mr. Waring, you should conduct our patient to a comfortable room where he may sleep away his weakness. Kathleen will share Agathe's apartment, that he may occupy hers."

All protestations to the effect that he could walk to his hotel being indignantly denied, the young man was immediately consigned to bed, and commanded to sleep as long as he could. For about half an hour the family sat up discussing the accident, and did not separate until its victim was unanimously pronounced handsome, elegant, charming!

The sun was many hours high next morning before our friends thought of stirring, and the two girls were yet sound asleep when their mother came tapping at the door. Her knock was so slight as to be scarcely perceptible, and, receiving no response, she entered. The change from bright sunshine to this darkened room at first made it impossible to distinguish clearly; but opening the blind a very little way, Mrs. Waring smiled to herself, as, glancing about the apartment, she murmured: "Those careless, careless girls! What is to be done with them?" Evidently, the careless girls had taken small trouble to arrange their things before retiring, and now a somewhat confused picture greeted the despairing mother's eye. The bureau appeared the favorite receptacle for almost all articles. A colossal brush, instead of properly supporting the rightful partner of its joys and sorrows, made desperate love to an ink-stand, a red bow, and a bottle of cologne, whose stopple had stepped over the way to consult an oracle of a watch about the probable comfort of the poor, deserted comb that patiently reposed on a prickly pin-cushion. The oracle, unwound and unmoved, refused utterance, and sullenly stared at a crowd of rings, bracelets, belts, reticules, hair-pins, false curls, and handkerchiefs indiscriminately gathered together. They were not interested in the watch, but bemoaned the sad fate of a coquettish gray hat with a scarlet plume, one string of which had caught in a tightly-shut drawer, and cruelly hung its fair possessor. A grand civil war had transpired in other parts of the room; the washstand implements were horribly mutilated and dashed about; the four shoes and stockings had taken leave of each other, and angrily stationed themselves in different corners; and, last, a huge trunk had brutally emptied itself of its contents, that now lay limp and helpless, here, there, everywhere.

Had not Mrs. Waring been well accustomed to such a display, it is possible she might have been dismayed; but as nothing is equal to habit, she preserved her equanimity, and, approaching the nearest bed, her attention was at once arrested by a tiny pair of beads which she perceived dangling from Kathleen's wrist. With a dark frown she retreated to the door, and cried:

"Girls! girls! it is time to get up. You have slept long enough even for weary travellers, and your patient has been waiting an hour to see the young ladies before taking leave. Do hurry and come at once to the parlor."

"Yes, mamma, we will," answered two very lazy voices.

"Yes, my dears, I do not doubt it," said Mrs. Waring; "but let me see you well out of those two comfortable beds, as you cannot be trusted in my absence."

In the midst of the commotion which followed Mrs. Waring escaped, and, slowly walking along the hall, murmured:

"Is it possible Kathleen still retains those absurd convent notions, and am I ever to regret having sent her to Mt. de C——? Surely, in three years she must have forgotten those ridiculous impressions; yet what does that rosary mean, and why should she sleep with it encircling her arm? Well, it will only make matters worse to discuss them, and, until I am certain what the poor child intends, I shall say nothing."

By this time the drawing-room was reached, and, entering, Mrs. Waring found her husband and their guest in hot dispute as to the best manner of sight-seeing in Rome. Mr. Waring expressed abhorrence of guide-books and his resolution never to use them. The stranger intimated such a resolve rash. Mr. Waring inquired why. The young man said guide-books being absolutely essential in a place so filled with objects of interest as Rome, he was willing to wager Mr. Waring would have three or four in his possession by the end of the week. Mr. Waring indignantly repudiated this idea, and the argument might have continued indefinitely had not the girls made an opportune appearance. In their wake came a delicious breakfast, after partaking of which the young man rose to depart.

"I cannot," said he, "pretend to thank you for such kindness to a stranger, for words are inadequate to express my gratitude. My obligations will be increased tenfold if you only permit me to continue an acquaintance so happily begun."

"My dear fellow," cried Mr. Waring, "don't mention gratitude; and as for an acquaintance happily begun, if you choose to consider as such one brought on by lightning, we are at your disposal, and nothing will delight us more than receiving you as our friend. But friends should know what to call one another, and, though my name is Alexander Waring, yours is still a dead secret."

"A thousand pardons! ' exclaimed the stranger. "My negligence is truly shocking; but it is Mr. and Mrs. Waring, with their lovely daughters, who have charmed me into a forgetfulness of Howard Lee, and it is they who must forgive him."

Of the two lovely daughters, Kathleen pouted bewitchingly at the foregoing speech, while Agathe gracefully inclined her head. The gentlemen shook hands most heartily, and Mrs. Waring cordially invited Mr. Lee to return often, assuring him of a sincere welcome. Thus, amidst compliments and acknowledgments on both sides, Howard Lee took leave of his friends, promising to see them very soon again.

It is scarcely necessary to add that the promise was observed, and during the next month or two he was almost constantly one of the gay little party which roved among the grand old ruins of Rome, wandered about its art-galleries and into its temples and churches, always consulting guide-books with a faith in, and a dependence on them that undoubtedly made Mr. Lee winner of his wager. It is very remarkable what wonderful things can transpire in a little while, though we are not certain whether you consider it remarkable that Mr. Lee soon manifested extraordi-

nary interest in the movements of Miss Kathleen. If that young person chose to stare an old statue out of countenance, she would not be long without the assistance of another pair of eyes that had suddenly remembered some never-before-known merit about the image, and were instantly intent on it. If Kathleen thought proper to sit among the ruins, he, completely overcome by fatigue, would rest by her side. We are much afraid this was not all that happened; for there were certainly some very ardent glances sent from his eyes to her sparkling black ones, that softened and glowed as they drank in the language of the blue ones. And at every new approach of the tall, manly figure didn't the gray hat with the scarlet plume droop lower and lower; didn't the round, dimpled cheeks beneath rival the feather in color; didn't the little hands clasp each other tightly, that their trembling might not make too bold a confession of her happy agitation? You cannot be surprised that, standing together by the beautiful Trevi fountain one moonlight night, to her was told in eloquent tones the old, old story which every woman hears once in her life, be she ever so poor, so ugly, so disagreeable. But this woman was lovely, bewitching; and the tale seemed exquisite harmony when softly, beseechingly it fell upon such ears. Long after the low voice had ceased telling what was music to her soul Kathleen stood silent. The water dashed from and over rocks in playful sport, defying the peaceful glance of the moon, which bade it be quiet. The church-bells rang out the hour of ten, and from the distance sounded Agathe's laugh, with the accompanying expostulation from several ladies and gentlemen who were begging her to sing. At last clear and full to these lovers came the sweet old song, " Kathleen Mavourneen." Howard waited till the music died away, then whispered,

> "Why art thou silent,
> Thou voice of my heart?
> Oh! why art thou silent,
> Kathleen Mavourneen?"

"Oh! spare me, spare me," cried Kathleen. "I cannot, cannot answer! If you but knew!"

"And do I not know you are what I love with all my heart, what I long to call my own? Have you not encouraged me? allowed me to believe you cared for me?"

"Oh! I never meant it. I would not have had you know that I cared for you. Have pity on me, Mr. Lee, and do not ask why! I can give no answer to your kind words. Believe me that it is best as it is."

"Miss Waring, your friends are coming—will interrupt us in one minute; can you give me *no* hope? Is there nothing you will say to comfort my yearning heart?"

"All I can say is, Wait; in a little while you will cease to wish for my affection when you have learned what it is essential you should know before I can give an answer to your question."

"Nothing can change my desire," pleaded Howard, gazing upon the tear-laden eyelashes and trembling lips. "Only tell me now what you think I must know, and then see if it makes the slightest difference."

"No, Mr. Howard," said Kathleen, regaining composure, "wait a few days; then I will either send for you or write what I have to communicate. With you will rest the decision. Remember always that I have cared for you, and that now it is a sad good-night I wish you, knowing it may be my last."

Here they were joined by their party, and Kathleen flying to the protection of her mother's arm, Mr. Lee took his place by Agathe's side, and thus they returned home. Poor Kathleen passed a miserable night, and awoke next morning with head aching so badly as to prevent her appearance at breakfast. Towards noon she improved, and by three o'clock presented herself in the drawing-room, where were her mother and sister. Telling them she was going out for a little fresh air, and to feel no uneasiness if she did not immediately return, she left the house, ran across the piazza, up the steps, and stood in front of the Trinità di Monte. Pausing a minute, "This is the 8th of December, the Feast of the Immaculate Conception, so certainly there must be Benediction here this afternoon, as they tell me the church belongs to the Ladies of the Sacred Heart. I'll try, anyhow."

The little portress, in her very ugly cap, informed *la signorina,* "Yes, benediction would be given in one hour from that time. Would she walk into the chapel now and wait, or would she prefer going away to return?" *La signorina* would wait; so she was shown into the church, and there left to her own reflections, which were one long struggle with feelings so contrary that to make them agree was impossible. The poor child had, ever since leaving the convent of Mt. de C——, been praying for courage to avow a faith which she knew would anger her father, distress that darling mother, and call forth words of bitter ridicule from Agathe. Now to these considerations was added the fear of losing Howard Lee's affection.

"Ah! Jesus, Mary, and Joseph," she cried, "help me in this my agony. Send down upon me your

blessing, that I may be strengthened in the path which has become
so difficult to my faltering feet!
Endow my heart with that courage
I once boasted I would ask for
when its need should be discovered. O my Father in heaven! look
upon thy child with pity, and heed
her earnest supplication."

For an entire hour she wavered
between the earthly devotion that
awaited but a word to be hers,
and the higher Love, that requires
many crosses and sacrifices before
it recompenses the heart. It will
never desert, never wound. The
sun sank lower in the heavens, and
the light in the chapel took a soft,
mysterious tone that lent supernatural quiet and stillness to the
place, greatly · soothing Kathleen's
restless mind. Her head leaning
on the railing in front of her, her
lips moving in unconscious prayer,
she fell into a deep, dreamless
sleep that was only disturbed
when over her senses stole the
faint sound of music, gradually,
gradually unclosing those delighted
eyes shining with blissful wonder,
as she supposed it all must have
been a dream, from which she waked to find herself safe in the dear
old convent. Surely, there was the
beautiful altar, the Blessed Sacrament exposed, many candles burning amid vases of exquisite flowers,
the venerable priest kneeling at the
altar's foot; above all, the convent
girls, in blue uniforms and white
veils, entering two by two, making
their genuflections, and standing
in their places till all were ready,
when tap! from the Sisters' bench,
and down they sat. From the or-
gan-loft the sweet litany she knew
so well came pouring into her ears
just as of yore; as of yore the
priest, the Sisters, and convent
girls sang in familiar tones:

" Mater Christi,
    Mater divinæ gratiæ,
    Mater purissima."

With happy heart and tearful
eyes she sang out the *Ora pro
nobis,* while many looked to see
from whence came the joyful
notes, so splendidly swelling their
chorus. Through the litany, the
O Salutaris! and the *Tantum Ergo*
her strong, young voice was clear and
sweet, and none guessed that in
the girl's heart a fearful struggle
had taken place, and that there
the good Lord had come and left
a gift which would never decay,
never be worthless, but ever bright
and glorious. A last prayer for
strength was uttered during Benediction, and Kathleen felt half her
difficulties were overcome when
she stood up at the *Laudate Do-
minum.*

That night she confessed to her
parents her intention of becoming
a Catholic, and besought their permission to take the step. Mr. Waring
was furious at first, and vowed she
shouldn't—not if he knew himself;
but three days' fussing and fuming
brought him to the conclusion she
might do as she chose, "but, for
heaven's sake, never expect him to
love her as much again," and en-
forced his resolution by hugging
and kissing her on the spot. Mrs.
Waring was very sad at the aspect
of affairs, but had so long anticipated it as to be little surprised.
Deeming a refusal of her sanction
worse than useless, she also said
her daughter might do as she pleased. Only Agathe was inexorable;
for, having begun by condemning
her sister's course, she considered
it incompatible with firmness ever
to change.

"How you can have allowed
yourself to be so wound about the
little fingers of those priests and

nuns I can't divine," she cried. "It indicates such contemptible weakness to turn from the religion in which you were born to that of a Papist—above all things, a Papist! Were I to live a hundred years, I could not do it."

"No, my poor sister," thought Kathleen; "with all your character, I fear you have not the daring courage required to combat the distress of parents, the anger of friends, the loss of a beloved object. No; it is a precious gift of God, and must be prayed for."

Next Kathleen wrote to Mr. Lee, informing him of all that had taken place, of her intention to become a member of the Catholic Church in a few weeks, and renewed her request that he would forgive the pain she had caused him in remembering the grief she herself endured; with many wishes for his future prosperity, she remained his true friend. No answer came to this at all, and the Warings saw nothing more of Howard Lee. Delicacy prevented their asking an explanation from Kathleen, and, as she proffered none, his name was never mentioned among them.

The days passed on, and Kathleen, being at last considered sufficiently instructed, had prevailed on the Sisters of Trinità di Monte to allow her retreat to be made with them, and her baptism and first communion to take place in their church. Christmas was the time appointed for the consummation of Kathleen's desire. The chapel had been beautifully decorated by the nuns and girls; and a little Bethlehem, removed some slight distance from the altar, was the emblem of the glorious feast. A new Mass had been learned, and, while the organ pealed forth its first tones, the white-robed girls filed in, followed by Mr. and Mrs. Waring and Agathe, who, by dint of persuasion, had been induced to appear on the occasion. Last entered Kathleen, and knelt in front of the altar. She was faint and trembling, but did not lose a syllable of the words that made her a Christian, a Catholic, and soldier of heaven. She was baptized, of course, before the celebration of Mass, and during it received for the first time the Holy Communion. Mr. Waring seemed much moved, his wife cried outright, and Agathe's flushed face and shining eyes belied the unconcern she tried so hard to assume.

No one noticed the tall, dark figure standing in the furthest corner of the church, nor saw the gaze riveted upon the fair, sweet girl at the altar. As everything here must have an end, so did the music, the lights, all that had brightened the chapel. The dark figure had hurried away, the girls in white had disappeared, the Warings were gone; only the little Babe of Bethlehem still lay in the manger, and one lamp shed its faint lustre in honor of that Blessed Sacrament which is for you, for me, for all who but seek it.

On the evening of the same day Kathleen was playing soft chords on the piano, and indulging in waking dreams, when she was greatly disturbed by the entrance of a man bearing in his arms a huge package of something very delicate, to judge from the care with which said package was deposited on the table. Before Kathleen could frame a question concerning the matter the man was gone. Approaching the very remarkable bundle, she perceived a card suspended bearing these words:

" A Christmas gift for Miss K. Waring."

Still wondering, she gently detached the paper cover, and there, delighting her eyes, was a tiny Christmas-tree literally filled with bonbons, colored candles, and children's toys, while two or three small papers concealed some more valuable presents no doubt. In perfect amazement she ran to the door and called father, mother, and sister, who, hastening to the room, uttered exclamations of pleasure at the sight. The candles were instantly lighted, and the tree admired from every point, though a thorough mystification ensued as to the donor. Each surmise only seemed to make the matter worse; so they instituted a search among the separate parcels. The first opened displayed a gold locket with the initials A. W. in pinheads of pearls; the next contained a handsome silver tobacco-box for Mr. Waring; the next, a musical work-box with Mrs. Waring's name; yet still there was nothing for Kathleen. More astonished than ever, they examined once again; and right on the very top of the tree, buried deep in its branches, was a round pasteboard box about the size of a lady's watch. Being opened, it disclosed a knot of hard-twisted note-paper, which Kathleen unwrapped and unfolded until she came upon an old, worn medal of the Immaculate Conception, from which hung a blue ribbon. As the paper in her hand had something written on it, she made haste to read, and here is the secret:

"Will my dear one take for a Christmas gift the little medal herein enclosed, which was put around my neck by my mother when I made my first communion eighteen years ago? I have kept away from you, that you might have a pleasant surprise for this Christmas day, though I went to communion for you this morning, and also saw the triumph of your brave spirit in the Church of the Trinità di Monte. If, when I come to you this evening, my little medal is about your neck, I shall know you accept me as your devoted   HOWARD LEE."

Kathleen stood looking at the words through gathering tears, and was not conscious of the quiet withdrawal of her parents and sister until the door opened gently to admit Howard, who, glancing quickly at the blue ribbon on her bosom, advanced eagerly, and, bending low, exultantly murmured:

" Why art thou silent,
   Thou voice of my heart?
 Oh! why art thou silent,
   Kathleen Mavourneen?"

LAST DAYS BEFORE THE SIEGE.

PART I.

AWAKENING.

BERTHE was holding a council about bonnets with her maid and Mme. Augustine when I went in. The complexion of the sky, it would seem, was a grave complication of the question at issue; it was of a dull leaden color, for, though the heat was intense, the sun was not shining outright, but sulking under a heavy veil of cloud that looked as if it might explode in a thunder-storm before the day was over.

"What a blunderer you are, Antoinette!" exclaimed Berthe impatiently. "The idea of putting me into pearl-color under a sky like that! Where are your eyes?"

Antoinette looked out of the window, saw the folly of her conduct, and proposed a pink bonnet to relieve the unbecoming sky and the gray costume. The amendment was approved of; so she left the room to fetch the bonnet.

"She is a good creature, Antoinette; but she is wonderfully absent-minded," remarked Berthe.

Mme. Augustine sighed, smiled, and shrugged her shoulders.

"What will you, Madame la Comtesse? Every one is not born an artist."

"Every one who is born with eyes in their head can use them if they have any sense," said Berthe; and she took up the ivory puff on her dressing-table, and began very deliberately shaking out delicate white clouds of *poudre à la violette* over her forehead and cheeks.

We were going together to a marriage at St. Roch, and we were to be there at *midi précis*, the *faire-part* said, so I had to remind Berthe that, if the business of powdering and puffing proceeded at this rate, we might save ourselves the trouble of the drive. With the sudden impulse that carried her so swiftly from one object to another, she dropped the puff, snatched her pink bonnet from Antoinette, put it on, fastened it herself, seized her gloves and prayer-book, and we hurried down-stairs and were off.

On turning into the Faubourg St. Honoré, we found a crowd collected in front of the *mairie*. Berthe pulled the check-string.

"It's news from the *frontière!*" she exclaimed eagerly. "If we were to miss the wedding, we must know what it is!"

She sprang out of the brougham, and I after her. The crowd was so deep that we could not get near enough to read the placards; but, judging by the exclamation and commentaries that accompanied the perusal by the foremost readers, the news was both exciting and agreeable.

Fallait pas nous effrayer, mes petites dames," said a *blouse,* who had seen us alight, and saw by our faces that we were alarmed. " We've beaten one-half of the Prussians to a jelly, and driven the rest across the Rhine."

" The *canaille !* I always said they would run like rabbits the first taste they got of our chassepots," exclaimed a lad of fourteen, who halted with arms akimbo and a basket of vegetables on his head to hear the news.

" And these are the chaps that marched out of Berlin to the cry of " *Nach Paris ! nach Paris !* The beggars ! They were glad enough to clean our streets—aye, and would have cleaned our boots in their moustachios, and thankful, just to turn a penny that they couldn't make at home," cried the first speaker.

" *Nach Paris* indeed !" cried the lad with the vegetables. " Let them come ; let them try it !"

" Let them !" echoed several voices. " We'll give them a warm welcome."

" Aye, that we will," declared a pastry-cook from the other end of the *trottoir ;* " and we'll treat them well ; we'll serve them up *aspic à la bayonette et petits-pois à la mitrailleuse.*"

This keen joke was received with hilarity and immense applause, and the pastry-cook, with his *bonnet de coton* perched on one side, strode off with an air of commanding insolence, like a man who has done his duty and knows it.

The remarks of the crowd, if not very lucid, were sufficiently conclusive as to the character of the placard that held them gaping before the *mairie.* The news was clearly

good news : so, satisfied with this broad fact, Berthe and I jumped into the brougham and continued our way to St. Roch.

But it seemed as if there was a conspiracy against our getting there. Before we came to the Rue Royale, we were blocked in front by a troop of recruits, marching down from the boulevards to the Rue de Rivoli. Flags, and banners, and bunches of tricolored ribbons hoisted on sticks floated at intervals above the moving mass, and the stirring chant of the " Marseillaise" kept time to the roll of drums and the broken tramp of undrilled feet. The shops emptied themselves into the street ; buyers and sellers rushed out to see the recruits and greet them with cheers and embraces, while many joined in the chorus, and shouted enthusiastically, " *Marchons, marchons, pour la patrie !* " the recruits every now and then, with an utter neglect of all choral harmony, relieving their pent-up patriotism by hurrahing and *Vive-la-France*-ing with frantic energy.

" Poor devils !" exclaimed a tradesman, who stood near us watching the stream flow past. " How many among them will ever set eyes on Paris again, I wonder !"

" Ah, indeed," said his wife ; " but, all the same, it's a proud day for them this, whatever may come of it. If our *gamin* were but a few years older, he would be stepping out with the best of them, and, who knows ? he might come home with a pair of gold epaulets to his coat."

" Tut, woman," retorted the man sharply ; " there is plenty of food for powder without him." And he went back to his shop.

" What a horrible thing war is when one comes to think of it !" said Berthe, turning suddenly round with a flushed face. " Every man going by there is the centre of another life

—some, perhaps, of many lives—that will never know happiness again if he is killed. It is a dreadful scourge. Thank God, I have no brothers!"

The way was cleared at last, and the carriages were able to move on. The noise and clamor that rose on all sides of us grew louder and wilder as we proceeded. One would have fancied the entire population had been seized with *delirium tremens*. The news of a victory coming unexpectedly after the first disasters of the campaign had elated the popular depression to frenzy, and, as usual with Paris, there was but one bound from the depths of despair to the wildest heights of exultation. Flags were thrust out of windows and chimney-pots, an eruption of tricolor broke out on the fronts of the houses, and the blank walls were variegated with red, white, and blue, as if by magic. Innumerable *gamins* cropped up from those mysterious regions where *gamins* dwell, and whence they are ready to emerge and improve the opportunity at a moment's notice; the bright-faced ragged young vagabonds mustered in force on the pavement, formed themselves into an impromptu procession, and marched along the middle of the street, bawling out the "Marseillaise" at the top of their voice; older *gamins* caught the infection, and bawled in response, and turned and marched with them. At the corner of the Place Vendôme, a citizen, unable to restrain the ardor of his patriotism, stopped a *fiacre*, and jumped up beside the driver, and bade him stand while he poured out his soul to the *patrie*. The cabman reined in his steed, and stood while the patriot spouted his improvisation, stretching out his arms to the column—the "immortal column"—and pointing his periods with the talismanic words, "*Invincible! Enfans de la France! Terreur de l'ennemi!*" and so forth.

No speaker in the forum of old Rome ever elicited more inspiriting response from his hearers than the citizen patriot from the motley audience round his cab. Again and again his voice was drowned in vociferous cheers and bravos, and when he was done and about to descend from the rostrum, the cabman, altogether carried away by the emotions of the hour, flung his arms round the orator, and pressed him to his heart, and then, addressing himself to the assembled citizens, defiantly demanded if their fellow-citizen had not deserved well of them; if there was any danger for the *patrie* while she could boast such sons as that! The appeal was rapturously responded to by all, but most notably by a native of the Vosges, who tossed his cap into the air, and caught it again, and cried vehemently: "*Prafo! prafo! Fife le pourgeois! fife la pâdrie!*"

If the words had been a shell scattering death among the listeners, their effect could not have been more startling. Like lightning the spirit of the crowd was changed; its joy went out like the snuff of a candle; for one second it swayed to and fro, hesitating, then a yell, a hiss, and a scream shot up in quick succession.

"A spy! a traitor! a Prussian! *A l'eau! à la lanterne!*" And away they flew in hot pursuit of the luckless Alsatian, whose German accent had raised the devil in them. The orator stood by the column alone in his glory, pelted by the jargon of cries that shot across him on every side from the boulevards and the many streets running out of the Place. "*Marchons! à l'eau! à Berlin! un espion!*" It was like the clash of contending tongues from Babel.

This was our last adventure till we reached St. Roch. As might have been expected, we were late. The wedding was over, and the bride was undergoing the ceremony of congratulations in the sacristy. We elbowed our way through the throng of guests, and were in due time admitted to embrace the Marquise de Chassedot, *née* Hélène de Karodel, and to shake hands with the bridegroom, and sprinkle our compliments in proper proportion over the friends and relatives on both sides.

At the wedding breakfast, the conversation naturally turned, to the exclusion of all other topics, on the happy event which had brought us all together; but as soon as the bride left the table, to change her bridal dress for a travelling one, everybody, as if by common consent, burst out into talk about the war and the news that had thrown the city into such commotion. The cautious incredulity with which the bulletin was discussed contrasted strangely with the tumult of enthusiasm which we had just witnessed outside. It was quite clear no one believed in the "famous victory." Some went so far as to declare that it was only a blind to hide some more shameful disaster that had yet befallen us; others, less perverse, thought it might be only a highly colored statement of a slight success. As to the authorities, it was who would throw most stones at them. The government was a rotten machine that ought to have been broken up long ago; it was like a ship that was no longer seaworthy, and just held together while she lay at anchor in the port, but must inevitably fall to pieces the first time she put out to sea, and go down before the wind with all her crew. The only exceptions to the rule were those government officials who happened to be present, and these were, of course, the life-boats that had been left behind by the stupidity of the captain. But this had always been the way.

In the downfall of every government, we see the same short-sighted jealousy—the men who might have saved it shoved aside by the selfish intriguers who sacrifice the country to their own aims and interests. Some allusion was made to the threatened siege of Paris; but it was cut short by the irrepressible merriment of the company. The most sober among them could not speak of such an absurdity without losing their gravity. It was, in fact, a heavy joke worthy of those beer-drinking, German braggarts, and no sane Frenchman could speak of it as anything else without being laughed at. As a joke, however, it was discussed, and gave rise to many minor pleasantries that provoked a good deal of fun. An interesting young mother wished the city might be invested and starved, because it would be so delightful to starve one's self to death for one's baby; to store up one's scanty food for the innocent little darling, and see it grow fat on its mother's *dénouement*. A young girl declared she quite longed for the opportunity of proving her love to her father. The Grecian daughter would be a pale myth compared to her, and the daughter of Paris would go down to posterity as a type of filial duty such as the world had never seen before. The kind and quantity of provisions to be laid in for the contingency gave rise to a vast deal of fun. One young *crevé* hoped his steward would provide a good stock of cigars; he could live on smoke by itself, rather than without smoke and with every other sort of nourishment; but it should be unlimited smoke, and of the best quality. His sister thought of buying a monster box of chocolate bonbons, and contemplated herself, with great satisfaction, arrived at her last *praline*, which she heroically insisted on her brother's accepting.

while she embraced him and expired of inanition at his feet.

"Do you intend to stay for the tragedy, madame?" said the gentleman who was to live on smoke, addressing himself to Berthe.

"If I believed in the tragedy, certainly not," she replied; "but I don't. Paris is not going to be so obliging as to furnish us with an opportunity for displaying our heroism."

"Not of the melodramatic sort," observed her Austrian friend, with a touch of sarcasm in his habitually serene manner; "but those who have any prosaic heroism to dispose of can take it to the ambulances, and it will be accepted and gratefully acknowledged. I went yesterday to see a poor fellow who is lying in great agony at Beayon. His mother and sisters are watching him day and night. They dare not move him to their own home, lest he should die on the way. He lost both arms at Gravelotte."

Berthe shuddered.

"Thank God, I have no brothers!" she murmured, under her breath.

"What is to be the end of it all?" I said. "Admitting that the siege of Paris is an utter impossibility, half Europe must be overhauled before peace is definitely re-established."

"So it will be," asserted the Austrian, coolly. "Wait a little, and you will see all the powers trotted out. First, Russia will put her finger in the *mêlée*, and then England's turn will come."

"I hope England will have the sense to keep out of it," said Berthe; "she would be sure to get the worst of it, fighting single-handed, as she would do now."

"That's precisely why Russia will take care that she does not keep out of it," remarked the Austrian.

"And what would Russia gain by England's being worsted?"

"She would gain the satisfaction of paying off old scores that have rankled in her side these fifteen years. Do you fancy that she has forgotten that little episode in the Crimea, or that she is less bent on revenge because she doesn't blast and blow and wake her enemy's suspicions by threatening to annihilate her and so forth? Not a bit of it! Russia doesn't boast and brag and put her victim on the *qui vive;* but quietly holds her tongue, and keeps her temper, and bides her time. When she is ready—and the day is not, perhaps, very remote—she will pick a fight with England; and the day the war is proclaimed, every pope and peasant in Holy Russia will light a candle to his holy images; and when the news comes in that England is thrashed, they will light as many as will illuminate the whole of Europe."

"*Après?*" I said.

"*Après* what, madame?"

"When they have thrashed her, as you say, what will they do with her?"

"Do with her? Annex her."

He looked me straight in the face without a smile on his; but I could not believe he was speaking seriously, and I burst out laughing.

"The position of the conquered territory might offer some difficulties in the way of annexation," I said, presently; "but we will assume that the obliging Providence of pious King William interferes in behalf of his Muscovite brother, and overcomes all obstacles by land or by sea, and that the doughty little island is constituted a colony of the czar's dominion: what would he do with it? What earthly use would it be to him?"

"Use!" echoed the Austrian, elevating his eyebrows with a supercilious smile. "In the first place, he might make it a little *succursale* of

Siberia. There is a whole generation of those unmanageable, half-mad Poles safely walking about this side of Europe, plotting and dreaming and rhapsodizing. Only think what a convenience it would be to their father, the czar, if he had a centre of action so near to them! He could catch them like rabbits; and then, instead of hawking them over the world to Nerchintz and Irkoutsk, he could sentence them to perpetual sciatica, or chronic lumbago, or 'a mild term of ten years' rheumatism, in the isle of fogs, *versus* the mines, and the knout, and all the rest of the paternal chastisements 'administered in Siberia. Then, over and above this immense accommodation, he might have his docks in England; he might make the naughty Poles learn of his English subjects how to build ships, till by-and-by the navy of Holy Russia would be the finest in the world, and big, top-heavy Prussia would shake in her shoes, and hot-headed France would keep still on her knees, and all Europe would bow down before the empire of Peter the Great. Use, indeed! Let Russia catch England, and she'll find plenty of use for her."

"Yes," I said; "just so; let her catch her."

It was near three when the wedding-party broke up and Berthe and I drove away. We found the excitement abroad still unabated. At many street corners, patriots were perorating to animated crowds; tongues innumerable were running up and down the gamut of noise with the most extraordinary variations. There is always something stirring in the sight of great popular emotion; but this present instance of it was more threatening than exhilarating. You felt that it was dangerous, that there were terrible elements of destruction boiling up under the surface-foam, and that the chattering and shouting and good fellowship might, in a flash of lightning, be changed to murderous hate and a madness beyond control. It was madness already; but it was a harmless madness so far. Was it nothing more? was there no method in it? I wondered, as we beheld the people haranguing or being harangued, rushing and gesticulating, and all showing, in their faces and gestures, the same feverish excitement. Were they all no better than a cityful of apes, chattering and screaming from mere impulse? Was it all quackery and cant, without any redeeming note of sacrifice and truth and valor; and would all this fiery twaddle die out presently in smoke and dumbness?

We had turned down to the Rue de Richelieu, and were coming back, when our attention was arrested by a body of volunteers marching past the Place de la Bourse. They were in spruce new uniforms, and they were singing something that was not the " Marseillaise," or " La Casquette au Père Bugeaud," or any other of the many chants we had been listening to ; altogether, their appearance and voices roused our curiosity, and Berthe desired the man to follow in their wake, that we might find out what kind of troops they were, and what they were singing. They turned up the Rue de la Baupe to the Place des Petits Pères, and there they entered the church of Notre Dame des Victoires, as many of them as could find room, for they numbered several thousand, and nearly half had to remain outside. The great front doors were thrown up, and remained open, so that those who were in the Place could see all that went on within. The soldiers were upon their knees, bare-headed, and a venerable old priest was speaking to them; but his voice was so feeble that what he said was only audible to those close to the altar-steps where he stood. There was no need to ask now who these men were, or whence they came. None but the men of Brittany, the sons of the men who went out to death against the ruthless soldiers of Robespierre, to the cry of *Dieu et le Roi!* were likely to traverse Paris, bearing the cross at their head, and make the ex-votos of Notre Dame des Victoires shake on the walls to the stirring old Vendean hymns. None but the descendants of the men " whose strength was as the strength of ten, because their hearts were pure," would dare in these days of sneaking, shamefaced Christianity to commit such a brazen act of faith. The volunteers were accompanied by a great concourse of people, mostly relatives and friends, but they all remained outside, leaving the church quite to the soldiers. It was a strange and beautiful sight to see all these brave, proud Bretons kneeling down with the simplicity of little children before the shrine of the Virgin Mother, and singing their hymns to the God of Hosts, and asking his blessing on themselves and their arms before they went out to battle. When they came out of the church, with the curé at their head, all the people of a common impulse fell upon their knees in the Place to get his blessing; the men received it with bare heads and in silence; the women weeping, most of them, while some lifted up their hands with the old priest and prayed out loud a blessing on the soldiers. Then he spoke a few words to them, not to the soldiers only or chiefly, but to all, and especially to the women. He bade them remember that they too had their part in the national struggle, and that they might be a noble help or a guilty hindrance, as they chose. Those who had hus-

bands, or sons, or brothers in the ranks would understand this without any explanation from him. But there were very many amongst them who had no near relatives in danger, and who fancied that this would exempt them from sharing the common burthen, and that they could stand aloof from the general anxiety and pain. It was a selfish, pagan feeling, unworthy of a daughter of France, and still more of a Christian. There could be no isolation at a time like this. All should suffer, and all should serve. Those who happily had no kindred of their own at the frontier should adopt in spirit the brave fellows who had left none behind. They should care for them from a distance like true sisters, helping them in the battle-field with their prayers, and in the camp and the hospital by their active and loving ministration; let such among them as were fit and free to do it, go and learn of that other sisterhood of the diviner sort how to serve as they do who serve with the strong, pure love of charity; let those who could not do this give abundantly wherewith the stricken soldier might be healed and comforted on his bed of pain; if they could not give their hands, let them give their hearts and their money; let them help by sacrifice—sacrifice of some sort was within the reach of all. He blessed them again at the close of his little exhortation, and then every one got up. The Bretons fell into rank, and, rending the welkin with one loud cry of *Dieu et la France!* set out to the Northern Railway. Berthe and I had been kneeling with the crowd.

" Let us follow and see the last of them," she said, and we got into the brougham and went on at a footpace.

The scene at the station was one that will never be forgotten by those who witnessed it. The pathos of those rough farewells, the lamentations of some of the women, the Machabean courage of others, the shrill crying of little children, the tears of strong men, who tore out their hearts, feeling it like men, but bearing it with the courage of soldiers and the exulting hope of Christians: it was a sight to make one's heart glad to rapture or sad to despair. Some of the volunteers were of the noblest families in Brittany, others were workingmen, farmers, and peasants; there was the same mixture of classes in the throng of people that accompanied them; the pure accent of the most cultivated French, crossed here and there with the coarser tones of the Vendean patois; side by side with the suppressed agony of the châtelaine, who strove to hide her tenderness and tears from the gaze of bystanders, you saw the wretched sorrow of the peasant wife, who sobbed on her husband's neck and clung to him in a last embrace. There was something more heart-rending in these humbler farewells, because one felt the sacrifice was more complete. If this was a last parting, there was nothing for either to fall back upon.

I lost sight of Berthe as soon as we alighted, and indeed I forgot her. My whole thoughts were absorbed in the scene going on around me. It was only when the bell rang, and the soldiers passed out to the platform, leaving the space comparatively empty, that I looked about for her, and saw her in the middle of the sidewalk with her arms round a young girl, who was sobbing as if her heart would break. It appeared that she was just a fortnight married to a Breton lad of her own age, nineteen; they had worked hard and saved all their little earnings these five years past in order to get married; and now, just as they were so happy, he had gone away from her, and she

would never see him again; he was certain to be killed, because he was so good and loving and clever. Berthe pressed the poor child to her heart, and committed herself to the wildest pledges for the safe return of the young hero, and finally, after evoking a burst of passionate gratitude from the girl, who half-believed her to be a beneficial fairy sent to comfort her, Berthe exacted a promise that she was to come and see her the next day, and we set our faces towards home.

We drove on for a little while in silence, looking each out of our separate window, our hearts too full for conversation. I saw by Berthe's eyes that she had been crying. I felt instinctively that there was a great struggle going on within her, but, though my whole heart was vibrating in sympathy with it, I could not say so. Presently she turned towards me, and exclaimed:

"And I was thanking God that I had no brothers! Blind, selfish fool that I was!"

She burst into tears, sobbing passionately, and hid her face in her hands. The change in her bright and volatile spirit seemed to make a change in all the world. I could not accuse the people, as I had done an hour ago, of being mere puppets, dancing to a tune and throwing themselves into attitudes that meant no more than a sick man's raving. It seemed to me as if the aspect of the city and the sound of its voice had quite altered, and I all at once began to hope wonders of and for the Parisians. One could not but believe that they were striving to be in earnest, that the mother-pulse of patriotism, so long gagged and still, was now waking up, and beating with strong, hot throbs in the hearts of the people, and that, once alive and working, it would break out like a fire and burn away the unreality and the false glitter and the tragic comedy of their lives, and serve to purify them for a free and noble future. No; it was not all cant and tinkle and false echo. There was substance under the symbolizing. There were men amongst them who worshipped God, and were proud to proclaim it. There were hearts that seemed dead, but were only sleeping. Paris was dancing in mad mirth like a harlequin to-day, but to-morrow it would be different—the smoke and the flame would go out, leaving behind them the elements of a great nation burnt pure of the corroding dross that had choked and held them captive so long.

On arriving at home, Berthe found a costume which had just come from M. Grandhomme's laid out on her bed. At any other moment, the sight would have claimed her delighted attention, but she turned from it with a feeling of indifference now, almost of disgust. Antoinette, who had been puzzling over some new trick in the tunic, took it up in a flurry and was for trying it on at once, to see how it fitted and whether the novelty became her mistress, but Berthe, with a movement of impatience, told her to put it away, that she was in no mood for attending to *bêtises* just then. The girl opened her eyes in astonishment. A costume of Grandhomme's, that cost eleven hundred francs, to be called a *bêtise !* It was flat profanity. She left the room with a painful presentiment that something very serious was amiss with Madame la Comtesse.

A soon as Berthe was alone, she began to think. It was a new experience in her life, this process of thinking, and she was hard pressed by it, for it was no vacant reverie that she was indulging in, but a sharp, compulsory review of her past and present existence—and the result was anything but soothing. Her life up to this day had been the life of a human butterfly, gay, airy, amusing, very enjoyable as regarded herself, and harmless enough as regarded her fellow-creatures. She had drunk her fill of the good things of life, enjoying herself in every possible way, but legitimately; she was incapable of wronging or hurting any one; she was extravagant in her dress and other luxuries, but her fortune allowed this, and she made no debts. So far, her life was blameless, and indeed, if she compared it with that of many of those around her, it was a very respectable one. But suddenly all her theories had collapsed, and her comfortable standard been upset. It turned out that she had a soul somewhere, though she had forgotten all about it, and been living, as if happily free from that incumbrance, in selfishness and folly, that were counted by this newly revealed standard little short of guilt. It was an unexpected discovery, and a most unpleasant one. That exclamation which had escaped her twice, and the thought of the great general sorrow, kept ringing in her ears like a warning and a reproach—"Thank God, I have no brother !" Who, then, were these men that she had just seen going forth in voluntary self-devotion to fight for her, and those who, like her, could not depend on themselves? Was there such a thing in Christendom as a woman or a man who had no brothers? Yet Berthe had believed herself to be this impossibility; she had been living up to it in utter forgetfulness of her brethren, ignoring them as a heathen might, or using them coldly for her own selfish purposes, to work for her and minister to her interests or her pleasures. There were some people whom she loved, but it was a love that narrowed to self; those who were disagreeable, or stupid, or bad she disliked, and, unknown to herself perhaps, despised. There were no wide sympathies in this discarded soul of hers for the great family of mankind; for the publicans and sinners and the lepers and the blind and the lame; she was kind-hearted, but suffering, to touch her, must be seen through some æsthetic coloring; the miseries and follies and infirmities of a prosaic kind that abounded on all sides of her she turned from in disgust, she avoided them like noisome things that belonged to creatures of an inferior clay and had no kinship with her more refined and privileged individuality. "Sacrifice is within the reach of all of you; you must help by sacrifice," that old man had said. What a strange sound the words had ! What did he mean ? Sacrifice! Was there any place in her life for such a thing ? She looked round at the azure hangings of her room, at the bright mirrors that reflected her figure in a dozen varying aspects, at the costly goods and trinkets that littered her dressing table, at the couches and chairs of every modern contrivance inviting the body to luxurious repose, and she saw that her nest was fair to look at, but too full for this unbidden guest called sacrifice to find a place in it. Her eye wandered absently from one object to another till it fell upon a pale ivory figure on a velvet background, fastened to the wall, and half-shrouded by the curtains of the bed.

"I am young; it is not too late; I will begin life afresh," said Berthe, rising and moving restlessly across the room; "I will begin to-morrow, no, to-day—now."

She went close up to the bed, and stood for a moment with clasped hands, her lips moving in quick, low utterances, and then fell upon her knees before the pale, thorn-crowned head looking down upon her.

They never knew it, but this conquest of a noble woman's life was perhaps the first victory won by the Breton soldiers who set out to battle that day !

PART II.

EXCELSIOR!

"GREAT news! Extra! Three sous!" The newsvender, a ragged little urchin who nearly collapsed under the weight and volume of his extras, was shouting out these three startling facts at the top of his voice as I went out early in the morning. Two rheumatic old rag-women, immediately suspending their investigation of the dust-heaps, dropped their crooks, and cried out to him to know the news. Was it a victory or a defeat, or was it anything about the siege? But the urchin, as hard-hearted as any editor, waved the momentous sheet majestically with one hand, and answered, "Three sous!" To the renewed entreaties of the rag-women he condescended so far as to say that it was well worth the money, that they never spent three sous more advantageously, for the news was wonderful news, but for less than three sous they should not have it. I did not altogether believe either in the extra or in the wonderful news, but the newspaper fever was on me like the rest of the world, so I produced the inexorable three sous and took the paper. The moment the two women saw this they came up to me, and, evidently taking for granted that I was going to give them the benefit of my extravagance, stood to hear the news. I read it aloud for them, as well as to a milk-boy who was passing at the moment and stood also to get his share of the three sous, and a remarkably sympathetic audience the three made. The

news was none of the best. The Prussians were at Chalons, and they might be at the gates of Paris before another week.

"That was MacMahon's plan from the first," observed the milk-boy, "and, if the Prussians fall into the trap, the game is ours."

The rag-women, not being so well up in military tactics and technicalities, meekly begged to be enlightened as to the nature and aim of the trap in question, and the young politician was so kind as to explain to them that the marshal had all along been luring on the Prussians to Paris, which was to be their pitfall; Mont Valérien and the fortifications would annihilate them like flies; not a man of them would go back alive; the only fear was that that rascally Bismarck would be too many guns for the marshal, and make him fight before Chalons, in which case, he observed, "it was all up with the marshal, and consequently with France."

Having delivered himself of this masterly exposition of the case, the milk-boy swung his cans, touched his cap to me, and, having achieved the most preternaturally knowing wink I ever beheld, strode off without waiting to see the effect of his words on the two old women. They looked after him aghast. Had they been talking to a confidential agent of the War Office, or to an emissary of the rascally Bismarck himself? A spy, in fact?

"One ought to have one's mouth sewed up these times," observed the more ancient of the beldames, casting a half-suspicious glance at me as I folded my newspaper and put it into my pocket. "One never knows whom one may be speaking to."

This remark was too deep and too fearfully suggestive to admit of any commentary from her companion; the only thing to be done in such a crisis was to take refuge in professional pursuits that offered no ground for suspicion, so seizing her crook the rag-woman plunged prudently once more into her rubbish.

A little further on, turning the corner of a street, I came on two gentlemen whom I knew, standing in animated conversation. I stopped to ask what news? None, except that the horizon was growing darker from hour to hour. The despatches from the frontier were as bad as could well be. As to pooh-poohing the siege now it was sheer stupidity, one of them declared, and, for his part, he only wished it were already begun; it was the last chance left us of rejecting the disasters of the campaign and crushing the remains of the enemy. His companion indignantly scouted both the certainty of the siege and the desirability of it. The city was not to be trusted; no great city ever was; there were hundreds of traitors only too ready to open the gates to the enemy at his own price. Look at the proprietors! Did any one suppose there were fifty proprietors in Paris who would not cry *Capitulons!* before one week was out?

"Well, let the proprietors be taken down to their own cellars, and kept there under lock and key, and let them sit on their money-bags till the siege is over!" suggested the advocate of the siege.

"Then you must lock up half the National Guard and the Mobiles," resumed the other, "for they are full of those money-loving traitors."

This was not very reassuring. I kept repeating to myself that public opinion at a moment like this was always an alarmist, and that the wisest plan would be to read no papers and to consult nobody, but just wait till events resolved themselves, as they infallibly do, sooner or later, to those who have patience to wait for them, and then act as they decided; but it was no use. I went home in dire perplexity, and began to wish myself in Timbuctoo or the Fiji Islands, or anywhere out of the centre of civilization and the fashions and chronic alarm and discontent. Things went on in this way for another week, the tide advancing rapidly, but so gradually that it was difficult for those on shore to note its progress and be guided by it. No one would own to being frightened, but it was impossible to see the scared faces of the people, as they stood in groups before every new placard setting forth either a fresh order from the Hôtel de Ville or some dubious and disheartening despatch from the seat of war, without feeling that the panic was upon them, and that the complicated problems of the great national struggle had resolved themselves into the immediate question: Shall we stay, or must we fly? When you met a friend in the street, the first, the sole, the supreme salutation was: "Do you believe in the siege? Are you going to stay?" The obduracy of the Parisians in refusing to believe in the siege up to the very last moment was certainly one of the strangest phases of the siege itself. They were possessed by a blind faith in the sacredness and inviolability of their capital, and they could not bring themselves to believe that all Europe did not look upon it with the same eyes; they thought that Prussia might indeed push audacity so far as to come and sit down before the gates, but beyond that Bismarck would not go; he would not dare; all Europe would stand up and cry shame on him, not out of sympathy for France, but out of sheer selfishness, for Paris was not the capital of France, but of Europe. So the walls were white with proclamations and advertisements and invitations to non-combatants to withdraw, and practical advice to the patriotic citizens whose glorious duty it was soon to be to defend the city; and the great exodus of the so-called poltroons and strangers had begun to pour out, and the much more inconvenient sort of non-combatants, the homeless population of the neighboring villages, poured in—a sorry sight it was to see the poor little *ménages*, the husband trundling the few sticks of furniture on a hand-cart, with the household cat perched on the top of the pile, while the wife carried a baby and bundle, and a little one trotted on by her side, carrying the canary bird in its painted cage—and still the real, born Parisian said in the bottom of his heart: "It will never come to a siege, they will never dare; England will interfere, Europe will not allow it."

On the morning of the third of September I went out to make some purchases on the Boulevards. Coming back, I saw the Madeleine draped in black, and a number of mourning-coaches drawn up in ghastly array on the Place. The solemn cortége was descending the last steps. I stood to let it pass, and then cast a glance round to see if there was any one I knew in the crowd. To my surprise I saw Berthe in the midst of a group of several persons who had broken away from the stream, and were standing apart in the space inside the rails; she was talking very emphatically, and the others were listening to her apparently with great

interest, and seemed excited by whatever she was telling them. When the crowd had nearly cleared away, I beckoned to her. She ran out to me at once.

"You are the very person I wanted to see," she said, clutching me by the arm in her vehement way. "I was going straight to your house. I have just been to the Etat Major, and met General Trochu there. He came down on account of despatches that had just come in, and have put them all in a state of terrible consternation. There is not a doubt of it now; the city will be blockaded in ten days from this. The Prussians are within as many days' march from us. I thought of you immediately, and I asked the general what you ought to do; he said by all means to go, and within forty-eight hours; after that the rails may be cut from one moment to another; he was very emphatic about it, and said it would be the maddest imprudence of you to remain; there is a terrible time before us, and no one should stay in Paris who could leave. Of course, you will leave at once."

I was too much taken aback to say what I would do. The news was so bewildering. I had never looked upon the siege as the impossible joke it had been so long considered, neither did I share the infatuation of the Parisians about the inviolability of Paris in the eyes of Europe, and for the last fortnight we had come to expect the siege as almost a certainty, that was now only a question of time, and yet we were as much startled by this cool official announcement of it as if the thing had never been seriously mentioned before.

"I don't know what I will do," I said; "if we had nerves equal to it, it would be the most fearfully interesting experience to go through."

"No doubt," assented Berthe;

"but it is an experience that will tax the strongest nerves; of that you may be sure; and unless one has duties to keep one here, I think it would be mad imprudence, as the general said, to run the risk."

"You mean to leave, of course?" I said.

"No; I mean to stay. I am pretty sure of my nerves; besides, as a Frenchwoman, I have a duty to perform; I must bear my share of the common danger; it would be cowardly to fly; but with you it is different. I don't think you would be justified in remaining for the interest of the thing. Only if you mean to go, you must set about it at once. Have you got your passport?"

"No; I had not gone that far in believing in the siege."

"It was very foolish," said Berthe; "all the foreigners we know have got theirs."

"I will go for it now," I said. "Come on with me, and let us talk it all over. Are you on foot?"

"No; but I shall be glad of the walk home; I will send away the carriage."

She did so, and we went on together.

"It is like death," I said; "no matter how long one is expecting it, it comes like a blow at the last; I can hardly realize even now that the siege is so near. Why, it was only the other day we were listening to those people joking about it all!"

"It was a sorry joke," said Berthe; "but that is always the way with us; we go on joking to the end. I believe a Frenchman would joke in his coffin if he could speak."

"And you really mean to stay, Berthe?"

"I do. I shall be of some use, I hope; at any rate, I will try my best. But we can talk of that presently. First about you; are you decided?"

"I cannot say; I feel bewildered," I replied. "I long to stay, and yet I fear it; it is not the horrors of the siege that would deter me, at least I don't think it is that; it is the dread of being taken up as a spy."

She burst out into one of her loud, merry laughs.

"What a ridiculous idea! Why on earth should you be taken for a spy?"

"There is no why or wherefore in the case," I said, "that is just the alarming part of it; the people are simply mad on the point; they have barked themselves rabid about it, and they are ready to bite every one that comes in their way. Twice on my way into town this morning I heard a hue and cry raised somewhere near, and when I asked what was the matter, a mad dog, or a house on fire, the answer was, 'Oh, no; it's an *espion* they've started, and he's giving them chase!' One man said to me, half in joke, half in earnest: 'Madame would do well to hide her fair hair under a wig; it's dangerous to wear fair hair these times.' I own it made me feel a little uncomfortable."

"Well, that is not very comforting for me," said Berthe, laughing, "my hair is *blond* enough to excite suspicion."

"Oh! your nationality is written on your face," I said; "there is no fear of you ever being mistaken for anything but a Frenchwoman."

On arriving at the Embassy, we found a throng of British subjects waiting for their passports, and considerably surprised at being kept waiting, and expressing their surprise in no measured terms. Surely they paid dear enough for the maintenance of their embassies abroad to be entitled to prompt and proper attendance when once in a way they called on their representatives for a service of this kind! The attachés were so overworked that it was impossible to avoid the delay ? Then why were there not special attachés put on for the extra press of work ? And so on. Some nervous old couples were anxious to have the benefit of his excellency's personal opinion as to the prudence of leaving their plate behind them, and, if he really thought there was a risk in so doing, would he be so kind as to suggest the safest mode of conveying it to London ? Also, whether it was quite prudent to leave their money in the Bank of France and other French securities, or whether it would be advisable to withdraw it at once at a loss ? Also, whether it would be a wise precaution to hang the Union Jack out of the window, those who had furnished apartments in Paris, or whether the present state of feeling between England and France was such as to make such a step rather dangerous than otherwise ? It was not for outsiders to know how things stood between the two countries so as to be able to guide their course in the present crisis, but his excellency being a diplomatist was well informed on the subject, and they would rely implicitly on his judgment and advice, etc.

Berthe and I were so highly entertained by the naïve egotism and infantine stupidity displayed by the various specimens of British nature around us, that we did not find it in our hearts to grumble at being kept waiting nearly two hours.

On reaching the Rond Point of the Champs Elysées, our curiosity was attracted by a silent, scared-looking crowd collected on the sidewalk in front of the Hôtel Meyerbeer. The blinds of the house were closed as if there were a death within, and a few *sergents-de-ville* were standing at intervals with arms crossed, staring up at the windows. The

owner of the hotel had been arrested with great noise the night before, on the strength of some foolish words which had escaped him about the possible entry of the Germans into Paris ; but we neither of us knew anything of this, and I asked the nearest sergeant if anything had happened. The man turned round, and, without uncrossing his arms, bent two piercing eyes upon me—piercing is not a figure of speech, they literally stabbed us through like a pair of blades—and, after taking a deliberate view of my person from head to foot, he growled out : " Yes, something has happened. A spy has been found !" There was something so diabolical in the tone of his voice and his expression that it terrified me, and I suppose my terror got into my face and gave it a guilty hue, for another *sergent-de-ville* who had turned round on hearing his colleague speak, strode up to me, and said nothing, but drove another pair of eyes into me with fierce suspicion. The crowd, attracted by the incident, turned round and stared at me, and I felt as if I had that morning posted a despatch to Bismarck or Bismarck's master betraying every state secret in France. Despair, however, that makes cowards brave, came to my rescue, and, putting a bold face on it, I said, with extraordinary pluck and coolness :

" Has he been arrested ?"

" He has."

" Ah, it is well !" I observed. And in abject fear of being pounced upon there and then, and done equally well by, I walked away.

When we had got to a safe distance, I looked at Berthe. She was as white as ashes. Indeed, if I looked half as guilty, it is nothing short of a miracle that we were not both seized on the spot and carried off to the *Préfecture de Police.*

"Let this be a lesson to us never to speak to any one in the street while things are in this state," said Berthe. "Indeed, the safest way would be not to speak at all, especially in a foreign language, for whatever they don't understand they set down as German, and to be a German is of course to be a spy."

After this we walked on in silence. Evidently Berthe no longer looked on my fears as chimerical or matter for laughter, and, puerile as the incident was, I believe it put an end to my hesitation, and decided me to leave Paris with as little delay as possible. She had not realized as much as I had, but the spy-fever had spread so alarmingly within the last few days that what had first been merely a recurring panic was now a fixed idea that had grown to insanity. You might read suspicion and fear written on the faces of the people as you went along. They walked in twos and threes without speaking, glancing timidly on every side, and trying to carry it off with an air of indifference or preoccupation. Every one was in mortal fear of being pointed at and hooted off to the nearest *poste*. No nationality was safe. A few Englishmen who had fallen victims to the popular mania, and been subjected to a night's hospitality at the expense of the government, had published their experiences, and described the sort of entertainment prepared for casual visitors, and it was anything but enticing: a *salle* crammed full of every kind and degree of sinner, from the imaginary spy whipped up on the pavement without proof or witness, to the lowest vagrants of the worst character, all put in for the same offence, and huddled up together without a chair to sit on or air to breathe. Those who were lucky enough to be set free after a short term of durance vile were

warmly congratulated by their friends, and retired into private life without further *éclat*. Some English subjects were simple enough to venture a protest against the unceremonious proceeding on the part of the police, and were politely reminded that the gates of the city were still open and trains ready to convey them to many places of more agreeable manners where the sacred person of a British subject ran no risk of being mistaken for a common mortal, but that, while they choose to remain within the gates, they must take the consequences. And this was, after all, the best answer they could make, and it behooved all sensible British subjects to abide by it. I parted from Berthe at the corner of her own street, and went home to pack up and start the next day by the twelve o'clock train.

I stopped on my way to the station to take leave of her. It was near eleven o'clock. Contrary to my expectations, I found her up and dressed, instead of lolling in dishabille on her couch. But this was not the only surprise awaiting me. The whole appearance of the house was changed. The *portières* and curtains were taken down; the two salons were emptied of their furniture, and four iron beds placed in the large one and two in the small one. A young woman was busy cutting out bandages with a great basket of linen beside her in Berthe's room—that soft, Sybarite room, so unused to such company and such occupation. Her face was concealed by a broad-frilled Vendean cap, but on hearing us enter she turned round, and I recognized the bride-widow of the Bréton volunteer.

"We are going to work very hard together," said Berthe, putting her hand on the girl's shoulder. "Jeannette is to teach me to make poul-ices, and to dress wounds, and to do all kinds of useful things that one wants to know how to do for the wounded. She is quite an adept in the service, it seems, so I hope our little ambulance will be well managed and comfortable for the dear soldiers."

Jeannette's eyes filled with tears, and she took Berthe's hand and kissed it. Just at this moment François came in to say there were some *Sœurs de Charité* who wanted to speak to madame. Berthe and Jeannette went out to meet them, and as they left the room Antoinette came in through the dressing-room. She threw up her arms when she perceived me, and looked toward the salon with blank despair in her face.

"The world is upside down," she said, "everything is going topsy-turvy; what between the war, and the siege, and the rest of it, one doesn't know what to expect next; but of all the queer things going, the queerest is what is happening in this house. To think of *le salon de la comtesse* being turned into a hospital! That I should live to see such things! Madame does well to go away; people are all going crazy in this country, and they say it's catching."

"So it is, Antoinette," I said, "and the best thing I can wish you is that you may catch it yourself."

Berthe wanted to come with me to the station, but I would not let her. I preferred to carry away my last impression of her as I saw her now. She was dressed in a plain dark silk, with a white apron before her, and a soft cambric handkerchief tied loosely round her head; the quaint, half-nunlike dress seemed to me to become her more than the most artistic of M. Grandhomme's combinations, and as I watched her going from room to room with a duster in her hand, changing the chairs and tables, and working as deftly as an accomplished housemaid, her face flushed with the exercise and bright with a new-found joy, I thought I had never seen her look so beautiful. So we parted in that blue chamber that was henceforth to have a new memory of its own to both of us. Before I had started from my own house, the news of Sedan had come in, and spread like wild-fire. All that I had previously witnessed of popular excitement was cold and calm compared with what I beheld on my way to the station. The city was like a galvanized nightmare, electrifying and electrified into hubbub and madness. Rage and despair were riding the whirlwind with suspicion tied like a bandage on their eyes. The cry of *Treason !* out-topped all other cries; every man suspected his brother and accused him; the air was filled with curses and threats, and there was no voice strong enough to rise above the popular tumult and subdue it. If there had been, what might not have come of it? If at that moment there had been a voice loud enough to speak to the hurricane, and compel those millions of tongues to be silent and listen to the truth, and then gather them into one great voice that would lift itself up in a unit of harmony and power that would have been heard, not only to the ends of Paris, but to the ends of France, what might not have been done? what might not have been saved? But it was not to be. Nothing came of the discord but discord. The strong hand that might even then have welded all these suicidal elements of hate, and fury, and suspicion into a vigorous bond of action was not forthcoming; the strife was to go on to the bitter end, till the soil of fair France was drenched with blood, and all her energies spent, and her youth and chivalry laid low in bootless butchery.

The blocks that stopped our progress in every street made it a difficult matter to get to the railway, and when we eventually did get there we were a quarter of an hour behind our time. But, as it happened, this was of no consequence; we had to wait another hour before the train started. Meantime the confusion was indescribable. Several wagons full of wounded had arrived by the last train, and a regiment of the line was waiting to start by the next. The Place was filled with soldiers, some were lying at full length fast asleep under the hot noon sun, others were smoking and chatting near their arms that were stacked here and there; some of the poor fellows had been out before, and were only just recovering from their wounds; they looked worn and weak as if hardly able to bear themselves; women were clinging to them, weeping and lamenting; inside the station, travellers were rushing frantically from bureau to bureau; then in despair at ever getting through the crowd that besieged every wicket, they would sieze some unlucky porter with a band on his hat, and implore him in heart-rending tones to help them to a ticket, and, when he protested that such a service was not in his power they would belabor him vindictively with hard words, and make another rush at the bureau.

At last we were off. It was an exciting journey, such as I hope never to make again. The lines were encumbered with trains full of wounded coming and troops going, and our pace was regulated with a view to avoid running into those ahead or being run into by those behind. Now we darted on at a terrific speed, the engine wriggling from rail to rail like a snake gone mad; then we would pull up spasmodically and crawl almost at a foot-pace, then off

we flew again like a telegram. Trains flashed past us on either side every now and then with a tremendous roar, and soldiers sang out snatches of war-songs, and we cheered them and waved hands and handkerchiefs to them in return. We had started an hour and a quarter behind our time, and we arrived three hours after we were due. For two hours before we reached Boulogne, the danger lights were flashing ahead, red and lurid in the darkness, and it was with something like the feeling of being rescued from a house on fire that we set foot at last on the platform. Once in safety, I was able to look back more calmly on the history of the last fortnight. It seemed to me that I had been standing on a rock, watching the tide roll in, creeping gradually higher and nearer to my standpoint till I felt the cold touch of the water on my feet, and leaped ashore.

And Berthe? She stood out like a bright star transfiguring the dense darkness of the picture. The change I had witnessed in her appeared to me like the promise of other changes, wider, deeper, universal. I had ceased to wonder at the choice she had made; the more I thought of it, the more I felt that she was worthy of it as it was of her, and the only wish I could form for her now was, that she might be strong to persevere unto the end. The course she had adopted was the noblest and the only true one for a Frenchwoman while France was suffering, and struggling, and bleeding to death. While the war-cry and the battle psalm were clanging around, it was not meant for the women of France to sit idly in luxurious ease, and watch the death-struggle of the nation in indifference or mere passive sympathy. We may none of us stand aloof from our brethren in such a crisis, or take refuge in cowardly neutrality. Neutrality in the brotherhood of Freedom is desertion, treachery. We have each our appointed post in the battle, and we cannot desert it without being traitors. We must all fight somehow. Not of necessity with iron or steel, but we must fight. Moses had neither bow nor arrow nor javelin when he got up on the mountain and watched with uplifted arms the conflict in the valley below, but yet he was not neutral. So to the end of time it must be with all of us. We must fight somehow; we may never abide in selfish peace or a sense of isolated security while the brethren around are at war; whithersoever the battle goes, to victory or defeat, to glory or humiliation, we must take our share in it, and let our hearts go on fighting faithfully to the end. We must love the combatants through good and evil alike; through the smoke and din we must discern every ennobling incident of the struggle, such as there abounds on every battle-field in every land, seeing all things in their true proportions, shutting our hearts inexorably to despair, making them wide to endless sympathy with the good, to inexhaustible pity for the wicked. The smoke must not blind us; the crash and the roar must not deafen us; through the agony of souls, despair, and hate, and sin, we must have our vision clear and strong to recognize the loveliness of virtue, the divine beauty of sacrifice, the infinite possibilities of repentance, the joy of the conquerors, the sweetness of the kiss of peace. Loving all love. Hating all hate. We must see angels outnumbering fiends in incalculable degree, light triumphing over darkness, and the breath of purity healing the blue corruption of the world.

ONE CHAPTER FROM HESTER HALLAM'S LIFE.

"AH! Hester, Hester, keep back your tears. Be the brave little wife and woman now. Have faith, hope, and courage; the year will soon speed by, and, lo! here shall I find you again! God grant it! And good-by, my wife, my children—my all and only treasures."

They are engraven on my memory—these last words of Henry Hallam, my husband, my beloved. They were spoken hopefully, cheerfully, though I knew they were intended to cover the sorrow of a heart that ached, even as did mine, at our final parting.

Henry Hallam was to go to South America as chief engineer of a proposed road from some inland city to the Pacific. After a marriage of eight years, this was our first separation. I never did consent to it. Better poverty and the humblest life together than that mountains and seas should divide us, I argued.

But Henry was proud, as he was tender and loving; he could not bear to see his wife, delicately reared, doing menial service; nor his little girls deprived of waxen dolls, because they would usurp the ragged dollar that must go for bread.

Our situation had fallen from bad to worse; an expensive law-suit had been decided against us, to liquidate the cost of which an out-West piece of land, that was to have been our children's fortune, had to be sold at a sacrifice; and when all was paid, except our scanty furniture, we had but three hundred dollars in the world. We lived in a rented house in the beautiful suburbs of Brooklyn; three months' rent would consume our all. Meantime, upon what should we live, and wherewithal should we be clothed? This was a serious question, which vexed my husband for many days. He suddenly answered it by accepting with alacrity this lucrative position in South America. My only living relative in all America was one sister, widowed and childless. She came from the West to abide with me during my husband's absence. She, too, had comparative poverty for her dowry, her only income arising from the interest of less than a thousand dollars.

No thought of poverty haunted us, however; heretofore all our wants had been supplied, and we had lived almost luxuriously, counting upon the fortune which had been for six years dwindling to less and less in courts of law.

It was with no dread of poverty, I repeat, that I saw my husband take his departure. I thought only how the light had gone from our house, and joy from existence. I am distressed whenever I read of the ever-recurring matrimonial quarrels and divorces which appear now the order of the day. I could have lived with Henry Hallam through the countless eternal years, and—God forgive me! —desired no other heaven.

We had no particular creed or faith. The Hallams had been Methodists; the Griffeths, my father's family over in Wales, had been members of the Church of England.

Henry and I, reading here and there indifferently, had become somewhat inclined to Swedenborg's theories. We read Dr. Bushnell and his colleagues with some faith and more interest. But we fashioned the great hereafter—the heaven we all talk of and dream so much of—after our own ideals. Those may have been in the right, thought we, from whom Shelley and many another poetical dreamer imbibed the idea that the Godhead was but the universal spirit pervading and animating nature; that man was immortal, and was to arise from the dead, clothed in purity and beauty, and was to wander endlessly in some limitless, enchanting paradise, where should be all things lovely to charm the eye, all sounds to entrance the ear, all spirits gentle, and wise, and good for communion of intellect and heart. In this heaven stood no stately throne upon which sat a God of justice, receiving one unto life, banishing another unto everlasting perdition. It was the same here as upon earth; the beauty, bloom, fragrance, and glory were permeated with an essence subtle, invisible, intangible, but present, the life and source of all—and this was God! The ancients had a heaven and a hell, which Christianity had adopted; but we lived in the XIXth century, and we need not pin our faith to such notions borrowed from the heathen. Were youth and health on earth immortal, we would prefer never to pass through the iron gate of death and the pearly gate of life; since, however, all must yield to the inexorable fiat, and *all men must die,* we would make a virtue of necessity, and be willing to go to that sensual heaven, which wore all the beauty of earth, with naught of its thorns and blight. Ah! we, Henry and I, were still in the glow of youth and hope; life seemed a beautiful vista, and the end far off! Of the great beyond we but carelessly dreamed—as carelessly as if our feet were never there to stand, nor our souls to tremble upon its awful brink.

With Henry gone, I was like a child bereft of its mother. I wept and would not be comforted. I counted the hours of every day; they seemed so inconsiderable, deducted from the almost nine thousand which the three hundred and sixty-five days yielded. I see now how foolish, weak, and wicked I was!

I was seized with a slow fever, which lasted me through the summer. In my weakness and wakefulness I saw visions and dreamed dreams which haunted me constantly. I began to fancy that I was to die. I would have been satisfied to have fallen in a sleep that should have known no waking until the dread year was over.

Early in September I heard from my room an unusual bustle in the house—the feet of men, and the unwonted sound of boxes or trunks laid heavily upon the floor. But why need I go into details?

Henry Hallam had died of yellow fever, and his trunks had been sent home!

In my despair, one thought overpowered me. I had made myself wretched counting over the hours until Henry should return. Now he would never, never come back, no matter how many hours; I might count for an eternity, and he would not come at the end. Oh! could he but some time come, even in the distant years, when his step was feeble and his hair was gray, how patient I would be, how hopeful, cheerful, in the waiting for that certain time!

Why had I not been happy when I knew that he still lived; when the fond hope was mine that, after a few months, I should again behold him?

We never know—alas! we never know! With my beloved gone, I fancied myself sunk in the lowest depth of desolation.

More than two years elapsed. My sister struggled bravely to keep a roof above our heads and the wolf of hunger from our door. Notwithstanding her closest economy, untiring industry, and fertile ingenuity, her small principal had become reduced one-half. Her zeal and energy were a reproach to me, and I had already commenced heroic endeavors to imitate and assist her. We might still have done well, educated my two little girls, and taken comfort in each other, now that my hopeless grief had become partially assuaged, and I had begun to take an interest in the management of our affairs. A fresh grief, however, was in store for me. Maria, my sister, upon whom alone I had come to depend, was stricken with an incurable disease, and, after lingering through months of pain, which often amounted to torture, died, and was buried.

I was not allowed to remain in my stupor of grief after I had beheld the cruel grave close over my only sister. The fact that but a trifle remained after all expenses had been paid aroused me to most painful apprehensions for the fate of my children. But for them I fully believe I should have adopted the advice of Job's friends to Job, the patient—curse God, and die! The dear little children, however, who had no friends but their unhappy mother, and who clung to me as if they had in me all that was sufficient and all the world, were an incentive to further endurance and fresh exertion.

In a moment of discouragement and gloom I wrote an unaccustomed letter of six pages to a lady who had been my friend while sojourning in the West. I had spent a year with my husband in a growing village upon the banks of the Mississippi where this lady resided. She had a delightful home in the midst of charming grounds, an indulgent, devoted husband, three lovely children, with wealth enough to command the desirable and good things of this world. We had corresponded for a time, but since my great affliction I had written no letters.

Without delay came Mrs. Bell's reply. In my selfish grief I had not thought that upon others also might be falling showers of the self-same woe. The thought of Mrs. Bell, with her happy surroundings, had formed a pleasant picture, comforting to dwell upon. Ah! how my eyes filled and my heart throbbed as I read her letter!

The beautiful home, with its pictures, books, its nameless household gods, was in ashes; the husband, really the handsomest, most elegant gentleman I have ever met, full of health, vigor, and cheerfulness, a year after the fatal fire had died suddenly, leaving his large property in an involved and unavailable condition; and my friend was living in a small cottage amidst the ashes and blackened trunks of trees—which stood like weird spectres about her former home. The letter, half read, fell from my nerveless grasp, and I clasped tightly my trembling hands, bowing down upon them my throbbing head, murmuring:

"Doth *all* of beauty fade to blight, and all of joy to gloom? Are *all* human loves so vain and transient? Are all hopes and dreams fleeting and unsubstantial as the goodly shadow of a summer cloud? Is it true of *all* beneath the sun, 'ashes to ashes, dust to dust'?" Gathering courage to finish the letter, another surprise awaited me. My friend had become a Roman Catholic. After giving brief details of her conversion, she thus addressed me:

"At this moment I feel more sorrow for you than for myself. My dearest earthly loves and hopes lie, like yours, in ashes. But out of *my* desolation hath sprung the green branches of heavenly peace. I weep not unavailing tears at the loss of what so charmed my heart as to separate my soul from God. Arise out of the ashes watered with your tears. Go to the nearest Catholic priest; ask him for books, counsel, and prayer that shall lead you upward and onward toward the kingdom of rest. Make the effort, I entreat you, in the name of God. If you find no peace to your soul, what will you have lost? If you find comfort and rest, will not all have been gained?"

Had I learned, in the midst of my happiness, that Miriam Bell had become a Catholic, I might have wondered, thought strange of it, but set it down as one of the unaccountable things, and not puzzled my brain by studying into it. But now it was different. Her afflictions, so similar to my own, brought her very near to me in sympathy. I would have as soon thought of myself becoming deluded by the snares of Popery as my friend, Mrs. Bell. Yea, sooner; she was more matter-of-fact, calm, philosophical, more highly educated, with a mind more thoroughly disciplined, and naturally more inquiring and comprehensive than my own. And she had heartily embraced this religious faith which, without ever having bestowed much thought upon, I had naturally regarded as one of superstitions and lies.

The sun went down, the twilight fell. Charlotte and Cora helped themselves to a slice of bread, and lay down to rest. The sewing-machine had for hours been idle, and the unfinished white shirt, suspended by the needle, looked like a ghost in the gathering gloom; and still I held my hands and deeply thought, or walked the floor with stilly tread.

And so Miriam Bell had found a balm for her sorrow, a light amid her darkness. How? By becoming a Catholic. And what was it to become a Catholic? To believe impossibilities, and to worship idols; to behold, in a tiny wafer of human manufacture, the body and blood, soul and divinity, of an incarnate God? Does Miriam Bell believe this? If she can believe it with all her heart and soul, then might she well be comforted! To fall upon one's knees before the relics of a saint, and beg his prayers, as if he could see and hear? To implore the Blessed Virgin to succor and defend, as if she were not a creature, but omnipotent and divine? To reverence the priest as a being immaculate, an angel with hidden wings walking upon earth, unto whose feet you must kneel, and unveil, as unto God, all the thoughts and interests of your heart? I pondered over this last suggestion. Standing in the white moonlight that silvered a space of the floor, I lifted up both weary heart and waiting hands, and, with eyes toward the unknown and infinite, I cried:

"Unto God would I pour forth the sins and sorrows of my soul; but I am all unworthy. He whom I have disregarded and failed to acknowledge is shut out from my vision and approach. Between him and me is the thick wall of my offences. Oh! if, in his infinite mercy, he could send forth one little less than an angel—who should have something of the human, that he might compassionate and pity; of the divine, that he might comprehend, guide, and assist—to that one I might yield in reverence. All the sins, and follies, and rebellions of my life should be poured into his ear; perhaps, oh! perhaps the hand of such an one might lift me into the light, if light there be indeed for soul so dyed as mine."

How this fancied being, uniting the human and angelic, became gradually, and by slow degrees, associated in my mind with the Catholic priest, I know not. Certain only I am that, after a few days of mental struggle, of resolve and counter-resolution, I complied with my friend's entreaty, and, accompanied by my little girls, sought the nearest priest.

I took this step not with faith, nor yet altogether with 'doubt. I went, not willingly, but as if irresistibly impelled. I was like one shipwrecked— floating in maddened waters, threatened death below, an angry sky above; and darkness everywhere. A friend in whom I trusted had pointed out to me a life-preserver.

"Stretch forth thy hand, hold it fast; it will save thee," she had said.

"It is but a straw," I murmured, clutching at it, drowning.

The priest entered the parlor a few moments after our admission by a domestic.

I scanned him narrowly as he walked straight up to us, rubbing one hand against the other, slightly elevating his shoulders. He was a middle-aged man, whose benevolent countenance wore the reflection of a happy, cheerful soul at peace with God and man.

My first thought on viewing him was of the woman who wished but to "touch the hem of our Saviour's garment"; and, when he uttered his first salutation: "And what can I do for you, my child?" I said involuntarily: "Oh! that I may be made whole."

"Ah! you would go to confession. Go into the church, and pray before the altar; I will be there presently." And he turned to leave the room.

I did not speak nor move. At the door he said:

"You are a stranger in the city?"

"No—yes—that is, I have lived here several years, but I have no friends; I am indeed a stranger."

"You understand and attend to your religious duties?"

"I have no religious duties; I have no particular religion. I am beginning to think myself a heathen."

"And have you not been brought up a Catholic?" he questioned in surprise, returning to where I still sat.

"The furthest from it. If you have time to listen, I will tell you what has brought me to you." And I went on to tell him of the advice of my friend, received in the depth of my afflictions and despair. If my conversion to the Catholic faith, entire, absolute, blessed, thanks be to God! was not instantaneous; if, being blind, I received not sight, being deaf, I received not hearing, in a moment, in the twinkling of an eye, as did those whom Christ himself touched and healed, still do I believe it to have been the work of Almighty God, and marvellous unto my own eyes. If God commissioned Miriam Bell, instead of his own holy angel, to direct me to the priest of his own anointing, I believe myself no less to have been sent to pious F. Corrigan than was Paul sent to Annanias, or Cornelius to Simon.

From regrets and lamentations, from dulness and despair, my heart bowed low unto God in rejoicing and thanksgiving.

Aside from this, the Catholic religion and the history of the church became to me an attractive, fascinating study. I seemed philosophizing with sages, praying with religious, meditating with saints. The whole world seemed newly peopled, unnumbered voices joining in that grand chant that the church for almost nineteen centuries hath sung: "Glory be unto God, and on earth peace to men of good-will."

F. Corrigan had sent a young priest to a new town in the interior, made by the opening up of new railroads. Here F. McDevitt had built a small church, and, in his report to his superior, spoke of having need of a teacher for a parish school. F. Corrigan offered me the situation, and in one week I was at Dillon's Station.

On the first day of our arrival, F. McDevitt asked my eldest little girl her name.

" Charlotte Griffeth Hallam," she replied promptly.

" Charlotte Griffeth ?" he repeated ; then turning to me:

" And for whom was she named ?"

" For my mother," I replied.

" And is your mother living ?"

" She died in my infancy."

" She must have been the person advertised." And taking a slip of paper from his memorandum-book, handed it me.

It was an advertisement for Charlotte Griffeth or her heirs in America, to whom an estate in Wales had descended, valued at one hundred thousand pounds ! And what interest had this possessed for F. McDevitt ? His brother had a short time previously married a Miss Griffeth, and it was to send in a letter to his brother that he had extracted from the paper this brief paragraph. Was not this too much ? I closed my eyes to keep back the tears, and pressed my hand against my side, to still the tumultuous throbbings of my heart.

God! my God! so long time from me hidden, giving me now the true faith, and then this unexpected fortune! What should I do with it ? A few months before, I would have purchased a splendid house, perfect in all its appointments. I would have gathered about me all that would have pleased the taste and gratified the senses.·

Now was it thrown in my way as a temptation ? Before the sun had set upon this wondrous change of fortune, my decision was formed. I would go on in the way I had intended. It had evidently been God's way chosen for me, and I would follow in it. I would go into a temporary cabin, and teach the children of the Irish laborers.

The fortune should be divided into three shares. My children should have two ; the third, which was mine, should go to build a home for widows and orphans.

And I ? Every morning, with my troop of little girls and boys, I go to the holy sacrifice of the Mass, where adoration is perpetually blended with thanksgiving—the latter one of the deepest emotions of my heart. I never expected to be so content and happy in this world.

Through thee I have found, O God! that " thou art the fountain of all good, the height of life, and the depth of wisdom. Unto thee do I lift up mine eyes ; in thee, O my God! Father of mercies, do I put my trust.

" Bless and sanctify my soul with heavenly benediction, that it may be made thy holy habitation and the seat of thy eternal glory ; and let nothing be found in the temple of thy divinity that may offend the eyes of thy majesty !"

AN ENGLISH MAIDEN'S LOVE.*

THE third Crusade had commenced. The cry, " God wills it," had gone forth from many a manly breast, and already Frederic of Germany, Henry II. of England, and Philip Augustus of France had received the cross from William, Archbishop of Tyre. But a more powerful monarch than Saladin, against whom their combined strength was to be directed, struck Frederic before he reached Palestine, and called Henry II., whom domestic difficulties had detained in England. Death gives not back that which he takes, and, for the want of a leader, the German army was broken up.

Richard, the brave Cœur de Lion, took his royal father's place, both on the throne and in the Crusade, and, with Philip of France, started on his glorious mission. Among those brave men who gathered around England's standard, joying to be led by so bold a king, who, with his lion's heart, dared every danger of sea, land, or fierce and cruel Moslem, was one of the oldest and proudest of Norman blood. His forefather, who had fought by the side of William the Conqueror, had distinguished himself by many a daring deed, and had won from his royal master, in recognition of his bravery, an earlship over a fair and smiling province of "merrie Eng-

land "; then, renouncing his Norman title in behalf of a younger son, and marrying his eldest to the daughter of a Saxon knight, he established his right to the soil of his adopted country. Much of his fearless nature seemed to have come down with the blood of Robert de Bracy, who, at the ripe age of fifty-five, had found himself unable to resist his monarch's call, and to whom Cœur de Lion himself owed much of wise counsel. Robert de Bracy was a man of stern aspect, but withal so compassionate and forbearing, that he won the love of every one who came in contact with him. His bravery had already been proved when, as a young man, he fought beside Henry II. during the war against France ; and, later, in that most dreadful invasion of Ireland—dreadful, because of the blow it gave to Irish independence, and for the gradual sinking of her people, from that time, from the eminence in erudition and lore for which they were renowned among the nations, and which, be it to their credit said, they are using every effort to regain. A man perfectly incapable of the least dishonorable action, he was revered as a knight " without stain or reproach." A fervent Catholic, his religion was his pride, and he never was ashamed of kneeling in church beside the poorest beggar, nor felt insulted because poverty's rags touched his velvet robes. But the good earl's heart received a terrible blow when he heard of the murder of Thomas à Becket. His faith in his king was shaken, and nothing but the stern duty of allegiance could have induced Robert

* Some years ago, a poem appeared in an English weekly with the same title, "An English Maiden's Love." The author stated that, when a mere girl, she read the incident in a very stupid old novel founded upon the same subject, and which she never could succeed in meeting with again. We have not seen the novel, but have ventured to borrow the incident, and offer it to the readers of THE CATHOLIC WORLD in its present form.

de Bracy to remain in England. So when the Crusade was preached, he gladly seized the opportunity to show his love for the crucified King—for him whose throne was a cross, and whose crown was of thorns—and enrolled himself among the Crusaders. He was joined by his only son and Sir John de Vere, who, like himself, was of Norman blood—a brave, honest man, of strict integrity, whose character will be better seen in the unfolding of the story. The earl was deeply attached to the young knight, and the highest proof he could give of his love was in his willing consent that, on their return from Palestine, Sir John should wed his daughter, Agnes de Bracy, whose heart was no less pure than her face was lovely. "An' we'll make an earl of thee, my lad!" cried the impetuous King Richard when the betrothal was announced to him.

The court of the earl's castle was crowded with armed retainers, knights, and esquires, who formed the retinue of De Bracy and De Vere. Even on and beyond the lowered drawbridge might be seen bands of neighing steeds, their impatience checked ever and anon by their riders, who awaited the earl to head and lead them to the rendezvous of the Crusaders. Court and castle alike resounded with the clank of steel and tread of armed men, while buxom waiting-maids and merry lads hastened to and fro in the bustle attendant on such a departure. Here and there stood a page giving the finishing polish to his master's sword, and, again, others assisted in the girding on of the armor. Every now and then might be heard the wailing of some fond wife or mother, contrasting somewhat strangely with the jests of those who had no tie to make the parting a sacrifice in the good cause. Apart from all this, in one of the inner rooms of the castle, were gathered the earl and his family. Lady de Bracy's loving eyes wandered sadly from her honored husband to the manly features of her son, kneeling by her side, and back again to the earl, who was soothing the grief of his youngest child, Mary, just old enough to know that her father was going over land and sea, and that she might never see him again. In the deep embrasure of one of the windows, partly concealed by heavy curtains, stood Sir John and his betrothed. Agnes had been weeping, but being calmed by Sir John, whose grief partook more of the nature of joy than fear, since on his return he was to claim her as his bride, she rested her head quietly against his breast, both her hands clasped around his neck, while her uplifted eyes sought to read every expression of his noble face.

"Beloved," he said in a low tone, "it will not be for long, please God, though I would that thou wert my wife e'en ere I go. And," he added, continuing his whispered tones, "I were no Christian knight to doubt thy faithfulness. I'll prove thee mine on our return from the holy wars."

Agnes looked steadily at the face so lovingly bent over her, and, unclasping her hands, she drew from her girdle a scarf, such as was worn in those days, and bound it on Sir John's sword-belt. Then, returning her head to its resting-place, and feeling his arm drawing her tightly to him, as though by the very motion to thank her, she said:

"An' there is thy love's guerdon; thou shalt wear it in battle, and, when thine eyes fall on it, remember that *one* is praying for thee in bonnie England."

Any further discourse was prevented by the earl, who cried:

"Sir John, we have no time to lose; the men are ready, the steeds drawn up, and our presence alone is needed for immediate departure. Come, Agnes, my daughter." And as he placed one arm around her, with the other he drew his wife gently to him. Raising his eyes to heaven, he exclaimed: "O God! protect these dear ones while I am fighting the good fight in thy name and for thee. And this child," he added, as, tenderly kissing his wife and Agnes, he loosened his hold and took Mary in his arms—"this child, Mother of God, belongs to thee; keep her pure, that thy name, borne by her, may be ever spotless!" Then, calling the knights, he hastily quitted the apartment, not daring to look back. The son tore himself from his mother's farewell embrace, and quickly followed; but Sir John still lingered. At last, summoning his courage, he strained Agnes to his breast:

"Farewell, my beloved! God have thee, my own, in his keeping for so long as it seems best to him that we be parted."

As the drawbridge was raised behind the retreating soldiers, Agnes stood at the loophole of the main turret, where, with her mother, she watched till the men, horses, and banners disappeared, shut from sight by the declivity of a distant hill, when she sank on her knees, and prayed fervently for the loved ones who had started on their perilous journey.

We have said that Agnes de Bracy was lovely; that word can hardly convey the true nature of her charms. Personal beauty she had, and much: dark eyes, a clear complexion, a perfect mouth, disclosing perfect teeth, and breaking into a smile of winning beauty, together with a graceful form; a character of womanly sweetness, and great strength of will. But as Spenser hath it·

"Of the soule the bodie forme doth take;
For soule is forme, and doth the bodie make."

It was the soul in Agnes de Bracy, rich in God's sweet grace, which gave her that wonderful expression; the pure heart, "without guile," which caused her eyes to gleam with a look that made Sir John once exclaim, "Methinks, Agnes, thine eyes would soften the stony heart of the Mussulman himself, and e'en make a Christian of him."

Nor was Sir John deficient in those qualities which would be apt to win the admiration and love of such as she. Like the earl, he was a most devout Catholic. With a full, heartfelt appreciation of his holy faith, he could not—as many, alas! do—put it on and off with holiday attire, but every word and action proved how thoroughly it was a part of himself, and how, without it, in spite of great natural talents, he would be—nothing.

To follow the Crusaders on their journey, every step of which was fraught with danger; to watch the course of events as they shaped themselves during the march of the two armies, is not the province of this story. About three years later, the earl, with wounds scarcely healed and a heavy heart, stood before the drawbridge of his castle, which was being rapidly lowered at the unexpected blast of his bugle. The clanking of the heavy armor was a joyful, long-looked-for sound to the inmates of the castle, who had assembled in the court to welcome back the earl and his followers. Weary and dustladen, they passed under the portal of the gateway, a sad remnant of their former numbers, greeting those who stood expectant with joy or fear. Suddenly a loud wailing arose, as many a mother looked in vain for the well-remembered form of her brave lad, who died fighting the

Saracen; and the sounds of glad rejoicing were hushed in the presence of the angel of sorrow. The earl and his son made their way rapidly to the same room that had witnessed their farewell, and there their loved ones awaited them. A thrill of terror passed through Agnes' frame as she missed the features of Sir John; and, seeing a strange look in her father's eyes, which were fixed so tenderly but sorrowfully on her, she clasped her hands tightly, and cried out: "My God! my God! thy will, not mine, be done; but, oh! if *he* is dead!"

"Agnes, my child, my precious child!"—and Robert de Bracy drew his daughter to him—"God knows my heart is heavy enough with the story I have to tell thee, yet it is not what thou dost expect. Sir John is living, strong and well, but"—and his lips quivered with emotion—"but he is Saladin's prisoner; and I fear me greatly that neither gold nor silver will ransom him."

"Saladin's prisoner, my father? Saladin's prisoner? And will nothing ransom him?" And bowing her face in her hands, she wept bitterly. But her violent grief was not of long duration; her nature was too thoroughly schooled. She checked its first outburst; and, trusting to Him who had always given her help in her troubles, she breathed a short, fervent prayer. Then, raising her head, she turned to the earl, and in her sweetest voice:

"Forgive me, my father," she said, "for that I have not been thy daughter, and, in my selfish sorrow for what God has ordained, I have forgotten to bid thee welcome home."

"Agnes! Agnes!" And the old earl nearly broke down under the weight of his sorrow—sorrow all the keener for the suffering of his daughter. "Agnes, we will not give up all hope. I would have begged of Sala-

din on my knees for *his* ransom, but it could not have been; I was ordered away, and no respite granted."

"Give up all hope? No, indeed, my father. Far from me be such a thought! God will help us, and my beloved shall be ransomed if it is his will; for he gave him to me, and he can take him away."

. . . . . .

Lo! Damascus is rising before us; not the Damascus of to-day, but the quaint, beautiful Oriental city of the XIIth century. The golden crescents of her domed mosques flash in the light of the Eastern sun. Her thoroughfares are crowded with men in their Turkish garb, and women veiled after the manner of their nation. Her shops are resplendent with jewels, pearls, and jacinths; fragrant with the perfumes of musk, ambergris, and aloes-wood; glittering with rustling silks and heavy brocades, interwoven with gold, and scarlet, and silver. Houses, beautiful in their quaint architecture, meet the eye at every corner, together with palaces, the residences of emir and vizier. But with naught of these have we to do. Our story takes us into the heart of the city to the palace of Saladin, Sultan of the Turks. As we enter, we behold banners unfurled. Shields, helmets, every species of armor decorate the main hall, along whose sides are ivory benches, where the eunuchs wait their master's orders. A great dome is overhead, and the sun, pouring down through its latticed windows, floods the hall with light, and causes the steel of the armor and the jewels of the hall to sparkle and flash with brilliancy. At the further end is a heavy curtain of brocade, richly wrought with various kinds of embroidery in white, red, and gold. Two tall armed men guard the corners. We will imagine the curtain lifted for us, and enter. There sits Saladin on his throne. His followers are around him. Rich are the robes which fall from his shoulders, well befitting the Sultan of the East. If the hall was gorgeous in its beauty, the room of the throne is no less so. The hangings on the walls are figured with various wild beasts and birds, worked with silk and gold. The sandal-wood work gives out its own peculiar perfume. In fact, all betokens a royal presence. And of what sort is Saladin? Great talents in him combine for mastery; great activity and valor. The severity and rigor, so inflexible as to make the bravest heart quail with fear before him, was often replaced by such kindness, such generosity, that the poor, the widowed, and orphaned did not hesitate to appeal to his mercy. And as he sits before us, we must draw back and continue our story.

An eunuch has presented the bowl and vase, and, having performed the ablution, Saladin turned slowly round, gazing steadily at the stern faces before him. "By Allah!" he exclaimed, as his eyes rested on the one nearest him—"by Allah! I trow, Moslem chiefs, you are brave, yea, very brave and very skilful. You have beaten back the Christians. You have proved yourselves true sons of Mahomet; but, for all that, I know a braver man than you. Eunuch! bid the Christian slave come forth." At his sultan's orders, the eunuch made a low bow, and retired behind one of the hangings. In a few moments he returned, followed by a guard of men, and Sir John de Vere in their centre. As they approached with him, Saladin waved them back, and bade the Christian only to remain before the throne. Then suddenly he made a sign—a sign dreaded alike by vizier and eunuch. It was obeyed, and a

soldier, stepping forward, waved a sharp and gleaming scimitar over the head of the captive; but he did not flinch, nor move a muscle of his face, but continued gazing with stern, unshrinking eye straight forward. The sultan, as if satisfied with the courage the prisoner evinced, motioned the soldier back. Then he said:

"John de Vere, thy father's land, thine ancient home, thou shalt see no more; but I have great need of men like thee. I command thee, forsake thy Christian faith; and, if thou wilt adore Mahomet and God, there is no favor thou shalt ask, by my royal word, that shall not be granted thee. I will set thee above all men. I alone will be above thee. I will make thee my son. I will give thee palaces, gold, and precious gems; and from all the queenly maidens thou shalt choose one and wed her as thy bride. Thou canst not refuse that which my caliphs strive for years to obtain, and which to thee is given in one day. I bid thee reply."

As Saladin finished, he sank back on his throne, and a quiet smile played around his lips as he awaited his captive's answer. Sir John listened to him calmly and patiently. Then having bowed low, he raised his head erect, and made the Christian's mark—the sign of the cross—upon himself.

"Saladin," he said, "Sultan of the Mussulmans, since thou dost bid me reply, I will first return thanks for all the favors I have received at thy hands. From the first day of my captivity till now thou hast loaded me with kindnesses; for these I am grateful, though gratitude may not seem to be in the answer I make thee. Know, then, I, a Christian, cannot renounce my faith. I am a sworn soldier of my God—of him who died for me. Dost thou think that I, who bear the cross upon my shoulder, could on that cross bring scorn? Thou dost promise me a Moslem wife. In that far-off land—which God grant I may see before I die!—I have a love, whom as my very life I love. To her sweet heart I will not be false. Saladin, I cannot bear a Moslem name nor wed a Moslem maiden."

"Ah!" cried the sultan, "thou dost not know woman's heart. Perchance she whom thou lovest so fondly is the bride of another; nor doubt me, that heart, fickle and false as any woman's, which swore such fealty to thee, belongs now perhaps to thy rival. Never yet was woman known to be constant. Ah! John de Vere, thou hadst better remain with me."

As he ceased, the curtain was raised, and two by two came those holy men vowed to ransom Christian captives from the hands of the Turks. They approached Saladin's throne, and, opening their bags, they poured out with lavish hand an untold treasure at his feet.

Then the chief monk said:

"The bride of Sir John de Vere, O Sultan Saladin! sends all she hath, gold and gems, and bids thee take them, but to restore to her her betrothed."

"The other captive knights may go with thee," replied the sultan; "but as for all these gems and gold, his lady-love would give them for a dress. Sir John de Vere may not go with thee. No wealth can ransom him, for I love him with a more than brother's love, and hope to win his in return. Why, I would give a hundred slaves, if he would renounce his Christian faith. So thus to thy lady this answer; for I will prove how Christian maidens love. Tell her that, before I yield my thrall, she must cut off her own right arm and hand, and send it hither to ransom John de Vere!"

"Saladin," said the captive, "thy permission for one word to say to these monks before they go. I bid you, brothers," he added, turning to them, "to speak of me as dead. For, O sweet-heart! my betrothed bride, well do I know that not only arm and hand, but even life itself, thou wouldst willingly give for me; and I cannot prove thy death, that I may live. Do not tell her the sultan's cruel words. O brothers! I beg you do not!"

As sole reply, they gathered up the useless treasure, and, returning to their ships, they sailed for England. With mournful hearts they landed on the shore, and travelled day and night till they reached De Bracy's castle. There they laid down their full bags, and told Agnes that for neither gold nor silver could Sir John be ransomed; but if it was still her heart's wish that he should see his native land again, the sultan had promised that for one gift her betrothed should go free.

"And that gift?" said Agnes.

"Is," replied the head monk slowly, "thine own right arm and hand, cut off for his sake. This is the ransom asked. Thou canst not prevail on Saladin to take a meaner thing."

Every face grew white at these cruel words. They shuddered as they listened to the monk; only Agnes preserved her usual calmness. The earl clutched his sword, and could hardly refrain from vowing death to every man of the Moslem race. Little Mary cried out, clasping her sister tightly, "Sure, Agnes, such a wicked man cannot be found." But quieting the child, she looked at Lady de Bracy. The face of the mother was marked with keen suffering. It was a dreadful moment for the brave spirit of Agnes; she knew she must make answer, and that at once. But how could she tell those, who suffered so much at the very thought of the deed, of her resolution? "My God! it is hard; but as we love in thee, thou must help me to do what is right," was the prayer which rose from her heart, as with her lips she framed her answer.

"My dear ones, your daughter need not say how much she grieves for your sakes that she must suffer. Cruel is the ransom asked; who could know it better than I? But God loves us, and did he not, because of his love, give his own beloved Son? And do we not see every day how churls and nobles give their lives for their king? 'Greater love than this no man hath, that a man lay down his life for his friends.' That, my father, we know from the holy Gospels. Wouldst thou have thy daughter shrink duty, thou, my lord and father, who hast bled by Cœur de Lion's side?" She hesitated a moment, then, her sweet voice growing clearer and stronger, she continued:

"I am John de Vere's betrothed, and to him I owe my fealty, even though it should cost my life. My lord and father, what is my life? Long years spent in pleading with God to end the banishment of my love. And at last he has heard, at last my prayer has been granted. Only it must be proved that my love is pure; so he sends me pain, and I will take it, grateful to endure; for is not the reward great?"

. . . .

Once again the holy friars found themselves in the beautiful city of Damascus. Eagerly they threaded their way through its broad but devious thoroughfares till they reached the palace of the sultan. Within, in the room of the throne, sat Saladin in royal state. By his side stood Sir John de Vere. He still retained the badge of slavery, for he was too true to give up his faith; but to Saladin's councils he was often summoned. When any measure to be taken against the Christians was the theme of debate, he remained respectfully but firmly silent. Against his brothers he could not in conscience speak; to do so, for them he knew would prove more than useless. But yet many were the subjects on which his knowledge and fine sense of justice could be brought to bear; and Saladin was not the man to fail in taking advantage of his wise judgment.

Some such serious business had called around the sultan his advisers, and, as usual, Sir John stood foremost among them. They had all but finished the subject under consideration, when the folds of the curtain were lifted, and a herald entered the royal presence.

"Sultan, our lord," he said, "the monks appointed to ransom the Christians stand without. They crave an audience again."

"Let them enter," was the command given, and swiftly obeyed. Again the curtain was lifted upon the holy men, and again it fell, shutting them from the outer hall, as they stood in the presence of Saladin. The superior stepped forward:

"We thank thee, sultan, for the favor thou hast accorded us in this audience. But we bid thee learn, O monarch! a lesson we bring thee— a lesson of how great, in a nobler faith than thine, is love's purity and power." A dim foreboding seized Sir John at the monk's words, and his whole form shook with ill-suppressed emotion, as he listened to the conclusion:

"Monarch! what are women to thee? Slaves, toys of an idle hour, the playthings of passion. What women of thine would do for thee as Agnes de Bracy hath done for him who stands beside thee—him whom thou callest thy slave? Thy cruel words have been heeded. Lo! the answer." And he laid at Saladin's feet a casket, richly wrought in gold and silver. Sir John looked as one frenzied, then seizing the casket pressed it to his heart:

"Why did you tell her, O cruel monks? Did I not ask you to speak of me as dead? O fair arm! O dear, sweet hand! that thou shouldst cut it off, my beloved, and for my poor sake!"

Saladin stretched out his hand to take the casket; but Sir John only pressed it the tighter, and sobbed aloud. At this, the superior of the monks, coming forward, said something in a low voice, which caused the young knight to lift up his face and look at the brother. Then, turning to the sultan, he placed the casket reverently before him. Saladin took it and opened it; as he raised the lid, the perfume of aromatic spices escaped therefrom. Lifting the linen, he looked steadily for a moment, then large tears were seen to escape from his eyes and roll down his cheeks. All the higher nature of the man seemed to be aroused. Calling his nobles around him, he held the casket silently for their inspection. Within it lay embalmed the lily-white right arm and hand of Agnes de Bracy. There was no mistaking the delicate form of the arm, the shape of the tapering fingers. Severed from the shoulder of that noble girl, they lay in all their beauty, a reproach to the cruelty of the sultan. In that throne-room not one man but was moved to tears. Then Saladin closed the casket, but, still keeping a firm hold on it, he cried out:

"Mahomet and God witness for me! with a deep brother's love I love John de Vere, and I thought I might retain him by me if I asked this ransom. But now I would give my kingdom to recall those words. Haste, John de Vere, haste to thy noble love. O fair arm! O fair hand! True, brave heart! Oh! that I could claim such love as thine! John de Vere, tell that noble woman that Saladin yields his selfish love. Take to her gold, gems; load the ship with all of wealth and beauty I have; but they would vainly prove Saladin's grief. She who has proved thee such a noble love will make thee a noble wife, John de Vere. But thou canst not take with thee this precious casket. Among my treasures I shall store it away. It will prove to future ages how Christian maidens keep their troth, and how pure is their love."

. . . . .

More than this the legend tells us not. But it is said that in a church in England may still be seen a statue of the knight and his noble, one-armed lady.

HOW I LEARNED LATIN.

WHEN I was young, I travelled a good deal, but travel then was very different from what it is now. My travelling was all obligatory, it was on business, and I sometimes found myself detained in places from which I would gladly have taken a quick departure. It happened once that, during my tour through France, I had to stay a Sunday at Lyons. The stages on Saturday were few, and did not suit me, and of course it was against my principles to travel on the " Sabbath." I had been brought up a very strict Presbyterian, and was very particular, especially in a foreign country, about attending service. I could hardly speak any French, which perhaps you will think strange, since I had business to transact in France, but my business was with English and American houses and their agents. You know, too, that in my time young people did not learn French as they do now, any more than young ladies learned to play on the piano. But I was determined I would go to church, and so set about finding out whether there was any English-speaking clergyman in Lyons. I could not find any, and, when I inquired after a church, I was deafened and confused by the number of St. Marys', St. Monicas', St. Vincents', St. Josephs', that were pointed out to me. If it had not been the " Sabbath," I think I should have been tempted to swear at the whole calendar and its Lyons representatives. I asked for a *Protestant* church. " Oh ! yes," said one (all the others looked blank), " there is a 'temple' (so they call them in France) in such and such a street," naming it,

and giving me directions by which I could not fail to discover it. I started, fearing I should be late. I had heard that the French Protestant religion was not unlike the Presbyterian, but I had never been to one of its churches before, having always been luckily within reach of some church where my own tongue was used. At last I found my " temple," and got in, rather behind time, to be sure. The people were singing. The church—meeting-house, I should say—was bare and whitewashed, large square windows lighted it with a painful exuberance of brightness, the seats were stiff and uncomfortable. I could not understand one word, and thought the voices rather nasal. The congregation sat down and the minister got up. This evidently meant a sermon. I tried hard to fix my mind on some Bible texts I knew by heart, so as to prevent my thoughts from wandering. As the preacher went on, his voice droning into my ear, I caught myself wondering whether I were in the right place after all, and whether his doctrine was the same as mine. I could not tell what he might be saying, but, of course, the hymns must be all right. I took up a hymn-book, and tried to make out from their analogy to some English words what these French words could mean. I could see the name of " Jesus " pretty often, and could make out " Saviour " too, but that was about all. The sermon was very long, and I was hardly quite awake at the end. Then the people sang again, and a harmonium joined in from somewhere. When it was all over, I felt very dissatisfied, an I somehow it did not seem to me as if I had been to church at all. I lost my way going back to my hotel, and happened to pass one of the " saints' " multitudinous shrines, just as the Catholic congregation were coming out. An acquaintance of mine, a young Englishman, was among them. He came across the street and shook hands.

" Why, where have you dropped from ?" he said.

" From church," I answered.

" What church ?" he asked, rather blankly.

"The Protestant 'temple,' of whatever religion that may be," I said, not in the best of humors. I told him my whole adventure, whereat he seemed very serious.

" My dear fellow," he said at last, " have you not often heard us Catholics abused for all sorts of mummeries, for muttering and mumbling in an unknown tongue, for bowing and scraping, and popping down, suddenly on one knee, and so forth ?"

" Of course I have," I said.

" Well, and what do you think of what you saw in the French Presbyterian church, this morning ?"

" Think ! I simply think it was unintelligible."

" Well, say, quite as unintelligible as our Latin, for instance ?"

" Yes, but not for the Frenchmen who were there."

" But if those Frenchmen had been in a Presbyterian church in America, they would have been as badly off as you were this morning. And if both you and they went to a German church, as Calvinistic as you could wish and as like your own in belief, would not you and your French friends be all at sea, as the saying is ?"

" Exactly so; but what are you driving at ?"

" Only this : that, when you go to the church, and know that the people believe pretty much as you do, you would like, I think, to be able to join in their devotions, and not feel yourself left out in the cold, as if you were a heathen or a Mormon, wouldn't you ?"

" Of course; but it can't be helped."

" I tell you it can, my dear fellow. Look at us, millions and millions of Catholics, all believing the same doctrine, all going to the same ceremonies, and taking part in the same devotions, because we have only one language for our services, one language that is spoken in Canton, in San Francisco, in London, in Africa, everywhere where a Catholic altar is put up and a Catholic priest says Mass."

"There is some convenience in that, I'll grant you."

" I tell you, my friend, when I come to a foreign city and find everything strange and feel very lonely in the hurrying crowd that has not one idea in common with me, I just find out a Catholic church as quick as I can, and hear Mass. See if every worshipper does not become a brother then, and if one's feelings don't change ! I take my chair, put it where I like, open my book, and follow the same old prayers that I heard long ago in little poky chapels in England. I feel quite at home."

" Well, it *is* pleasant : but that is not all one wants."

" But is it not a great deal ? What do you think of a religion that meets you everywhere, just the same, dear old familiar faith, never changing among the mandarins of China, the Red Indians of your own territories, the blacks of South Africa, and the traders of London and Birmingham ? Don't you call it comfortable, homely, to say the least ?"

"Yes, but I suspect it is all sentimentalism: you like the sound of the old words, but you don't really understand them. A baby would like the same cooing it was used to at home, supposing it got lost and picked up somewhere, but there would be no sense in the cooing, for all that."

"But, my dear fellow, we *do* understand our Latin. All of us who can read have the translation of it plainly printed alongside of the text in our books of devotion, and the greater part we are already familiar with on account of its being taken from the Gospels and the Psalms."

"No, really? Is that so indeed?"

"Indeed it is. And, now, what do you think of this? You see the priest 'pop down suddenly on one knee, and pop up again,' as you would put it. Well, he has been saying, 'The Word was made flesh and dwelt among us.' Is not that in the Bible, in St. John's Gospel? Of course you are well up in texts, you know where *that* is. And, again, when you see the priest beat his breast three times, and you call out 'Superstition!' do you know what he is saying? 'Lord, I am not worthy that thou shouldst enter under my roof; but say the word, and my soul shall be healed.' Is not that in the Bible (with the substitution of 'soul' for 'servant'), where the centurion begs our Lord to cure his servant? And so on through the greater part of the Mass. When you see the priest wash his hands, he repeats a whole Psalm, the Twenty-fifth; and at the very beginning, when you see him stand at the foot of the steps, he 'is also repeating a Psalm, the Forty-third. Further on he repeats the 'Our Father,' and there are other parts of the Mass, whose names would only confuse you, which change according to the ecclesiastical seasons, but are always exclusively composed of Scripture texts, aptly chosen for the different solemnities of the year. So, you see, we know all about what we hear said in Latin."

"Well, you surprise me; all that mumbling seemed to me so childish."

"Do you think these Frenchmen childish when they speak their own tongue, and do their business in it, and their courting, and their literature?"

"Well, no, of course that would be absurd."

"And the Italians, the Germans, the Greeks, the Spaniards, don't they all talk foreign languages, yet you don't think them childish, or call their conversation *mumbling?*"

"No; I simply say I am sorry I cannot understand them."

"Then don't you see that as a Catholic you would be even better off, for though the Latin would be a foreign language, yet you *would* understand it?"

"Certainly, if all you say is true, the Latin is by no means a bad contrivance."

"Do you know that, up to the twelfth and thirteenth centuries at least, most books were written in Latin, no matter to what country the author might belong, and that till even later than that all law business was transacted in Latin all over the civilized world?"

"Was it indeed? Well, I have learnt something this morning, and it is really worth thinking over."

"Come this afternoon to St. Vincent's, and I will show you at Vespers how well every one understands the service."

"All right! agreed."

And so we parted, and in the afternoon my English friend and I went to a Catholic church, and sat down among a crowd of very attentive worshippers, all of whom were reading their prayer-books. My friend opened his, and pointed out the Psalm the choir was singing; it was one I knew very well: "The Lord said to my Lord." The people about us were all French; their books had the same Latin Psalm on one column as my friend's book showed, while the French translation was in the place of the English one which he had on the opposite page. Many of the congregation were singing alternately with the choristers at the altar. My friend sang too; he did not mumble, but said the words distinctly, so that I heard each syllable, though I could not understand the meaning. He gave me his book presently, and chanted by heart. As we came out, there was a group of dark-skinned men, talking eagerly near the door. They were Spaniards; they too seemed quite at home. The next day, I was curious enough to go to Low Mass with my friend; as the ceremony went on, he showed me every word, and made me follow everything, even the introit, collects, gradual, communion, which he looked out for me in a missal he had with him. I was puzzled by all these names then, though they are A B C to me now. My friend had to leave in a day or two, but I had bought a book like his in the meanwhile at an English library, and continued through curiosity to go to the different Catholic services, just to assure myself that the Latin was not gibberish. It struck me as strange that three-quarters of the prayers should be my own Bible texts!

Well, to make a long story short, I left Lyons soon after, and travelled to many other places, European and Asiatic. At last one day I was in Canton, in high spirits, for I was to go home soon and be a partner

in the firm whose foreign business I had been managing. Sunday came, and I went to church; I was just as anxious as ever about my Sunday duties, but somehow it was not for a Presbyterian church that I was looking. I knew my way very well to *my* church, and my church had a cross on its gable end, and was called "The Church of the Holy Childhood." There were plenty of Chinese there, a few English, a few Americans, and a good many French people. They all had the Latin on one page of their books, and their respective languages on the opposite page. But I did not need to look at my English translation, for I knew the Latin by heart now. I am sorry to say I had distractions, and during one of them I suddenly perceived my old friend of Lyons. When Mass was over, I went to him and called him by name; he stared and did not recognize me; we had never met since, and I had a beard of many years' growth. I told him my name, and asked him if he had forgotten St. Vincent's Church at Lyons? I can tell you we had a good long talk over the past, and he congratulated me heartily, while I thanked him eagerly for the best lesson I ever learned in my life.

And that, boys, was how I learned Latin.

But I have only told you about one reason which our church has for keeping to the Latin tongue; that particular reason struck me most, because it was through that I was converted; but of course, when I came to examine things thoroughly, I learnt all about the other very good reasons assigned by the church for this practice. You know how modern languages are always changing, and how the same word will mean a different thing in two separate centuries; there is the word "prevent," for instance, which now means to hinder, but which formerly was used in the Anglican liturgy in its Latin sense, to succor and to help. Well, it would not do for the dogmas or the rites of the church to be subject to these apparent changes, which would lead most likely to misunderstandings and perhaps heresies, so the church chose to fix her liturgy in a language whose rules and construction undergo no alteration from century to century. You know the law, also, has Latin terms, probably used for the same reason. Then, besides, it is not necessary for the people to be able to join in the absolute words of the Mass and other services, provided they join heartily in the *intention* of the sacrifice and prayers. As I have told you already, the *fact* is that most Catholics do understand the words themselves, and not very imperfectly; still, the *theory* remains that such comprehension (which after all is more a grammatical accomplishment than a devout necessity) is not absolutely required. If it were otherwise, you see, the doctrine of intention would suffer. In the old days, the Hebrews—on whose ritual all non-Catholics claim to take their stand, or by which at least they measure their standard of adequate worship—used to stand outside the temple, where they could neither see nor hear, though they knew that by their presence alone they were participating in the sacrifice and receiving the blessing attached to it. Then, again, we forgot, when as Protestants we used to object to the Latin liturgy, that the Catholic ceremony of Mass is essentially a *sacrifice* offered to God *for* the people, the priest being the sole representative of the people and interceding in their name. Long ago, at the English court of the Plantagenet kings, French was the language universally spoken, while the Saxons, the subjects, adhered to their own tongue. The petitions of the people were offered to the king in the language of the court, that is, French; but the result was identical with that which would have been the consequence had the prayer been in a tongue the people could understand. So in the church it is sufficient for God to hear the petition of his children; they themselves would not be benefited the more for understanding every word of the pleading of the priest. The things that are said *to* us, not *for* us, the sermons and instructions which are to explain God's will and our duty to us, are always in the tongue common to each particular country; and when there is a large foreign settlement in a town, it has a church of its own where such instruction is administered. Look at this large city of New York: have we not German churches and a French church besides our English-speaking churches? The Mass is identically the same in each, but for those who are to be taught the language is varied according to their nationality. And so for all offices which the priests perform toward us, as, for instance, confession. In the great church of which you have all heard, St. Peter's at Rome, there are confessionals where priests of every nation are ever ready to receive and console the sinners of every clime, while above each box is plainly written "For the English," "For the Spaniards," "For the French," "For the Germans," "For the Greeks," "For the Poles," etc., etc. So, you see, the church, after all, is quite as wise as she is loving, and indicates her claim to be our mother in every way. Take my advice, and always look well into things before you condemn them; for, if *I* had done so when a boy, I should have saved myself a great deal of trouble in getting rid of prejudices which every year increased and deepened, till it needed a miracle of the grace of God to strip the tightening garment they were wrapping round my fettered soul.

.

www.ingramcontent.com/pod-product-compliance
Lightning Source LLC
Chambersburg PA
CBHW030328270326
41926CB00010B/1543